# TRUSTS AND ESTATES SIMULATIONS

## Second Edition

**Danaya C. Wright**
*T. Terrell Sessums and Gerald Sohn Professor in Constitutional Law*
*University of Florida, Levin College of Law*

**Silvia Menendez**
*Master Legal Skills Professor*
*University of Florida, Levin College of Law*

BRIDGE TO PRACTICE SERIES®

WEST ACADEMIC

860 Blue Gentian Road, Suite 350
Eagan, MN 55121
1-877-888-1330



Published in the United States of America

**ISBN:** 978-1-63659-370-8

# TABLE OF CONTENTS

# TRUSTS AND ESTATES SIMULATIONS

## Second Edition

# INTRODUCTION

## WHY SKILLS PRACTICE

For many years, Trusts and Estates courses have been taught at law schools in a single way, as a doctrinal course through which students learn the general principles and theory of estate planning by studying case law and the relevant statutes. While this exploration is often fascinating (the *In re Estate of Rothko*[1] case comes to mind immediately), it has only limited applicability when a law student transitions to law practice. In many Trusts and Estates courses, students rarely see a will or trust document, and they never know more about the facts of leading cases than what are reproduced in the opinion itself. However, from the moment a new practitioner walks into a law firm, he or she is asked to provide real life clients with plans and documents that meet the clients' specific needs.

Moreover, societal changes over the last 50 years have greatly changed how estate planning practitioners need to practice. Divorce and remarriage, families without a defined legal status, non-marital children from non-spouses, disabled adults who are able to live independently, and reproductive technologies are just a few examples of the changes that have made modern estate planning more complex than ever. Plus, there is no end of fancy new trusts or other mechanisms for transferring property at death, that are designed to avoid probate, avoid litigation, avoid title changes, avoid conflict among beneficiaries, or avoid having to come back to an attorney for updates. New practitioners and students should be able to identify the complexities of a client's situation, the various options for estate planning, and understand the considerations necessary to know how and when to use them. This book is intended to bridge that gap between doctrine and practice, and start the student and new practitioner on the road to becoming an advisor and planner who is able to facilitate the smooth succession of estates.

Within these pages you will meet your new client(s) and work through drafting a complete, albeit simple, estate plan. And you will have an opportunity to amend the plan in light of some more complex considerations after you have mastered the basic elements. We will also introduce you to some of the minefields you will need to negotiate just to represent your client appropriately. In each chapter, we will introduce you to the relevant facts, provide a basic discussion of the law, review the issues that need to be addressed, and then provide any documents necessary to complete the exercises. Finally, each chapter concludes with a discussion of the lessons learned, practice problems, and additional factors that a planner may have to address. For this second edition, we have updated the scenarios to better reflect the current state of the law but still provide the practical skills the T & E students require.

We begin our approach with the most basic question—who is your client? It may be easy to know who has hired you when that person walks in your door, papers in hand, is of sound mind and has the intention to execute a will. But rarely does life, or the practice of law, seem to operate with such straightforward intentions. That client who claims to be a single man may still have a life partner, children, a former spouse with whom he owns property, or a parent or sibling who he supports. He may be in debt up to his eyebrows, or he may be the next richest man after Bill Gates.

[1] 43 N.Y.2d 305, 313 (N.Y. 1977) in which the co-executors of Mark Rothko's estate entered into contracts with companies and galleries which they owned to dispose of Rothko's vast collection of abstract expressionist paintings subject to large commission fees. The Court of Appeals of New York found that the conduct of the executors was "manifestly wrongful and indeed shocking."

You won't know until you get all of the information you need from him, and he is unlikely to provide it unless you know how to ask for it.

Who your client is can become especially difficult if two people walk in your door: a husband and wife, a parent and child, an elderly individual and a caregiver, two siblings, or two relative strangers. Are they there to make a joint estate plan, or is one person simply assisting the other? If the latter, is that assistant directing the plan, or is she simply chauffeuring the client to his meeting with you? If the former, do they want similar reciprocal plans, leaving all to the survivor, and then upon the survivor's death everything to the kids? Or does one have secrets from the other, secrets that might jeopardize your ability to represent both clients in an ethical and professional manner? Often before the appointment is even made, you will need to negotiate some of these issues, and you won't even have a client yet!

Once you have identified your client, you will next need to determine what property your client owns, and has the right to transfer on death. That house that your client bought for a child may still be in the client's name, or there may be property over which your client has a power of appointment that is still titled in his mother's name. Your client may have joint bank or securities accounts, life insurance, or a vacation house in a different state or country. All of these can make determining what property your client has into a difficult calculation. In Chapter 2, we figure out what property your hypothetical client has and examine some of the different ways in which it can be titled and/or managed both before death and after death. Some of this property can be given away now, while some should be held onto until death. Some of the property can continue without much management or control, while other property may need periodic attention from a trustee, guardian, or account manager. Deciding what estate plan your client needs depends heavily on what property your client has.

In Chapter 3, we will discuss the family protections that most states have adopted. These protections include homestead property, family allowance, exempt property, and the elective share. These statutory entitlements may require that certain sums of money, or particular items of real or personal property, must pass to a surviving spouse and/or minor children. In many cases, the homestead, family allowance, and exempt property come out of an estate first, before debts are paid and before we even need to think about whether the client has a will or died intestate. Part of a good estate plan consists in making sure that this property is available right away, in relatively liquid form. The elective share, which is the minimum amount that most states require be given to a surviving spouse, must be accommodated within an estate plan for any married persons. Although there may be ways to avoid these mandatory statutory shares, we will plan within their constraints here. There is no point learning the different ways to manage these, however, until you know what effect they likely will have on your client's estate.

Next we will draft the basic documents your client will need to adequately prepare for a period of incapacity before death. You will draft a living will and durable power of attorney for health care, which are readily available documents on the internet or in statutory form books. But your client will need to have these documents customized for his or her particular needs. It is also a good time when your client is young and healthy to think about bodily disposition, funeral arrangements, organ donation, and who is up to the job of carrying out the final wishes. Chapter 4, therefore, focuses on the period leading up to death, and death itself.

In Chapters 5 and 6, you will turn to the disposition of your client's property after his or her death. In these Chapters you will draft a basic will and a revocable trust, but unlike that English Literature paper you had to write in freshman composition, you can plagiarize from other wills and trusts if you find language that appropriately accomplishes your client's goals. We provide some samples and certain facts and preferences for your client and ask you to draft these documents as you think best, focusing primarily on making the language clear evidence of your client's intentions.

In order to draft these documents, you will need to know who the client's beneficiaries are, both in the mind of your client and at law. Although a client will likely come into your office with a clear set of who she intends to receive her property, you will need to make sure that there are no surprises, either for your client, her executor, or her beneficiaries.

The famous case of *Will of Moses*[2] led to the failure of a will because the lawyer did not thoroughly determine who the potential beneficiaries might be and adequately discuss their claims with his client. Thousands of wills have been voided on the grounds of incapacity in large part because the moral, if not the legal, claims of beneficiaries were not adequately accounted for and they contested the wills of the decedents. Throughout the planning exercises, therefore, you will explore your hypothetical client's possible beneficiaries and discuss why you need to do a thorough job identifying all the potential claimants to your client's estate.

One of the most important skills, as you will quickly discover from your Trusts and Estates course, is drafting instrument language that actually expresses your client's intentions. Poor drafting of future interests, savings clauses, and even basic bequests could fill hundreds of casebooks with examples of what not to do. Without sound drafting practices, the other skills addressed in this book will not make a difference to an estate plan. As you draft the important provisions in Chapters 5 and 6 you will need to focus carefully on the words you are using to express your client's intentions and check that you have covered all the possible contingencies. These exercises are meant to ensure that all readers of the document come away with the same understanding of the plan.

In Chapter 7 you will go through an execution ceremony, draft a final letter to your clients explaining what you have done and, most importantly, what changes in their lives will require them to come back to you for adjustments to their estate plans. You will make sure that all the appropriate documents are executed, filed, and are in place, and you will close out your representation by sending a final bill.

As is frequently the case, however, closing out the initial representation is not the end of your relationship with these clients. In Chapter 8, we introduce a set of facts that further complicate the estate plans you drafted. In this chapter, you will have the opportunity to consider the impact of various changes to your clients' lives, including a child with special needs, grandchildren from nontraditional relationships, and inheritance of significant assets from a parent. For each of these changes, you will amend the existing documents, in order to meet your clients' needs.

We are going to be careful throughout this book and the exercises not to involve any issues that might raise actual estate tax or income tax concerns. As of 2023, the decedent's estate must be worth over $12.92 million to trigger any estate or gift taxes. And that number is expected to climb to keep pace with inflation. At that rate, fewer than 1% of decedents will have estate tax considerations to deal with in their estate plans. Income taxes are payable on virtually all levels of income, regardless of whether the person is alive or dead. Michael Jackson's estate is currently generating millions of dollars of income every year, which is fully taxable. But income taxes are a topic far beyond the scope of this work. In our exercises and hypotheticals, therefore, we will work with estates that are smaller than the trigger for estate taxes, and we leave the calculation of income taxes to tax accountants. But for those of you who are pursuing advanced work in estate planning, we have included some important exercises on drafting tax apportionment language and Crummey provisions in Chapter 9. These don't require that you draft to minimize estate taxes, but rather that you think about how you would draft certain standard tax-related provisions that would be appropriate if you were planning for a potentially taxable estate.

When you have completed these exercises, you will have done a large percentage of the work that many clients of modest estates require. And you will have encountered some tricky situations

[2] 227 So.2d 829 (Miss. 1969).

and have had to think about how to address them as best you can given what you know about the law and their unique needs. We hope that you enjoy these exercises and that you enter into them in the spirit of being fully engaged estates attorneys. If you only half-heartedly fill out the forms or only write a brief retainer letter, you will find yourself far less comfortable on that first day of practice when you have your own real-life clients. But even if you do it all, you are likely to face new issues and unique situations every day in your practice that we obviously have not covered here. For those situations you should turn to other lawyers, drop into the library, and don't be afraid to ask for assistance.

To make these exercises more like the real practice of law, we also want you to keep track of your time by recording everything you do for your clients and how much time you spend. In your initial interview you will need to discuss your fees for the representation, which you do as either a flat fee or an hourly fee. Your clients will need to agree to the fees you are charging if they are going to hire you. So be sure to discuss with them all of the work you intend to do and provide them with an estimate of the total cost. At the end of the book, you can tally up your time to see whether you were appropriately compensated. As with most client arrangements, you are likely to spend more time than you bill. But this exercise will help you to see which of your activities should be paid for by the client, and which ones you should just chalk up to expanding your legal education.

We would be remiss not to discuss the emerging technologies of artificial intelligence and their role in lawyering practice. Some of these chatbots and open-source AI tools have the potential to transform the practice of law. But no matter how good these tools become, the insight of the trained lawyer will be necessary to ensure that a client's individual needs are being met and their intentions are manifested in these instruments. At the same time, lawyers should not have to reinvent the wheel every time they write a will or a trust. There are great boilerplate terms that should be included in all, or nearly all, instruments. But a good lawyer must know why to add certain terms and which ones to customize to your client's needs. Your professor will establish rules on copying from other wills, trusts, or estates documents and whether you can use a chatbot or other artificial language tool in this class. It would be counter-productive in a drafting class to tell you that you can copy all of these assignments or feed them into ChatGPT. This is an ideal course to explore the appropriate role of these language tools in both law school and law practice.

We hope that you enjoy this area of legal practice as much as we do. A client who walks out your door with a well-crafted estate plan has a peace of mind that few other lawyers can instill. Most people just think about lawyers and their palms sweat and they feel defensive or miserable. But the estate planning lawyer is often the one lawyer a client truly trusts and feels comfortable being dependent upon. And clients are usually happy with the result of the interaction. Even clients in the midst of death, divorce, bankruptcy, or other crises are likely to feel more comfortable if they know that their beneficiaries are properly provided for and their intentions about the succession of their property will be carried out. You will still need supervision with estate planning documents even after this course, but you should have a much better understanding of what these documents look like, and what provisions you should be paying special attention to when you are drafting them to fulfill your client's needs. At the end of the day, the client will be happier the better you know your job, and you will be happier the more comfortable you feel with the quality of your work product. Thus, let's get on our way toward gaining the skills and confidence you need to satisfactorily represent your client.

## MEETING YOUR CLIENTS AND THEIR FAMILY

We have set up the exercises in this book with a relatively traditional client and his family. Meet Henry Higgins and his wife Wanda Doolittle Higgins. Henry went to an Ivy League University and received a liberal arts degree in Sociology, but his parents urged him to get a practical degree, and so he went to the local State University where he received an MBA with a specialization in economics. He works as a mid-level manager for a Public Utility Consulting Firm (they write a lot of reports and papers about energy prices, patterns of consumption, and government regulation). He married his first wife, Janet, when he was in college, and they had two children, a son Steve, and a daughter Doris. Steve is now 25 and never went to college. He is a "professional" musician. He wants to open a record label after he makes it big playing string bass with a local garage band. Doris is 20 and is still in college. She is studying biology, because she can't decide whether to be a surgeon or an environmental ecologist. She lives out of state during the school year, in an apartment that Henry subsidizes. Steve still lives at home and does odd jobs, working at the local pizza parlor for spending money until his band makes it big.

Henry and Janet divorced when Steve was 12 and Doris was 7. They shared custody equally and Janet lived about 4 streets away while the children were growing up. Once Doris reached 18, however, Janet married her yoga teacher, and they moved to Tibet. Henry met Wanda the year after he divorced Janet when Wanda got a job at his firm as a mail clerk. Wanda was the daughter of the senior partner of his firm, but she had a hard time deciding what to do with her life, especially since she was used to living a life of luxury in the home of her wealthy parents. Wanda was 21 when she started working at the firm, but Henry and Wanda didn't start dating until she was 25 and he was 38. By that time Steve was 17 and Doris 12. They didn't actually get married until Doris had reached 18 because Wanda's father didn't want her to be legally responsible for Henry's children. However, Wanda and Henry had two children before they married. The first year after they started dating, they had a daughter, Gillian, and two years later they had a son, Benjamin. Gillian was 5 and Benjamin 3 when their parents married.

The following timeline should help us keep track of Henry and Wanda's immediate family.

1974—Henry is born

1977—Janet is born

1990—Wanda is born

1996—Henry and Janet marry

1998—Steve is born

2003—Doris is born

2010—Henry and Janet divorce

2011—Wanda begins working at the firm and meets Henry

2015—Wanda and Henry begin dating

2016—Gillian is born

2018—Benjamin is born

2021—Janet moves to Tibet

2021—Henry and Wanda marry

2023—Henry is 49, Wanda is 33, Steve is 25, Doris is 20, Gillian is 7, Benjamin is 5

Henry and Wanda both have large extended families, each has three siblings, and Wanda's parents are still alive. Henry's father died in 2019 but his mother is still alive and living in Des Moines.

Henry and Wanda live in the proverbial State of Sunshine, a state that has adopted the Uniform Probate Code in its entirety, and has kept up with most of the updates to the UPC. To the extent any special statutes or common law rules are important for our exercises, we will discuss those in each Chapter.

As we go through the exercises in this book, you will be introduced to additional family members, and new facts and information will arise about Henry, Wanda, and the four children that will influence the drafting of some of Henry's and Wanda's estate documents. The facts in each chapter will build on the facts from prior chapters. We have included a variety of factual scenarios in the practice problems at the end of each Chapter. These facts do not follow through. These provide additional drafting opportunities but are not part of the estate plan you will be creating for Henry and Wanda.

# CHAPTER 1

# IDENTIFYING THE CLIENT AND THE NATURAL OBJECTS OF HER BOUNTY

While each attorney-client relationship has its own unique story, there are certain elements that are common in estate planning circumstances. At a first meeting with a client, the attorney may have only a limited understanding of the client's circumstances. This first meeting is intended to give the attorney some of the background necessary for developing a sound estate plan. An attorney will often have the client complete an intake form of some sort. A good intake form can give the attorney a lot of information before the parties ever meet. Useful information includes:

- Name, age, occupation, and health situation of the client
- Client's marital or relationship status
- Names and ages of any dependents, including special health or other circumstances
- Names and ages of other relatives who might be recipients of the client's property, including parents, siblings, nieces and nephews, and the like
- Organizations to which the client belongs or which might be likely recipients of charitable gifts
- Basic information concerning the client's assets and debts

There is always a potential downside to providing a client with a questionnaire before the first meeting—scaring a client away. If you ask your friends why they do not have a will, the answer almost always comes down to the same things—it's too much work, and it's scary. Few people think of the possibility of a world without them, or what will happen to their children in the event of their death. And, the work involved with identifying all of a person's assets can be an excuse for ignoring the need for a plan. If the task of planning appears too arduous, many will choose not to plan at all. Therefore, in the first meeting with a client, the best strategy may be to ask for somewhat general information, but to avoid overwhelming the client with demands to see every check stub or I.R.A. statement.

Generally speaking, your job is to determine what your client's goals are for the client's estate, and to determine if those goals are appropriate, given the client's financial and familial situation. A solidly middle class client may come to an attorney with a desire to minimize "death taxes" that he is unlikely to ever pay, but without a plan for dealing with an adult child who has a substance abuse problem. As the attorney, your job is to point out any misconceptions that your client has concerning any aspect of estate planning and administration, and bring up matters that your client hasn't thought about and that can be addressed in an estate plan.

We are not ready to focus on your client's assets or her likely estate plan in this first Chapter. Instead, we are going to work on ascertaining who your client is, including your client's family and friends. That is, we are going to do some in-depth digging to figure out who is likely to be the natural objects of the client's bounty from a client or clients who may not even know who those people are or whether they want to benefit any of them.

In your Trusts and Estates class you probably read the case of *Will of Moses*[1] in your study of undue influence. In that case, the decedent, Mrs. Fannie Moses was a 3-time widow with no children

---

[1] 337 So.2d 829 (Miss. 1969).

and a modest estate. Shortly after the death of her third husband, a young lawyer, 15 years her junior, began spending time with her. The trial court chancellor characterized the relationship as one of "dubious morality." It appears that the young lawyer, Clarence Holland, had begun doing legal work for Mrs. Moses and, over time, their relationship developed into one of friendship, and perhaps more. Mrs. Moses managed all of her property quite competently during her life and, when she decided to make a will and leave everything to Holland, she found her own estate lawyer who had no prior relationship with Holland. She drove herself to her meetings with the lawyer, explained the distribution of her estate that she wanted, reviewed numerous drafts of the will, and returned to the lawyer's office to execute the instrument. Her will gave most of her estate to Holland. When her will was probated after her death, an older sister successfully challenged it, alleging undue influence. The will was voided and the older sister took the majority of Mrs. Moses' estate under a prior will.

This case is usually discussed in the context of whether Clarence Holland had unduly influenced Mrs. Moses into executing a will that passed most of her estate to him. What is often overlooked is what her lawyer did wrong. Consider how easy it would have been for Mrs. Moses' lawyer to ask about her prior will, which left all to her sister, and include a sentence explaining why she was changing her plan. If her lawyer had indicated that she was disinheriting her sister who never visited to leave all to Holland, who had helped her manage her affairs since her husband's death, he might have avoided the will contest and his own ignominy.[2]

When a client comes to your office stating that she is childless and wants to leave everything to her unmarried companion, the lawyer's job is to explore the identity of all the people who might have standing to challenge that will and would be in a position to upset your client's estate plan. By not adequately considering prior will beneficiaries, or intestate takers, the lawyer who drafts a plan conforming to a client's wishes may be setting the client off with a ticking time bomb. Even though the client may shrug aside the likelihood of a will challenge by a disinherited child or remote relative, the lawyer must take that possibility very seriously. If you don't know who those people are, and discuss them with your client, you may very well find your estate documents being litigated and ending up in case books, which definitely would not be in your client's best interests.

In broadest terms, you want your client to provide you with information concerning the *who* (the family or other beneficiaries) and the *what* (the assets) of the estate plan. Once you have this information, you can focus on the *how*. Keep in mind, however, that simple answers may not give the entire picture. Consider for instance—

Attorney: Are you married, and do you have any children?

Client: Yes, I'm married, and I have 4 children.

On first glance, the answer seems very straightforward, and one is likely to assume that the children are the children of both the client and his or her spouse. But what if the spouse is incapacitated? What if one of the children is from a prior relationship and one is a foster child who was never formally adopted? Your client's *who* may not have changed, but your basic estate plan has.

One of the first issues that an estate planning attorney needs to address with clients is dual representation. It is not unusual for an attorney to represent both spouses or partners in creating estate plans. In fact, it can be very advantageous. Each party can maximize the tax planning aspects of estate planning, assets can be held separately to maximize the marital deduction, and charitable giving can be coordinated. Dual representation is always less costly than sole representation and the plans can be designed so that one spouse's assets cover certain obligations while the other

[2] See Deborah Gordon, Browne Lewis, and Carla Spivack, eds., Feminist Judgments: Rewritten Trusts and Estates Opinions, 39-64 (2020).

spouse's assets cover other obligations. This helps avoid over-providing for some and under-providing for others. It is imperative, however, that the clients understand that in order to do so, they must waive their rights to your sole loyalty. Any sign of disagreement over the estate plan may be a sign that the parties need separate representation. And unfortunately, it has happened that marriages crack when the parties disagree about the final distribution of their collective and individual assets.

Another fault line often arises around the appointment of a guardian for minor children. If both parents die simultaneously, they may have different expectations of who would best raise their children. If one parent dies first, he or she may have no problem with the surviving parent raising the children alone, but may have significant fears about a step-parent coming into the picture. Discussing the appointment of guardians for minor children may reveal conflicts of interest that will force you to stop the meeting and advise them to seek separate counsel.

For centuries, married women were not entitled to own their own separate property or make wills to dispose of any property they brought to a marriage. The husband was deemed to own all the wife's personal property outright during the marriage under the doctrine of coverture. The husband was also entitled to a life-estate in any real property the wife brought to the marriage and, following his death, it would pass to their children, or back to her collateral relatives if they had no lineal descendants. Only if the wife outlived her husband could she freely dispose of her estate, and only if the husband devised some property to her out of his estate would she have anything to give away.

The law of coverture was been substantially abolished, along with primogeniture (the right of the eldest son to take the entire estate), in the twentieth century. But vestiges still remain. Although the spouse is now deemed to be the principal heir in most states, the law permits spouses to limit a surviving spouse's share. You will learn all about the surviving spouse's mandatory elective share in your Trusts and Estates class, and we will cover the elective share later in this book. At this point, you need to be very aware that gender differences, cultural norms, and family expectations are likely to operate in ways that limit a wife's power over property often deemed by others to be morally, if not legally, her husband's. Thus, when wives have their own property or assert their right to control that property, or have opinions about the disposition of marital property the couple acquired during the marriage through their joint efforts, tensions may quickly escalate. You need to be sensitive to gender or class dynamics within your client's family without making stereotyped assumptions about who "owns" what, who "earned" what, and who is "entitled" to make a decision about its disposition.

Many clients will not be married precisely because they are uncomfortable with the legal constraints that marriage places on them and their power over property. Although marriage triggers certain rights and responsibilities, you need to be especially sensitive to the infinite ways in which people choose to structure their own intimate relationships. Many commentators criticized the outcome of the *Will of Moses* case, asserting that it promoted a sexist stereotype of gender relations. Had Fannie Moses been Fred Moses, and Clarence Holland been Clara Holland, and Fred had gone out of his way to draft an estate plan that would benefit his intimate younger partner, few imagine that the court would have voided Fred's plan on the grounds that young Clara had unduly influenced him to leave his estate to her. Norms of marital roles and earnings, expectations about the appropriateness of male authority over property, and stereotypes about male aggression and female passivity in relationships can all cloud our view of what is an appropriate distribution of a client's estate. And those views have changed very little, as a recent case in San Diego reveals.[3]

You will be practicing law during a period of profound social change, especially with the growth of non-traditional families. Over half of all children today are being raised in a non-traditional home,

---

[3] See http://m.utsandiego.com/news/2014/nov/28/charities-challenge-womans-estate/ (this is a virtually identical case to Will of Moses, only in this case an estranged husband was still living).

usually a blended family that involves divorce and/or step-parents. But a large percentage of same-sex couples are parenting children, and many children are being reared by single parents, grandparents, or other relatives. Single parent families make up the majority of children in poverty, which have their own very important estate planning needs. These non-traditional relationships are only growing as demographic patterns change. You will need to be comfortable with the choices your clients make in order to represent their interests appropriately. And you will need to be sensitive to their needs and the stereotypes within the legal system that may derail their plan so you can help them steer clear of likely problems.

### Exercise 1—Determining the Nature of the Representation

You were at a dinner party last summer with some of the partners and clients of your firm, as well as potential new clients. You met Henry and Wanda Higgins at that party, but you did not speak long with either of them. However, Wanda knows one of the partners in your firm quite well, and that partner recommended you when she asked the partner for advice about preparing their estate plan. They have no estate planning documents, although Henry had an old will executed back when his children Steve and Doris were small, in which he left everything to his first wife, Janet. Now that he is divorced, remarried, and has minor children again, he is in a hurry to get these things in order. Henry and Wanda called your office and set an appointment to speak with you about their current situation and future goals and to decide if they want to retain you to draft their estate plan.

For this exercise, we want you to make a decision after your initial client interview as to whether you can appropriately represent Henry and Wanda together, or whether you will need to recommend that they seek separate representation. To make that decision, you need to collect enough information about them and their wishes to understand whether a conflict exists. Only then can you flesh out the contours of your representation by preparing a retainer letter. We will prepare the retainer letter in the next exercise. For now, we want you to get to know your client(s). But first, you need to understand a few basic legal rules.

### The Law of Joint Representation

The ABA Model Rules of Professional Conduct (MRPC) recognize that conflicts of interest arise, and so they must be managed well in order for the conflict not to get in the way of ethical representation. Clients can waive their rights to undivided loyalty if they have appropriate information, and the parties can define the scope of their representation as they choose. As you can see, in most instances, disclosure to the client and obtaining the client's permission is enough to manage a typical conflict reasonably well. The Conflict of Interest provision of the Model Rules states:

**MRPC Rule 1.7 Conflict of Interest: Current Clients**

(a) Except as provided in paragraph (b), a lawyer shall not represent a client if the representation involves a concurrent conflict of interest. A concurrent conflict of interest exists if:

(1) the representation of one client will be directly adverse to another client; or

(2) there is a significant risk that the representation of one or more clients will be materially limited by the lawyer's responsibilities to another client, a former client or a third person or by a personal interest of the lawyer.

(b) Notwithstanding the existence of a concurrent conflict of interest under paragraph (a), a lawyer may represent a client if:

(1) the lawyer reasonably believes that the lawyer will be able to provide competent and diligent representation to each affected client;

(2) the representation is not prohibited by law;

(3) the representation does not involve the assertion of a claim by one client against another client represented by the lawyer in the same litigation or other proceeding before a tribunal; and

(4) each affected client gives informed consent, confirmed in writing.

The MRPC have also identified a number of specific instances that often give rise to conflicts, like having sexual relations with your client or investing in your client's business. The one most linked to the practice of trusts and estates is MRPC 1.8(c), involving gifts, especially testamentary gifts, to the lawyer. But other specific conflicts can easily arise in a trusts and estates practice, and you are likely to see them in your Trusts and Estates casebook. Consider how the specific rules of the MRPC 1.8 interact with the general rule just presented.

**MRPC Rule 1.8 Conflict of Interest: Current Clients: Specific Rules**

(a) A lawyer shall not enter into a business transaction with a client or knowingly acquire an ownership, possessory, security or other pecuniary interest adverse to a client unless:

(1) the transaction and terms on which the lawyer acquires the interest are fair and reasonable to the client and are fully disclosed and transmitted in writing in a manner that can be reasonably understood by the client;

(2) the client is advised in writing of the desirability of seeking and is given a reasonable opportunity to seek the advice of independent legal counsel on the transaction; and

(3) the client gives informed consent, in a writing signed by the client, to the essential terms of the transaction and the lawyer's role in the transaction, including whether the lawyer is representing the client in the transaction.

(b) A lawyer shall not use information relating to representation of a client to the disadvantage of the client unless the client gives informed consent, except as permitted or required by these Rules.

(c) A lawyer shall not solicit any substantial gift from a client, including a testamentary gift, or prepare on behalf of a client an instrument giving the lawyer or a person related to the lawyer any substantial gift unless the lawyer or other recipient of the gift is related to the client. For purposes of this paragraph, related persons include a spouse, child, grandchild, parent, grandparent or other relative or individual with whom the lawyer or the client maintains a close, familial relationship.

* * *

(h) A lawyer shall not:

(1) make an agreement prospectively limiting the lawyer's liability to a client for malpractice unless the client is independently represented in making the agreement; or

(2) settle a claim or potential claim for such liability with an unrepresented client or former client unless that person is advised in writing of the desirability of seeking and is given a reasonable opportunity to seek the advice of independent legal counsel in connection therewith.

* * *

Note how some of these activities listed in MRPC 1.8 are absolutely prohibited, and others are prohibited unless certain things happen, like the business relationship is fair or the client consents. Consider the ACTEC[4] Commentary on MRPC 1.7 involving multiple representation.

**ACTEC Commentary on MRPC 1.7**

**General Nonadversary Character of Estates and Trusts Practice; Representation of Multiple Clients.**

It is often appropriate for a lawyer to represent more than one member of the same family in connection with their estate plans, more than one beneficiary with common interests in an estate or trust administration matter, co-fiduciaries of an estate or trust, or more than one of the investors in a closely held business. See ACTEC Commentary on MRPC 1.6 (Confidentiality of Information). In some instances the clients may actually be better served by such a representation, which can result in more economical and better coordinated estate plans prepared by counsel who has a better overall understanding of all of the relevant family and property considerations. The fact that the estate planning goals of the clients are not entirely consistent does not necessarily preclude the lawyer from representing them: Advising related clients who have somewhat differing goals may be consistent with their interests and the lawyer's traditional role as the lawyer for the "family". Multiple representation is also generally appropriate because the interests of the clients in cooperation, including obtaining cost effective representation and achieving common objectives, often clearly predominate over their limited inconsistent interests. Recognition should be given to the fact that estate planning is fundamentally nonadversarial in nature and estate administration is usually nonadversarial.

Before you begin Exercise 1, be sure to read through and discuss among yourselves the limitations related to conflicts of interest so that you can solicit information from your clients if you begin to see a conflict arise. The goal of this exercise is to elicit the appropriate information to represent your client well and then to determine if you can represent Henry and Wanda together, or whether you need to advise them to seek separate counsel. The important rule of thumb regarding conflicts of interest is that they often arise, but most can be *managed*. Learning how to manage the conflict is one key to being a good lawyer.

In the following hypothetical, we have presented you with some facts that don't sit well with certain stereotypes, and do accord with others. As you go through this exercise, ask yourself what

[4] ACTEC is the American College of Trusts and Estates Counsel and is the leading professional organization for lawyers in this field. Because a typical trusts and estates practice raises many unique ethics issues, especially because the norm is for lawyers to represent the family, or a couple, ACTEC has produced a series of Commentaries on the Model Rules of Professional Conduct that are available online at: https://actecfoundation.org/trust-and-estate-professional-resources/professional-conduct-rules-for-trust-and-estate-practitioners/. You will want to have this website bookmarked for easy access during your practice.

assumptions you are making about Henry and Wanda's relationship and the appropriateness of their likely estate beneficiaries.

We would like for you to divide up into groups of four. Two of you will act as attorneys, meeting with your client(s) for the first time. The two attorneys should think of themselves as a single lawyer having an initial client interview. But two heads are better than one, and you two can collaborate on and discuss the matters of the meeting, and catch each other or help each other out as you try to extract as much relevant information from your clients as you can, without sending them running off to hide their heads in the sand. If, at the end of the initial meeting, you determine that you cannot represent both clients together, you will split up, and each will represent one party to the marriage.

The other two of you will act as Henry and Wanda, who have finally decided that they should get their financial house in order in case anything unexpected happens. In this exercise, you will receive from your professor some additional information (private facts) about Henry's and Wanda's relatives, circumstances, and relationships. This information is not meant to be withheld from your attorney, but rather is information similar to what many people have in their lives but about which they might not think to tell their attorney. You should not lie if your attorney asks you directly about some of these facts, but you might not want to offer it up immediately. The point of this exercise is to see how much information the lawyers get, and whether they anticipate potential problems or landmines that require further investigation.

Spend 30 or 40 minutes in a mock interview together. The lawyers should use the following client intake sheet to collect relevant information about Henry and Wanda and their family and friends. The lawyers should take notes, as those notes are going to be very important in drafting the client retainer letter. After the interview, the lawyers should decide, based on the law described above, whether they can jointly represent Henry and Wanda, or whether they need to insist on separate counsel. Henry and Wanda should also decide whether they think a single lawyer can still represent their interests after they have begun to realize that they may have some different intentions.

Regardless of their decision, the attorneys will need to draft an appropriate client retainer letter (Exercise 2), and the clients will need to review that letter to determine whether they are comfortable with the scope of the representation. For this exercise, we have provided the portion of a client intake sheet covering the clients' family, relatives, and friends (the natural objects of the client's bounty), as well as circumstances involving these people that may likely affect the future estate plan. We provide the second half of the client intake sheet in Chapter 2, for our exercises on identifying the client's property. At this point, therefore, don't worry about the *what* so much as the *who*.

## The Public Facts

Henry and Wanda come to their lawyer feeling very secure in their relationship and believing that their intentions for their estates are identical. On the phone with the attorney, they discussed the following:

- They wish for one another to be the primary beneficiary of each estate.
- They wish for their children to inherit following both of their deaths.
- They wish to have one or two additional family members receive small bequests.
- They would like for a family member to be named guardian of the minor children Benjamin and Gillian, if Wanda and Henry both die while one or both of the children are underage.

— They would like to use some portion of the estate to make charitable bequests.

In addition to this information, they will also present all of the biographical information listed in the introduction to this book.

While meeting with Henry and Wanda, the attorneys use the following intake sheet to make sure that they have the necessary information. This intake sheet, however, is incomplete. As you interview your clients, you will find that the answers to these basic questions may lead to additional questions. The additional questions will help you get the private facts that Henry and Wanda are holding back, understand the estate planning needs of Henry and Wanda, and determine if dual representation is appropriate. It also makes sense for you to open a file on Henry and Wanda where you will keep all of their confidential information, copies of their estate planning documents, your invaluable notes, and your time sheets. A good, thorough, organized file is critical in all law practices, but is especially important here where you might be called as a witness after your client has died to provide evidence about his or her intentions regarding the estate plan you created.

Lawyers today do a lot of work on their computers. Gone are the days of the manilla folder and top-hole punch. Think about how you will be keeping track of your time, but also how you will organize this information about your clients so you can easily find it when you need it.

As you go through this exercise, be sure to write out any supplemental questions and the answers you get from your clients.

| **Family Information** | **Henry** | **Wanda** |
|---|---|---|
| Names | | |
| Date of birth | | |
| Address<br>physical & electronic | | |
| Phone number | | |
| Occupation | | |
| Marital status | | |
| State of residence | | |
| Any prior marriage | | |
| Children—ages and birthdates | | |
| Names of proposed guardian | | |
| Names and addresses of living parents | | |
| Names and addresses of siblings | | |
| Identify children of siblings | | |
| Preferred charitable beneficiaries | | |
| If no parents, children, or siblings, what other relatives does the client have? | | |
| Any unrelated friends the client intends to benefit | | |
| Identify special circumstances of any potential beneficiaries (financial, physical, mental, incarcerated, etc.) | | |
| Names of proposed primary and alternate executor/personal representative/trustee | | |
| Future concerns—Is there anything you would like to address that we have not mentioned? | | |

After you have completed your role play, and the attorneys feel comfortable that they have adequate information to make a decision about dual representation, you might want to go out for a cup of coffee and discuss among yourselves what information you believe creates, or might create, a potential conflict of interest. A conflict doesn't necessarily exist just because Henry and Wanda have different desires for who will be the guardian of their children or who should be the executor of their estates. The conflict comes in if the parties are not able to work out their differences, especially if each client goes home secretly hoping he or she will outlive the other so the survivor can restructure the plan to suit his or her own wishes.

You will want to discuss the benefits of joint representation, from a smaller fee to an integrated plan that works together. You will also need to assess whether Henry and Wanda are going to be comfortable with joint representation. They do not have to have an integrated plan. The key to whether you can represent them both is whether they are comfortable with the fact that you cannot keep secrets from the other. If Henry is fine that Wanda has her own ideas about how to dispose of her property and Wanda is fine that Henry might be able to appoint his own guardian if she predeceases him, then joint representation is possible. Not only will separate representation be more costly, it is likely to engender more suspicion and distrust between your potential clients. Did you have that conversation with them?

Take notes about any conflicts you see, and the potential conflicts that might come up if you continue on with dual representation. With those notes in hand, turn to Exercise 2.

### Exercise 2—the Client Retainer Letter

In this exercise, you will put to work what you learned in Exercise 1. In order to properly manage conflicts, and especially in order to provide dual representation, you want to be very clear in your retainer letter who you represent and what you will be doing for each client.

Any retainer letter should be clear about at least four things: 1) explain who your client(s) is, 2) explain what documents you will prepare for them and what other services you will provide (like recording deeds, notifying accounts holders of beneficiary changes, etc.), 3) explain what you expect your client to do (provide appropriate information and documents promptly), and 4) explain how you will handle conflicts if they arise.

If you determined in exercise 1 that Wanda and Henry should have separate lawyers, then we want each of the lawyers to represent one client, and to separately prepare a client retainer letter. In this exercise, we have provided two sample retainer letters. The first letter is provided by ACTEC and envisions representation of both a husband and wife who have not waived their rights to confidentiality. ACTEC is an organization with tremendous reach and resources for assisting trusts and estates lawyers. ACTEC has a entire guide on engagement letters, available at: https://www.actec.org/assets/1/6/ACTEC_2017_Engagement_Letters.pdf?hssc=1 that you might want to bookmark. The second letter is one that envisions joint representation but can be easily modified to represent a single client. Of course, you will need to modify either one you choose carefully to reflect the unique character of your representation of Henry and/or Wanda.

As you prepare your retainer letter, decide how explicit you want to be about any possible conflicts or arrangements you will make in case the parties disagree. Did you think during your client interview to ask who would be paying your fees? Did you discuss the scope of your representation in terms of keeping confidential information from the other spouse? Feel free to go online and look up other client retainer letters. There are many on the web, and you should have no problems finding some that are much more detailed about the scope of the representation. Do you want a more detailed letter? If you decided to undertake dual representation, prepare the letter with your partner lawyer. As you do so, discuss whether you anticipate future conflicts arising that will be irreconcilable and what you will need to do if such a conflict does arise.

**ACTEC Client Retainer Letter**

[Date]

[Name(s) and Address(es)]

Subject: [Subject Matter of the Engagement]

Dear [Clients]:

You have each asked me to [scope of representation]. I have agreed to do this work and will bill for it on the following basis: [DESCRIBE ARRANGEMENTS PERTAINING TO FEES, BILLING, ETC.]. If I am asked to perform tasks not described in this letter, an additional engagement letter may be required for that work.

It is common for a husband and wife to employ the same lawyer to assist them in planning their estates. You have taken this approach by asking me to represent both of you to [scope of representation]. However, each of you wants to maintain your right to confidentiality and the ability to meet separately with me. I have agreed to do this work on this basis and will bill for it on the following basis: [DESCRIBE ARRANGEMENTS PERTAINING TO FEES, BILLING, AND WHICH OF THE PARTIES, IF NOT BOTH, WILL BE RESPONSIBLE FOR PAYMENT.]. If I am asked to perform tasks not described in this letter, an additional engagement letter may be required.

I will represent each of you separately and will not discuss with either one of you what your spouse has disclosed to me. Each of you releases me from the obligation to reveal to you any information I may have received from the other that is material and adverse to your interest. Furthermore, I will not use any information I obtain from one of you in preparing the other's plan, even if the result is that the two plans are incompatible or one plan is detrimental to the interests of the other spouse. In short, the representation will be structured so that each of you will have the same relationship with me as if each of you had gone to a separate lawyer for assistance in your planning.

While I have agreed to undertake this representation on a separate and confidential basis, you should be aware that there might be disputes between you now or in the future as to your respective property rights and interests, or as to other issues that may arise between you. Should this occur, I would not be able to represent either of you in resolving any such dispute, and each of you would have to obtain your own representation. After considering the foregoing, if each of you consents to my representation of each of you separately, I request that each of you sign and return the enclosed copy of this letter. If you have any questions about anything discussed in this letter, please let me know. In addition, you should feel free to consult with another lawyer about the effect of signing this letter.

Sincerely,

[Lawyer]

CONSENT

We have read the foregoing letter and understand its contents. We consent to having you represent each of us on the terms and conditions set forth.

Signed: ____________________, 20___

________________________________________ (Client 1)

Signed: ____________________, 20___

________________________________________ (Client 2)

Here is the second sample retainer letter designed expressly for a husband and wife.

**Re: Estates and Trusts Representation by [Lawyer Name]**[5]

Dear __ and __ [NAME]:

[5] Reproduced with permission of Professor Lee-Ford Tritt.

Thank you very much for you recent phone call. I am indebted to [Name] for referring you to me and am honored that you have asked me to work on your family's estate planning matters. I believe that I can only be effective, though, if I have your full confidence. Therefore, I seek to make the basis for my legal fees perfectly clear at the outset of our relationship. Accordingly, please review this fee proposal and sign the agreement if it meets with your approval.

**Nature of Representation**

This letter confirms that I will draft Wills, Trusts [state] Health Care Proxies, [state] Living Wills and [state] Durable Powers of Attorney for both of you. I look forward to assisting you in these matters. Please understand that my representation will be limited to the above-mentioned matters. Of course, I would be delighted to assist you with other estates and trusts related matters as well, if the need arises. Attending to any additional matters, however, may require a separate fee agreement.

**Fees and Costs**

Generally, my fees for legal services are based on the time spent working on a particular matter. Time is recorded and charged based on 1/10th hour increments. Presently, my hourly rate is $[RATE]. In addition to fees for legal services rendered, I will bill for reasonable disbursements incurred from time to time including postage costs, photocopying charges, telephone tolls, the costs of using computerized legal research services, court filing fees, messenger delivery fees, transportation charges and other reasonable and necessary out-of-pocket expenses, in accordance with customary practices. I will bill you quarterly, or, if you wish, more frequently as our work progresses. Payment of invoices is due within **10** (ten) days of receipt. Of course, if you have any questions about any invoice, please do not hesitate to let me know. Upon request, I will be happy to provide additional information.

**Retainer**

As I have mentioned, before rendering any services in this matter I require a retainer in the amount of $_____ (________ Thousand Dollars). I will keep this retainer as a positive balance and as a credit against the final bill for costs and fees in this matter. In the event that payment of your invoice is not received on the due date and a written inquiry regarding your invoice has not been received, all or part of the retainer may be applied toward payment of your invoice. Should this become necessary, you will need to provide our office with sufficient funds to replenish the retainer and bring its balance back to $_________. Any amount of the retainer remaining after crediting the same toward the final bill will be promptly reimbursed to you. Please enclose your retainer when you return this executed letter.

**Additional Terms**

In addition, although it is customary for spouses to employ the same trusts and estates lawyer to assist them in their estate planning, the Rules of Professional Conduct limit my ability to represent multiple clients in certain situations. For instance, I may not represent multiple clients who have conflicting interests. The converse, however, is that I may represent multiple clients who do not have conflicting interests. I must, however, advise you of any reasonably foreseeable adverse effects that may arise in my representation of both of you. In addition, I must obtain the consent of both of you to such representation.

Because you do not seem to have conflicting interests at this time, I may represent you subject to your consent. Please be aware, however, of the following adverse effects from my joint representation of you:

1. Since I will be representing both of you, each of you will be my client. As a result, matters that one of you might discuss with me might not be protected by the attorney/client privilege from disclosure to the other of you. Therefore, for clarity's sake, I will not agree with either of you to withhold information from the other. Of course, anything either of you discuss with me is privileged from disclosure to third parties.

2. If the two of you have a difference of opinion concerning your proposed estate planning activities, I will thoroughly point out and explain the pros and cons of such differing opinions. I will not, however, advocate one of your positions over the other.

3. Although I doubt that it will happen, if conflicts do arise between the two of you of such nature that it is impossible in my judgment to perform my obligations to each of you in accordance with this

letter, it would become necessary for me to withdraw as your joint attorney and to advise one or both of you to obtain independent counsel.

If this letter satisfactorily sets forth the understanding of my joint representation of both of you, I would appreciate each of you signing this letter and returning it to me along with the retainer check.

I sincerely appreciate the opportunity to represent you and I look forward to a pleasant and successful relationship.

With best regards.

Very truly yours,

__________________

Lawyer Name

Agreed to and accepted by:

________________________ Dated: ______________, 20__

[Name #1]

________________________ Dated: ______________, 20__

[Name #2]

Once you have prepared your client retainer letter(s), give it to Henry and Wanda and ask them to sign it. Although in real practice you are most likely going to mail the retainer letter to your clients, and will look for a signed copy back by return mail, complete with a check, for this exercise we want you to meet with your clients to go over the terms, especially if perhaps you didn't get all of the information you now realize you needed. Sit down for 20 minutes and discuss the various provisions (in groups of 2 if you are doing single representation and a group of 4 if you settled on dual representation). Explain to your client what the various provisions mean and, especially, why you settled on either single or joint representation. Give them some idea of what kinds of conflicts may cause you to have to alter your representation in the future so that they can get out now if they anticipate they might arise.

Henry and Wanda: now that you have read your private facts and you know some of the differences in your expectations, read through this letter and decide if you are comfortable with a single lawyer representing both of you, or whether you prefer two lawyers. If they are suggesting two lawyers, do you think the separate representation is appropriate? Remember, you are the clients, and you are the ones paying for legal representation to provide you with your estate plan. Do you like the way things are going?

### Exercise 3—Keeping Track of Your Time

You will want to keep very good notes of all of your interactions with your client, as well as the work you do on their behalf. If they lose their wills in a tornado or hurricane, you may be called upon to give testimony as to their intentions and desires for the succession of their property. Although you are likely to have a clear copy of their wills in your computer, you also want to have good notes about why they chose to leave nothing to Steve or why they put cousin Susan's property in a trust. Taking good notes will also be invaluable when you are drafting the various documents, as it can be quite embarrassing to have to call up your client because you forgot whether they finally agreed on Doris or Susan as guardian. Take your notes in a separate document, either electronically or on paper, and keep the pages well organized in a file folder. Then, keep track of all the time you spend on their case on the following time sheets. Come back to these time sheets every time you read through their documents, research the law in a particular area relevant to their situation, or spend time drafting or executing any of the instruments in the book. At the end of the semester you will be asked to tally up your time and compare the time spent with what you discussed with your client should be a reasonable fee. How much did you earn per hour? Assuming that a modest estate plan, without a trust, would normally be in the range of $2,000–$3,000 and one with a trust would be in the range of $5,000–$10,000 depending on how much retitling you have to do, are you likely to be over-paid or under-paid?

| Date | Activity | Time Expended |
|---|---|---|
| | | |
| | | |
| | | |
| | | |
| | | |
| | | |
| | | |
| | | |
| | | |
| | | |
| | | |
| | | |
| | | |
| | | |
| | | |
| | | |
| | | |
| | | |
| | | |
| | | |
| | | |
| | | |
| | | |
| | | |
| | | |
| | | |
| | | |

| Date | Activity | Time Expended |
|---|---|---|
| | | |
| | | |
| | | |
| | | |
| | | |
| | | |
| | | |
| | | |
| | | |
| | | |
| | | |
| | | |
| | | |
| | | |
| | | |
| | | |
| | | |
| | | |
| | | |
| | | |
| | | |
| | | |
| | | |
| | | |
| | | |
| | | |
| | | |

| Date | Activity | Time Expended |
|---|---|---|
| | | |
| | | |
| | | |
| | | |
| | | |
| | | |
| | | |
| | | |
| | | |
| | | |
| | | |
| | | |
| | | |
| | | |
| | | |
| | | |
| | | |
| | | |
| | | |
| | | |
| | | |
| | | |
| | | |
| | | |
| | | |

## Lessons Learned

We hope that these exercises made you think a lot more about your likely expectations regarding Henry's and Wanda's relationship, and their likely estate plan. Do you feel comfortable that they know, and you know, who they want to have receive their property at their deaths? Do you feel confident that you understand the big ticket items, like guardianship, the primary beneficiaries of the estates, or the size of non-family bequests? Do you know who might be likely to challenge their estate plan or will be disgruntled enough to cause problems during probate? Are Henry and Wanda on the same page?

### *PRACTICE PROBLEMS*

Did you think to ask Henry what his obligations were to Janet, his ex-wife? Assuming he said something like "oh—I send her some money now and then and I'm supposed to provide for Steve and Doris at my death," how would your plan change if he sent you a copy of the divorce decree and you found the following stipulations? (These are just hypothetical problems and should not be carried forward into later chapters.)

1. Henry is required to provide *appropriate* support for Janet's health, maintenance, support and welfare, if Janet is unemployed or disabled at any time prior to Janet's death.
2. Henry is required to leave one-third of his probate estate to Janet if, at Henry's death, Janet has not remarried.
3. Henry is required to execute a will that leaves a minimum of one-half of his estate to Steve and Doris if they are minor children at the time of his death, or one-third of his estate to Steve and Doris if they are not minors at the time of his death.
4. Henry is required to appoint Janet the legal guardian of Steve and Doris if he dies while they are minors and Janet is still alive. He is also required to nominate Janet's sister Beverly their guardian if they are minors and Janet has predeceased him.
5. Henry is required to maintain a life insurance policy on his life, naming Janet the beneficiary.

---

It goes without saying that an estate planning lawyer cannot adequately represent a divorced client without seeing the divorce decree. And you would be surprised how many divorce lawyers include elements of property succession in the divorce agreement without having a clue how property can and should be managed under these circumstances. At the time of the divorce, Janet's lawyer just wanted to make sure that Henry would adequately provide for Janet and their children. And Henry's lawyer probably wasn't thinking about Henry remarrying and having a second family.

As you go on to Chapter 2, where we will collect information on Henry's and Wanda's property, be thinking about their prior obligations and whether that property is already committed to pass in a particular way. Be sure to ask to see the property settlement agreement. What clients think or say is very often vague at best and often completely wrong.

# CHAPTER 2

# IDENTIFYING THE CLIENT'S PROPERTY

Now that you know something about your clients and their likely beneficiaries, you will need to determine what property is available, or is likely to be available, for distribution to those beneficiaries. Some of Henry's and Wanda's property may be titled in such a way as to pass automatically at death. Other property may be available and best distributed via a will or put into a trust before or after they die. And other property may have designated beneficiaries who are identified through documents provided with insurance or securities companies, and not through a typical will (will substitutes).

This Chapter will introduce you to the documents that show how different property is held, and will help you to determine what property can be distributed at death. Before you can even begin to plan an estate, you will need to know what property there is and see if there are any limitations on its alienability. We also will assume that you are working through this book simultaneously as you take a regular course in Trusts and Estates, or have already taken it. That means you might not have a firm grasp on powers of appointment or the different kinds of trusts that are possible, but you already know a lot about wills and will substitutes. At this point, therefore, we are going to focus primarily on typical kinds of property and the various ways in which it can be held. These should all be familiar to you from your first year Property class. But if it isn't, we provide a brief summary of the different ways of holding property here. If you need more information, read ahead in your Trusts and Estates casebook, or in a Trusts and Estates treatise.

## The Law of Property (Revisited)

As you should remember from your first year Property course, property can be held in many different ways: it can be held in a fee simple absolute, a defeasible fee simple, a life estate, a term of years, as joint tenants, tenants in common, tenants by the entirety, and tenants by the community. One could also have only a future interest in the property, like a reversion, a remainder, or a power to appoint the property. One might hold it as a trustee on behalf of a beneficiary, or one might be the beneficial title holder, while a trustee holds legal title to the property. We'll go over the basic categories of present estates and concurrent ownership interests here, leaving trusts and powers to a later chapter.

### *a. Present Estates and Future Interests*[1]

#### *i. Fee Simple Absolute*

The most common and most alienable way to hold property is to hold it in fee simple absolute (typical for ownership of land, the family car, personal property, and the like). Property conveyed in fee simple absolute will be granted with language like, *O grants Blackacre to A and his heirs forever.* Although modern statutes dispense with the *and his heirs* language, most modern deeds either will use the *and his heirs* term, or will state that the land is being held in fee simple absolute. Personal property that you purchase from a store, like your stereo, sofa, and iPad, will be held completely and absolutely, even if you still owe payments on your credit card used to purchase the property. The only time you might need to think about any lesser interest with regard to personal property might be if the property was purchased with a bank loan (like a car, boat, or RV in which case the

[1] For a thorough discussion of present estates and future interests, see Danaya C. Wright, THE LAW OF ESTATES AND FUTURE INTERESTS: CASES, EXERCISES, AND EXPLANATIONS, Foundation Press, 2015.

bank usually retains the title documents until you've paid off the loan) or if the property was given to you in a will from a relative and you were only given a life interest, or some other lesser interest in the property.

### *ii. Defeasible Fee Simple*

Land and personal property also can be held in some form of a defeasible fee simple. A fee simple determinable is a fee interest in property, but it is limited in some way. If the triggering event occurs, the possession and ownership of the property will revert automatically back to the original grantor of the property who retained a possibility of reverter. A fee simple determinable is usually conveyed using language like: *O grants Blackacre to A for residential purposes only, and if A or his heirs ever use Blackacre for non-residential purposes, the land reverts back to me or my heirs.* A fee simple determinable is freely alienable, devisable, and descendible so long as doing so does not trigger the limitation. The possibility of reverter is also freely alienable, devisable, and descendible in most states. Thus, if your client's grandparent transferred land subject to a limitation, and retained a possibility of reverter, your client may own that possibility of reverter and not even know it. So you might want to ask your clients about family property that may have transferred subject to a future interest.[2]

Land and personal property also can be held in a fee simple subject to a condition subsequent or a fee simple subject to an executory limitation. Both of these are fully inheritable and alienable fee interests, but they are subject to either a condition subsequent which has a power of termination in the grantor, or an executory limitation which cuts short the possessory fee and causes it to transfer automatically to a third person if the condition is triggered. A fee simple subject to a condition subsequent is transferred with language like: *O grants Blackacre to A so long as used for residential purposes, but if A or his heirs or successors fail to use Blackacre for residential purposes, then I or my heirs or successors have a power to terminate (or a right of re-entry) to reclaim possession.* A fee simple subject to an executory limitation is conveyed with language like: *O grants Blackacre to A so long as used for residential purposes, but if A or her heirs or successors fail to use Blackacre for residential purposes, then it shall pass to the City of Sunshine.*

### *iii. Life Estates*

Land and personal property can also be held in a life estate, although it's generally a bad idea to create legal life estates in real property. But many people may hold life interests in trusts, which usually entitle them to the income off the trust property for life, or the right to live on the land or use the property for life. A life interest does not include the right to devise the property by will, however. For once the life tenant dies, the property passes to the remaindermen, or the reversioner, who will then have the right to receive the income or use the property. A life estate can easily be created in personal property, like paintings, although gift letters or documentation are usually needed to confirm the grantor's intentions about creating a life interest.[3] A typical life estate is created with language like: *O conveys Blackacre to A for life, and upon A's death to B and his heirs.* More likely, however, the life estate will be created with language like: *O conveys Blackacre to T as*

---

[2] This might seem like an unusual thing to keep in mind, but remember *Evans v. Abney*, 396 U.S. 435 (1970) from Property (or T&E). In that case, a gift of land to the City of Macon, Georgia, for a whites-only park reverted when the discriminatory condition could no longer be upheld. Senator Bacon's living heirs acquired title to a priceless city park as a result of the Senator's reversion.

[3] The famous case of *Gruen v. Gruen*, 496 N.E.2d 869 (N.Y. 1986), involved a father who gave to his son a valuable painting upon the son's graduation from college. The father sent his son a letter stating that he was giving him the painting, but he (the father) wanted to retain possession of it until his death. But the letter clearly indicated that the son was to have full ownership of the painting when his father died. The court held that the father had given his son an absolutely vested remainder in the painting, and that the father had retained a life estate. Even though the painting was personal property, and there was no deed recorded down at the courthouse, the gift letter served as evidence of the father's intent when he made the gift. The property rights thus attached based on the intent of the donor, and upon his giving up suitable possession to the grantee (in the form of the gift letter since giving up actual possession conflicted with his retention of a life estate).

*trustee to hold Blackacre for the benefit of A for life, and upon A's death to convey Blackacre to B.* If O is giving personal property to A for life, she might use language like: *I give to my wonderful daughter, A, my Picasso for her life, but at her death, the painting shall pass to the Metropolitan Museum of Art.*

In all of these instances, A has a life interest that will terminate upon A's death. Thus, if A is your client, she may not control where the property goes upon her death if she only holds a life interest. Such property will pass according to O's will, or the deed in which O conveyed the property, or according to the *inter vivos* gift to A and the Metropolitan Museum of Art.

*iv. Term of Years*

A grantor may also convey a term of years, which is the right to possession of the property, either real or personal, for a set period of time. A term of years is often created in trusts, where a beneficiary gets the income off the trust until the beneficiary reaches a certain age, and then the beneficiary may be entitled to the trust corpus. Such an interest would be created with language like: *O gives the rest of my estate to T, as trustee, to give the income off the trust corpus monthly to my daughter D and my son S until each reaches 35 years of age, and to distribute half of the corpus to each child when each reaches 35.* Or, an owner of real property may transfer a term of years to a grantee, and retain a reversion upon the termination of the present estate. Such a term of years would be conveyed using language like: *O conveys Blackacre to A for 25 years, at which time Blackacre shall return to me or my heirs.* Like the legal life estate, terms of years in real property are rarely created.[4]

Although there are plenty of differences between vested and contingent remainders, shifting and springing executory interests, and reversions and remainders, for our purpose here you need to focus on what interests your client might have in certain property and, if it is not held in fee simple absolute, whether your client has an inheritable estate. Life estates are not inheritable, but most future interests are, as are all fee interests and terms of years (to the extent the grantee predeceases the term). This means they have property that you need to consider in planning their estates.

### *b. Concurrent Estates*

Concurrent estates are interests in real or personal property owned by two or more individuals at the same time—i.e., they share ownership between themselves. The common concurrent estates are:

- The joint tenancy with right of survivorship
- The tenancy in common
- The tenancy by the entirety
- The tenancy by the community.

Not all states recognize all of these concurrent estates, especially the tenancy by the entirety and the tenancy by the community. Both of these latter two estates are held only by married couples and the tenancy by the community is available only in the nine community property states.[5]

---

[4] Although many property professors and treatises treat the term of years like a leasehold, the modern day leasehold is so different from the old common law term of years that, for our purposes, it is better to think of the term of years as similar to the life estate, only it terminates after a predetermined period of time rather than at the grantee's death. In both cases, the interest will definitely terminate and possession and ownership will transfer back to the grantor in the case of a reversion, or to a third party in the case of a remainder. For a more thorough discussion of the term of years, see Danaya C. Wright, THE LAW OF ESTATES AND FUTURE INTERESTS, Foundation Press, 2015 at 176–178.

[5] Those states are: Arizona, California, Idaho, Louisiana, Nevada, New Mexico, Texas, Washington, and Wisconsin. Alaska allows married couples the option to hold marital property as community property but it is not the default rule.

The most important tenancies for estate planning purposes are the joint tenancy with right of survivorship and the tenancy by the entirety (where recognized) because they allow the survivor to take the entirety of the property immediately upon the death of the co-tenant, without requiring any probate of the property or any subsequent conveyance. The tenancy by the entirety has the added benefit of creditor protections in certain states which prevent the property from being seized by creditors of the decedent.[6] But it is limited to married couples, thus excluding its use for inter-generational transfers. With any tenancy with a right of survivorship, however, a co-tenant may not devise property held in a joint tenancy by will unless she is the survivor and owns it individually. The four estates have the following characteristics:

- The *Joint Tenancy with Right of Survivorship* is owned by two or more co-tenants, each having equal shares that were created by the same instrument and at the same time. These are called the four unities of time, title, interest, and possession. Upon the death of each co-tenant, the remaining tenants' shares increase proportionately. The joint tenancy can be destroyed by any co-tenant transferring his or her share to a stranger during the tenant's life, which converts that tenant's interest into a tenancy in common, but it does not affect the shares of the other co-tenants vis-à-vis each other. A joint tenancy with right of survivorship cannot be destroyed by a testamentary transfer.
- The *Tenancy in Common* is owned by two or more co-tenants, they may have unequal shares, and each has an inheritable interest that passes to his or her heirs or devisees upon death. The tenancy in common can be freely alienated without the consent of the co-tenants and does not require the four unities. Tenants in common have co-equal rights to possession. If your client owns a one-half interest in a family business as a tenancy in common, she can freely devise her half at her death; not so if it is held as a joint tenancy.
- The *Tenancy by the Entirety* is owned only by a married couple in a form that closely resembles the joint tenancy with right of survivorship. The marital unit is deemed to own the tenancy and, upon the death of the first spouse to die, the survivor takes full individual ownership. The tenancy by the entirety cannot be easily destroyed. It can be converted to a tenancy in common or a joint tenancy by mutual agreement and transfer by both spouses, or it will be converted to a tenancy in common upon divorce. But unlike the joint tenancy, which can be destroyed by the unilateral action of one co-tenant, the tenancy by the entirety cannot be destroyed by the unilateral action of one spouse, except by divorce.
- The *Tenancy by the Community* is a form of holding property in community property states in which each spouse is deemed to hold an undivided one-half share of most property acquired or earned by either spouse during the marriage. Upon divorce, community property is converted into a tenancy in common, and upon the death of the first spouse, that spouse's share is freely devisable and descendible. Some states permit married couples to hold community property with a *right of survivorship* which would result in the surviving spouse taking the decedent spouse's half at death. But most community property states provide that each spouse may freely devise his or her community property, just as a tenant in common may do.

It is very likely that any client you have will hold some property in some form of a concurrent tenancy. The client may have inherited the family home with his or her siblings in a tenancy in common. The client may have bank accounts or the marital home held in a joint tenancy with right of survivorship or a tenancy by the entirety. The client may have moved from a community property

[6] See *Sawada v. Endo*, 561 P.2d 1291 (HI. 1977).

state to a common law state, or vice versa, and personal property that moves from one state to another does not necessarily lose its identity just because it has been taken from one jurisdiction to another. Some common law states have statutes that treat community property coming into the state as quasi-community property, with many of the characteristics that would govern community property. Most community property states, however, do not have provisions to treat property earned by spouses in common law states as community property, although all new property acquired by the couple in a community property state will be deemed community property.[7]

### c. *Joint Bank Accounts*

Many clients will have joint bank accounts, usually either as a joint tenancy with right of survivorship or as a tenancy by the entirety. But they may also have added a second person's name to their checking accounts to assist them with paying bills, without any intention that that person would have any ownership interest in the funds in the account. Similarly, many people may add a child's name to an account with the idea that the child will take the funds upon the primary account holder's death, but have no control over the funds while the primary account holder is alive. Property interests in bank accounts can be quite complicated to determine, and they are usually based on the intentions of the person who contributed the funds. Thus, if a husband and wife each put equal amounts into the household checking account that is held as a joint tenancy, each will be deemed to own half. But if dad puts his son's name on his account, which dad fully funded, then it will depend on whether dad's intent was that the son receive a gift of half the value of the account at the time son's name was added, or whether dad's intent was to make only a testamentary gift to his son if the son survived him. The three primary bank account interests are:

- *True Joint Tenancy Account*—this account is established with the intention of giving each co-tenant an immediate right to an equal share of the funds in the account during life, and a survivorship right to the funds in the account for the surviving co-tenant. A tenancy by the entirety account will function in the same way, giving each co-tenant a right to the property during life, and sole ownership at the death of the first spouse.
- *Agency Account*—this account is established by a single account holder who adds someone's name to the account in order to permit that person to act as an agent for the primary account holder. Caretakers, persons with powers of attorney, and family members are often added to bank accounts to assist with paying the bills. Although the agent has the power to withdraw funds, they are to be used for the benefit of the primary account holder and the agent receives no right to withdraw funds at any time for his or her own benefit. At death, the funds in the agency account belong to the primary account holder's executor and not the agent.
- *Payable on Death Account*—this account, also called a *Totten Trust,* is established by a primary account holder who wants to give whatever funds remain in the account at her death to her co-tenant, but does not want to give that co-tenant any control over the account during her life. POD accounts function like other beneficiary accounts. Until the primary account holder dies, she can change the beneficiary designation and she has full and complete control over the funds in the account. But upon her death, the account will transfer to the designated co-tenant/beneficiary automatically and is not a part of the decedent's estate.

These various ways of holding bank accounts are not always clearly identified by the bank's documents and you may be required to investigate who contributed the funds to the account, and what the intentions were of the primary account holder when a second or third name was added to

[7] See Danaya C. Wright, Michael J. Higdon, Bridget C. Crawford, WILLS, TRUSTS, AND ESTATES: AN INTEGRATED APPROACH, 2021 at 105–110.

an account. You will learn about these different types of accounts in your regular Trusts and Estates class, but for now you need to understand how the co-tenant's rights vary based on the different types of account.

Thus, if Henry and Wanda have a joint checking account for paying bills, it will most likely be in a form that includes a right of survivorship. But if Henry's name is on his mother's bank account as her agent, he will not have any interest in those funds and his estate plan will not need to include that account. However, if Henry's name is on his mother's bank account as a beneficiary, then, although he may not have any immediate property rights to the funds in the account now, it may be likely that he will inherit that account someday, most likely before his own death. If the account only has a few hundred dollars in it, it's not a big deal. But if his mother's bank account happens to hold $4 million, you will need to be thinking about how to dispose of that property if Henry's mother predeceases him and he doesn't have the time or the inclination to spend it all before he dies.

With this short summary of the basic ways in which individuals can hold property, let's go on to our first exercise: reviewing the clients' property.

### Exercise 1—Ascertaining the Client's Estate

In Chapter One, Henry and Wanda answered questions about who they are and indicated some of the likely beneficiaries of their estates. In this chapter, we look at what they have to pass to their beneficiaries. Most estate planners will provide the client with a questionnaire to determine the extent of the clients' property, or they will ask their clients to come to a client meeting with a list of all their property.

For this exercise, once again, break into groups of four (or two, depending on the outcome of the exercises in Chapter One) to continue the client representation of Henry and Wanda. Assuming that Henry and Wanda have decided to retain your services, you will need them to provide to you information regarding their property. Henry and Wanda will work with you to fill out the Asset Questionnaire, and they will bring some papers to your office as well. As you discuss the property during your client meeting, fill in the asset review form as best you can. And as you discuss the property, also discuss with your clients who they would like to have receive this property at their respective deaths.

The students who are playing Henry and Wanda will receive from their professor a list of additional property in which they have some type of property interest that you will need to ascertain (the Private Facts) and some additional documents that are not reproduced here in the book. As you go through the property with your clients, try to ascertain if there is any property they wish to pass to certain designated beneficiaries.

### The Public Facts

- Henry and Wanda "own" a home in Lovelyville, Sunshine (see copy of warranty deed below), valued at approximately $500,000, and subject to a mortgage of $300,000. For purposes of the property calculations in this and the next Chapter, you can use just the amount of equity they have in the home, which is $200,000.
- Henry owns a 401(k) plan retirement account through his employer, which he contributes to on a monthly basis, and which is currently worth $1,225,000. Wanda is the primary beneficiary, and the 4 children are the secondary beneficiaries.
- Henry and Wanda each have joint checking and savings accounts which they individually funded, and they treat as their own, but they have the other's name on them for convenience' sake and with the expectation that the survivor would own both upon the death of the first spouse. They are held as joint tenants with rights of

survivorship. Henry's checking account has $10,000 in it and his savings account has $30,000. Wanda's checking account has $4,000 in it and her savings account has $40,000.

- Wanda has an investment account with her father, Alfred Doolittle, through which they own stock currently valued at $375,000. They hold it as a joint tenancy with right of survivorship. Wanda and her father have each contributed equal amounts to the account.
- Henry drives a car worth $10,000; Wanda drives a car worth $15,000.
- Henry, through his current employer, has a $500,000 life insurance policy on his own life, of which the four children are the primary beneficiaries.
- Wanda is likely to inherit a substantial amount from her father at his death. She also has inherited a substantial amount of jewelry and silver from various family members, but she is not fully aware of their value.
- Wanda's father has executed a beneficiary deed for his vacation cabin in Montana which, if not revoked, will result in Wanda taking the property at her father's death. It is currently worth $700,000. See TOD beneficiary deed below.
- Henry and Wanda have household furniture, artwork, and other furnishings worth $150,000. They would hold these as joint tenants with rights of survivorship.
- Henry's mother has told him that she put his name on her "accounts," but he does not know what type of interest he has, and his siblings have told him that "he's getting everything because mom always liked him the best."

Now meet with your clients and fill out the asset questionnaire, being careful to identify the value of the property and the true ownership. Use additional paper if necessary, and be sure to take very good notes. As you go through this exercise, be sensitive to your clients' body language and whether they are comfortable letting each other know about their assets. One of the principal points of contention between spouses arises when one spouse thinks of the property as "ours," and the other thinks of it as "mine." If both think of it as ours, or both think of it as mine, you are less likely to be walking into a conflict situation. But if they have very different understandings about decision-making regarding assets, you may have to move to separate representation.

---

### Sample Asset Questionnaire

**Henry and Wanda**

1. Personal residence:

    Address:

    Description (e.g., single family, condo, or co-op, similar description):

    Do you own or lease?

    If you own, how you hold title:

    Fair Market Value:

    Mortgage balance:

2. Other residences, vacation homes, or additional real estate (add additional pages if necessary):

    Address:

Description:

How you hold title:

Fair Market Value:

Mortgage balance:

3. Personal and household effects:

State your best estimate of the value of each kind of property and how you hold title.

Automobiles:

General personal and household effects such as furniture, furnishings, books, and pictures of no special value:

Valuable personal and household effects such as jewelry, artwork, collections (indicate if insured):

Other personal property, including clothes, tools, personal electronics, etc.:

4. Cash, cash deposits, and cash equivalents:

(a) Checking accounts, including money market accounts (indicate value in each):

You:

Spouse:

Jointly with:

(b) Ordinary savings accounts:

You:

Spouse:

Jointly with:

(c) Certificates of deposit or Money Market Accounts:

You:

Spouse:

Jointly with:

5. Pension & profit-sharing plans, IRAs, 401(k), 403(b), ESOPs or other tax-favored employee-benefit plans:

(a) Defined benefit or Defined contribution plans.

You: Current value: ____________

Spouse: Current value: ____________

(b) Individual Retirement Accounts (IRAs).

You: Current value ______________

Spouse: Current value ______________

(c) Other types of employee benefit plans.

6. Life Insurance on your life and your spouse's life:

Who owns it?

What is the value?

Who are the beneficiaries?

7. Investment assets. Includes: Publicly traded stocks and corporate bonds, municipal bonds, U.S. Treasury Notes and Bonds, Limited partnership interests, college savings plans, and other investments, including mutual fund accounts.

   How are they held?

   Who is the owner?

   What is the value?

8. Other interests of current or future value:

   (a) *Interests in trusts.* Describe any trusts created by you or any other person, in which you or a member of your immediate family has a right to receive distributions of income or principal, whether or not such distributions are actually being received or anticipated in the future. If possible, submit a copy of the trust agreement. State the approximate current value of the trust and the annual income from it.

   (b) *Anticipated inheritances.* If you or any other members of your immediate family are likely to receive substantial inheritances in the foreseeable future from persons other than yourself or your spouse, describe your best estimate of the value and the nature of each inheritance.

   (c) *Business Assets.* Describe any interests you hold in any businesses, farms, or non-work related entities, including the real and personal property assets of the entity, and your proportionate share.

9. Liabilities:

   Describe here substantial financial liabilities not reflected in the asset information you have provided above. Indicate whether you have insured against any of these obligations in the event of your death, or if the obligations do not survive your death.

---

After you have successfully filled out the Asset Questionnaire, and think you have a pretty good grasp of Henry's and Wanda's estates, look at the documents, reproduced below, that they have brought to your office for this meeting. Do any of these documents call into question the information Henry and Wanda provided to you about their assets? If so, can you ask about them without potentially breaching any duty of confidentiality?

You should also ask to look at any other documents they may have brought which came from the private facts you have discovered. As lawyers, you should have a good sense of what certain legal language means in these various documents and can therefore assess whether changes should be made to how they are titled. One of the most important services estate-planning lawyers provide is advice on how to title assets, and secondly helping to ensure that retitling actually happens. Countless estate planners have sent their clients home with a lovely file of documents and explicit instructions of which items need to be retitled or which beneficiaries need to be changed, only to discover years later, when the beneficiaries bring mom or dad's will or trust documents to you for probate after their death, that they didn't do any of the things you instructed them to do. If they are going to pay you for your advice, you want to be sure they get the value of that advice, and that may very well mean lots of follow-up with them after you send them home with that nifty packet of estate documents.

Now you also need to ask Henry and Wanda about how they want their property to pass at their deaths. At this point you want to ascertain the broad parameters of their intentions about their property. Most likely they will want the other to take the house, and the personal furnishings and perhaps even the personal property. Ask them about the cars, the cash in the bank accounts, the jewelry and silverware, the securities accounts, and the painting. Ask about family heirlooms or certain items of personal property they might want to give to specific individuals. Take notes on how they indicate they want that property to pass, especially if they want to make some provisions for anyone besides their surviving spouse and/or children.

We have not provided any specific instructions for how Henry and Wanda want their property to pass other than the broad wishes mentioned in the private and public facts. Students role-playing the clients should think about their possible beneficiaries and work out the effects with their lawyers throughout the exercises in this book in accordance with what they think would be appropriate for someone in Henry's or Wanda's position. Although this Chapter is about ascertaining the relevant property, you will need to craft an actual plan that works for the clients' needs, however they define them.

## WARRANTY DEED

This document was prepared by:
Lawyer Lederman
55 Main St.
Lovelyville, Sunshine 45678

This Indenture, made this 28th day of June 2004, between COLONEL PICKERING, GRANTOR, whose address is stated below and who resides in Lovelyville, Sunshine, and HENRY and JANET HIGGINS, a married couple as tenants by the entirety, GRANTEES, whose address is post office box 123, Lovelyville, Sunshine, 45678.

Witnesseth: That said grantor, for and in consideration of the sum of Ten and no/100 Dollars ($10.00) and other valuable consideration to said grantor in hand paid by said grantees, the receipt whereof is hereby acknowledged, have granted, bargained, sold, and conveyed, to the said grantees, and grantees' heirs and assigns forever, the following described land, situate, lying and being in Wheeling County, Sunshine, to wit:

Lot 23 in the Begonia Park subdivision, more precisely described as follows:

Commencing at the northwest corner of lot 28 of the plat of sections 16 and 17, township 12 south, range 21 east, known as the property of the heirs of N. Smith, as shown in plat book E, page 35, of the public records of Wheeling County, Sunshine, thence S. 89°59'14" E along the north boundary of said lot 28 a distance of 102.43 feet to the point of beginning; thence continue S 89°59'14" E along said north boundary 135.13 feet to the northwest corner of the east 279 feet of said lot 28; thence S. 00°06'27" E along the west boundary of said east 279 feet of said lot 28 a distance of 278.63 feet; thence departing from said west boundary S. 89°57'19" W 1135 feet; thence N. 00°16'26" E 278.86 feet to the point of beginning.

Containing 1.03 acres, more or less.

The street address of said property is 12345 45th Pl., Lovelyville, Sunshine. Tax ID # 000-345-6789-X

Subject to restrictions, reservations and limitations of record, if any, and prorated taxes for the year 2004 and taxes for all subsequent years.

And said grantor does hereby fully warrant the title to said land, and will defend the same against the lawful claims of all persons whomsoever.

IN WITNESS WHEREOF, grantor has hereunto set his hand and seal the day and year first above written.

Colonel Pickering

COLONEL PICKERING
12345 45th Pl.
Lovelyville, Sunshine

WITNESSETH: We the undersigned witnesses attest that the foregoing instrument was freely signed by the grantor.

| | |
|---|---|
| Julie Jennings | Julie Jennings |
| Signature | Name |
| | 45 18th St., Lovelyville, Sunshine |
| | Address |
| John Jacobs | John Jacobs |
| Signature | Name |
| | 1717 NW 82nd Pl., Lovelyville, Sunshine |
| | Address |

State of SUNSHINE )
County of Wheeling ) ss

The foregoing instrument was acknowledged before me this 28th day of June, 2004, by COLONEL PICKERING.

Larry Lederman
Notary Public
My commission expires:

(Seal)

## BENEFICIARY DEED

This document was prepared by:
Lawyer Farr
57 Main St.
Lovelyville, Sunshine 45678

This Indenture, made this 12th day of January, 2019, between ALFRED DOOLITTLE, GRANTOR, whose address is stated below and who resides in Lovelyville, Sunshine, and WANDA DOOLITTLE HIGGINS, as GRANTEE, whose address is 12345 45th Pl., Lovelyville, Sunshine, 45678.

Witnesseth: That said grantor, does hereby grant and convey to grantee, effective only on my death, the following described land, situate, lying and being in Elk County, Montana to wit:

160 acres, more or less, in Elk County, Montana, more precisely described as follows: the SW corner of the SE corner of section 14, township 23 E, range 41 S.

Subject to restrictions, reservations and limitations of record, if any, and subject to any mortgage and taxes owing on said property.

And said grantor does hereby fully warrant the title to said land, and will defend the same against the lawful claims of all persons whomsoever.

If the grantee beneficiary predeceases the grantor, the conveyance to the grantee beneficiary shall become void.

IN WITNESS WHEREOF, grantor has hereunto set his hand and seal the day and year first above written.

Alfred Doolittle
ALFRED DOOLITTLE
43 Mansion Circle
Lovelyville, Sunshine

WITNESSETH: We the undersigned witnesses attest that the foregoing instrument was freely signed by the grantor.

Sally Smith — Signature
Sally Smith — Name
27 E. Cypress Circle, Lovelyville, Sunshine — Address

Scott Sondheim — Signature
Scott Sondheim — Name
4 W. 14th St., Lovelyville, Sunshine — Address

State of SUNSHINE )
County of Wheeling ) ss

The foregoing instrument was acknowledged before me this 12th day of January, 2019, by ALFRED DOOLITTLE.

Frank Farr
Notary Public

My commission expires:

(Seal)

Alfred Doolittle Enterprises

43 Mansion Circle
Lovelyville, Sunshine 45678

December 25, 2015

Dear Wanda:

I know how much you like the Jean-Michel Basquiat painting that mom and I have in the living room. I picked it up in a small gallery in New York City back in 1987, just before he died, for only $1,500.00. Because you have always admired it, I want to give it to you now, so you will always know how much we love you. However, your mom really loves the painting too, so we want to retain possession of it until mom dies. At her death, however, the painting is yours.

Since Basquiat's death in 1988, the painting has appreciated greatly in value. We had it appraised five years ago, and it appraised for $185,000. That was quite a surprise to us. The market in Basquiats hasn't increased that much in the past five years, but who knows what it will do between now and when your mom dies. If, at my death, it is worth more than $300,000, then I want you to be sure to deduct anything over that amount from your share of my estate so that all you kids get basically the same size shares. I don't want there to be any hard feelings between you all after mom and I are gone.

I hope you enjoy the painting as much when you finally get possession of it as you do now, and know that mom and I will love you always.

With hugs and kisses,

*Dad*

Once you student attorneys have completed the asset questionnaire, and asked additional questions to ascertain the extent of Henry's and Wanda's property as reflected in the private facts, you should work together to do the following:

a. Create a list of Henry's and Wanda's individual and joint assets (you can go ahead and use the chart in Exercise 2 for this purpose).

b. Determine how each asset is held.

c. Decide what would happen on either of their deaths if the type of ownership changes. For instance, what if Henry and Wanda added each other's names to their individual bank accounts, or changed the beneficiary designation of the life insurance or investment accounts.

d. Determine if the current ownership of the assets helps to fulfill their plans for their estates, as they described in your meeting with them, or does it make those plans more difficult?

e. Decide if Wanda and Henry were to die today, what would be the value of each of their estates?

f. Do you anticipate any problems based on the current and future ownership of their assets?

### Exercise 2—the Probate and the Non-Probate Estate

The only property that Henry and Wanda may dispose of by a will is property they own outright. Property in joint tenancy, property already in trust, property in an account with a POD designation, life insurance, or other people's property in which they might have a power of appointment or on which they are designated beneficiaries, is not fully devisable by them at their deaths. It is only property they own in their own names, free and clear, that can be disposed of by a will, or by intestacy if they have no will. This is property that will likely have to be administered with court supervision as part of the probate process unless you retitle it to pass through a probate-avoiding will substitute, like a revocable trust or joint tenancy.

Identifying the probate property, therefore, is an important exercise necessary for developing a sound estate plan. It is particularly important to compare a client's probate estate with the rest of the property that will pass via a will substitute or is already set to pass to others automatically at death. Some forms of property you may not be able to adjust without the consent of joint tenants or others who might have a stake in the property. Other property can be retitled or transferred in order to maximize the benefits of avoiding probate. But debts are usually paid out of the probate estate, so you will either want to identify a different source for paying certain debts or ensure that there is enough property in the probate estate to pay the bills. Otherwise, the probate estate may be eaten up by the debts and the will beneficiaries will receive nothing.

In order to determine how best to plan Henry's and Wanda's estates, you will first need to identify what property (and its value) will pass automatically without reference to a will, and what property (and its value) is owned outright and may be devised by will. You will need to determine what property is already set up in such a way as to pass automatically, and which neither Henry nor Wanda can alter, and what property may be put into a different form, either so it passes outside probate via a will substitute, or passes via a will. Before you can make recommendations, however, you need to know how everything is currently set up and whether Henry and/or Wanda have the power to change its current form. You will also need to know how much property each would have in their respective probate and non-probate estates so that you can determine what each spouse's respective elective share would be, or intestate shares if they died without a will. We will determine the elective and intestate shares in the next Chapter, but to do that we need to know what property is in the probate estate, what property is set to pass to the surviving spouse outside of probate, and what property is set to pass to others outside of probate.

In this exercise we have listed all of the property owned by Henry and/or Wanda, but you need to fill in the value and how it is owned.

In the last column identify whether the property is:

A. Henry's sole property that will pass through probate—HP

B. Wanda's sole property that will pass through probate—WP

C. Henry's property that will pass outside probate to Wanda—H2WNP

D. Wanda's property that will pass outside probate to Henry—W2HNP

E. Henry's property that will pass outside probate to others (including children)—H2ONP

F. Wanda's property that will pass outside probate to others (including children)—W2ONP

| Property | Value | Ownership | Probate/ Non-Probate |
|---|---|---|---|
| House | \$500,000 (–\$300,000 mortgage) =\$200,000[8] | | |
| Henry's 401(k) retirement account (he contributed all the money) | | | |
| Henry & Wanda's joint checking and savings accounts | | | |
| Wanda's investment account | | | |
| Henry's Ford Explorer | | | |
| Wanda's VW Passat | | | |
| Steve's 1984 Volvo 240 | | | |
| Doris' 2022 BMW | | | |
| Life insurance policy with Allstate on Henry's life provided by his employer | | | |
| Life insurance policy with Prudential on Henry's life required under the divorce agreement | | | |
| Wanda's jewelry and silverware | | | |
| Wanda's father's Montana cabin | | | |
| Henry's IRA (he contributed all the money) | | | |
| Henry's private bank account | | | |
| Wanda's private bank account | | | |
| Henry's 529 Plan for Steve | | | |
| Henry's 529 Plan for Doris | | | |
| Basquiat painting | | | |
| Henry's personal property/clothes/ electronics, etc. | | | |
| Wanda's personal property/clothes/ electronics, etc.[9] | | | |
| Henry and Wanda's joint household furnishings | | | |
| Henry's mother's bank accounts | | | |
| Henry's mother's condominium in Des Moines | | | |

[8] We'll go ahead and deduct the mortgage from the house to indicate only Henry's equity in the house.

[9] Does not include the Basquiat painting or Wanda's jewelry and silverware, which are included separately.

After you have gone through and identified what property would be part of Henry's probate estate, what part passes directly to Wanda outside probate, what part passes to others outside probate, and the same for Wanda's estate, there will be a few items of property you won't quite know what to do with (Wanda's father's cabin, Henry's mother's condominium and bank accounts). These don't seem like they are Henry's or Wanda's property at all, and yet it is quite possible that some or all of this property will be given to Henry or Wanda before they die. What should you do with it?

Right now, you can put it to the side, as the property isn't theirs yet but these items of property will come back into play in later Chapters. Instead, let's think about two other things that you may find confusing.

### 1. How Do You Allocate Jointly Held Property?

As you saw above, Henry and Wanda have joint checking and savings accounts. Whose property is it? The rules on how to attribute jointly held property can be confusing. But, for our purposes here, we are going to use two simple rules. The first is that **property held in a joint account is deemed to be owned by the person who contributed it**, until that person dies and a right of survivorship gives that property to someone else. Thus, Henry's mother's condo and her bank accounts are not relevant and should be deemed owned entirely by her because, even though Henry's name might be on the title documents, he did not contribute any of the property. But the investment account Wanda shares with her father should be divided equally since both she and her father have contributed equal amounts to the account. In valuing her property, you want to give her only half the value until such time as her father dies, and she gets his share either through his will or through a right of survivorship. Although the account is currently held in a joint tenancy, it might make sense for them to change that designation.

The second rule is that **property held jointly by a husband and wife will be considered to be owned equally by each spouse,** regardless of who contributed the funds or bought the property. That means that Henry and Wanda should each be deemed to own half of the other's bank account. The same is true of the household furnishings that are owned jointly by them. But their clothes, personal bank accounts, cars, and even the house are deemed to be owned individually (unless you live in a community property state in which case you will allocate those as belonging half to each). Also, when considering whether there are non-probate assets passing to the surviving spouse, you should treat each spouse's share in joint tenancy property as passing to the survivor at death. Thus, Wanda and Henry each own half of the other's bank account, but at the death of the first to die, that person's share will pass to the surviving spouse. So for figuring out Henry's estate, you should consider his share of his accounts as being non-probate transfers to his surviving spouse, and his share of Wanda's accounts as also being a non-probate transfer to Wanda. And the same goes for Wanda's shares of his and her bank accounts. Her half of each would pass to Henry as a non-probate transfer to her surviving spouse. Feel free to combine the checking and savings account values and attribute half to each.

If you are studying in a community property state, or are likely to be practicing in a community property state, then you want to treat all property acquired during the marriage as community property. For purposes of this exercise, treat community property as a tenancy in common between Henry and Wanda, with each having the right to fully devise his or her half unless the property is expressly held jointly with a right of survivorship. And since they have been together quite a while, you can consider the cars, their furniture, their personal clothing, and the investment and bank accounts that were funded after their marriage as community property. Property that they owned before they married and property they acquire through inheritances or family gifts are generally not considered community property. Thus, the Basquiat painting, Henry's retirement account for Janet and his two older children, and Wanda's jewelry should not be considered community property. The house is probably not community property, but there may be homestead rights in it.

So you will want to have a conversation with your professor about how to treat the house in this and the following exercises.

## 2. How Do You Value Life Insurance and Future Interests and What Do We Do with Debts?

As you will no doubt learn in your Trusts and Estates course, how to value life insurance, various future interests, and what you do with debts can be downright confusing. For instance, the IRS treats life insurance payouts as part of a decedent's taxable estate for determining if estate taxes will be owing. A few million dollars in life insurance can quickly put a decedent's estate over the line for estate taxes. And some states consider all life insurance in the decedent's estate for elective share purposes. Some states do not include life insurance in a decedent's estate for elective share purposes, but do consider life insurance payable to a spouse as part of the decedent's non-probate transfers to the surviving spouse to offset the elective share. So for some purposes it may be considered part of an estate, and not for other purposes. Because that can be terribly confusing, we are going to treat life insurance the way the Uniform Probate Code[10] treats it, as part of the elective estate both for determining the elective estate and for purposes of identifying the amount of property that is being given to the surviving spouse. At this point, therefore, consider all the life insurance as part of Henry's estate, regardless to whom it is payable.

Some states consider only the present value of a life insurance policy for certain purposes. If your state statutes mention the *present value*, then it is only including the present value of *whole life* policies, and not *term life* policies. Whole life policies are similar to a bank account. You pay sizable premiums and are guaranteed a payout at death, regardless of when you die. If you die before your account reaches the full value, the company will pay you the full contracted-for benefits. If your account reaches the full value before you die, you will get the amount of the policy benefits, and some but perhaps not all additional accumulations in value. Term life policies, however, have much smaller premiums and they only pay out if you die during the term of the policy. If you have a $500,000 term life policy for 20 years, and you die 21 years after taking out the policy, you get nothing. Term life policies, therefore, have no present value. For our purposes, assume that Henry's two life insurance policies are **term** life policies.

That future interest in the Basquiat painting is a bit more difficult. There are all sorts of actuarial tables that help determine the value of a life estate in certain property. Obviously, if the life tenant is in his 80s, the value of the life estate should be rather small compared to the value of the remainder. But if the life tenant is relatively young, and the property isn't likely to appreciate in value significantly during the next fifty or so years, the present estate may be worth more than half the value of the entire property, especially if it is property that might decline in value (like cars, clothes, and most consumer goods). For our purposes, let's assume that the present estate in the painting is worth 30% of the full value, and the remainder is worth 70%. And we won't make your life really miserable by creating a few contingent remainders and vested remainders subject to divestment in the painting, all of which would have to be valued. Assume that Wanda's remainder interest in the painting is worth 70% of $85,000.

Now what about those debts? Debts are a bit difficult. It used to be that debts would be paid out of the estate on property that was specifically devised to others. That meant that if Henry devised the house to Steve and Doris, and the remainder of his estate to Wanda, Gillian, and Benjamin, the residuary devisees would have to liquidate assets to pay off the mortgage for the house from the residuary property. Today, however, the opposite is true. Property, especially real property, passes with the mortgage, property taxes that might be due, and other debts associated

[10] See UPC § 2–205(1)(D) and § 2–206(3).

with it. Big debts attach directly to the property to reduce its value for the estate and the beneficiaries.

However, few administrators are going to cull through the credit card bills to determine if Grandpa actually paid off that 64″ flat screen television, or if there is still some debt owing on it. So for our purposes, we will only attach the debt to property that is clearly associated with it. Car loans, mortgages for real estate, the home equity line of credit that is attached to the house, will all pass with the property. This means that we should value Henry's house as only $200,000 because the mortgage will go with the house. But if Henry and Wanda also owe some credit cards, some medical bills, or have other general debts, then we will take those debts out of the residue of the probate estate before we calculate the value of each estate and will not try to reduce the value of his new socks, the milk in the refrigerator, or even the iPad Henry bought on credit just before his death.

Consider these debts that Henry and Wanda have identified. Determine what category of property (HP, WP, H2WNP, W2HNP, H2ONP, W2ONP) will be charged with these debts.

| **Property** | **Creditor** | **Amount** | **Category of Property from which debts are payable** |
|---|---|---|---|
| House | Bank of America Mortgage—in Henry's name | $300,000 | |
| Wanda's student loans | Wells Fargo | $25,000 | |
| Doris' car | BMW of America Car Loan—Loan is in Henry's name only | $40,000 | |
| Henry's mom's condominium | Bank of America Mortgage—in mom's name | $25,000 | |
| Henry's credit cards | Sunshine Credit Union | $10,000 | |
| Wanda's credit cards | Citicorp | $20,000 | |
| Henry's hip replacement surgery | Sunshine County Hospital | $20,000 | |

Now that you know what debts each has, and what property each can be considered to own now, calculate the value of Henry's and Wanda's estates by dividing the property into the six categories:

| **Henry's Property** | **Value** | **Wanda's Property** | **Value** |
|---|---|---|---|
| Henry's Probate Estate (HP) | $ | Wanda's Probate Estate (WP) | $ |
| Henry's non-probate transfers to Wanda (H2WNP) | $ | Wanda's non-probate transfers to Henry (W2HNP) | $ |
| Henry's non-probate transfers to others (H2ONP) | $ | Wanda's non-probate transfers to others (W2ONP) | $ |
| **Henry's Total Assets** | **$** | **Wanda's Total Assets** | **$** |
| Henry's Probate Property Debts | –$ | Wanda's Probate Property Debts | –$ |
| Henry's H2WNP Debts | –$ | Wanda's W2HNP Debts | –$ |
| Henry's H2ONP Debts | –$ | Wanda's W2ONP Debts | –$ |
| **Henry's Net Estate (total assets minus total debts)** | **$** | **Wanda's Net Estate (total assets minus total debts)** | **$** |

These numbers are important, and will follow through the rest of the exercises. So make sure they are correct. We will be using them when we consider the elective share and homestead allowances in the next Chapter. In particular, be sure to deduct the probate property debts from the probate property to determine the **net probate estate**.

| | | | |
|---|---|---|---|
| Henry's Probate Estate (HP) | $ | Wanda's Probate Estate (WP) | $ |
| Henry's Probate Property Debts | –$ | Wanda's Probate Property Debts | –$ |
| **Henry's Net Probate Estate** | **$** | **Wanda's Net Probate Estate** | **–$** |

Now before you finish, be sure to fill in your time sheet in Chapter One with the time you spent determining Henry's and Wanda's property, how they want it allocated at their deaths, and how it is currently held, if you haven't already done so. Make a list of their basic plan for the succession of their property, and make a list of property issues you might need to discuss with them, like that house that is still titled in Henry's and Janet's name.

## Lessons Learned

Go back and look at the chart on the bottom of page 44. What is your gut reaction about these numbers? Should some of them be changed? These exercises should give you a good foundation for evaluating a client's current estate, give you a sense of what property issues may arise in the future (like inheritances, debts, or college expenses for the children), and where the conflict points may be. Is the current asset distribution lop-sided? Are there good reasons for the differences, or does it seem to be simply inertia that has left certain property the way it is? Are your clients amenable to changes?

Combining what you now know about their wealth, with what you know about their personal situations and personalities, you should be able to judge whether your representation is likely to result in a unitary plan that puts most of the wealth into a joint, or mutual trust. Or is it likely to result in two separate plans that may be different but are understood and accepted by each to be different? Or is it likely to result in two separate plans that work at cross purposes with the other? Only the third situation is likely to require separate legal representation. How much does each know about the other's assets and intentions and how much is each comfortable telling the other? If they are open about their assets, and each is comfortable that the other can control his/her assets as they choose, then separate plans can be crafted without running into a conflict. If both want to pool their assets or at least have them flow together into a plan that is mutually reinforcing, then joint representation is critical. But if they each want to turn their back on the other and create a plan without reference to the other's assets or financial needs or conditions, then separate representation is preferable.

### *PRACTICE PROBLEMS*

For a little more practice, try to classify the following property: [This is not property that will carry forward in later chapters, but is here for you to practice thinking about ownership interests in property that often crops up in a client's estate.]

1. Wanda takes out a $1,000,000 life insurance policy on her life, payable to Henry as primary beneficiary, and Gillian and Benjamin as secondary beneficiaries.
2. Henry's brother, Bob, puts Henry's name on his business as a joint tenant with right of survivorship, but Bob contributed all the value to the business and continues to exclusively operate the business. The business is worth $3,500,000.
3. Wanda has a general power of appointment over the $2,000,000 principal in her grandmother's trust.
4. Wanda's grandmother conveyed a 20-acre parcel of land in Lovelyville to the City to be used as a public park only, and if not so used the land was to automatically revert back to her. She then devised her possibility of reverter in this park land to Wanda and her three siblings.
5. Wanda and Henry own a sailboat as tenants in common worth $30,000.

Now that you know the scope of your representation (separate or joint), and you know your client's current assets, you can begin the next phase of your representation, which is to advise them of their legal rights and obligations to each other, their children, and other family members, and craft an estate plan that best fits their needs and wishes.

# CHAPTER 3

# FAMILY PROTECTIONS: CALCULATING HOMESTEAD, FAMILY ALLOWANCE, EXEMPT PROPERTY, INTESTATE SHARES, AND THE SPOUSAL SHARE

## HISTORY OF THE FAMILY PROTECTIONS

In this chapter we will be focusing primarily on the portion of Henry's and Wanda's estates that will pass to each other as surviving spouse. The law treats marriage, and the rights of the surviving spouse, far more generously than the rights of children or collateral kin. But that was not always the case.

Historically, upon marriage a husband took ownership of all of his wife's personal property, managed all of her real property, and owned all property acquired during the marriage under the law of coverture. She owned no property and could not make a will so long as her husband was still alive. She was deemed to be legally dead, while he owned and managed the couple's combined wealth. As a result, husbands and wives were very differently situated when one died. The surviving husband simply continued to own all of the couple's property which he could then take with him to a new marriage, devise to their children, or spend as he chose. The only limitation on his rights was that he only held a life estate in the real property she had owned before the marriage, and at his death it passed to their children or back to her side of the family.

A wife who survived her husband, however, had no personal property of her own and, although she reacquired sole ownership and management over lands she had brought to the marriage, she did not own any real property they acquired during the marriage. The law, therefore, sought to provide her with some property interests in her deceased husband's estate so she would not be destitute and become a burden on the parish in her widowhood. Hence, she received a life estate in one-third of all lands acquired by the couple at any time during the marriage as her *dower*.[1] At one time she had received outright ownership of most or all of her husband's movable property, but that was reduced in 1677 by the (ironically titled) Act for the Better Settling of Intestate's Estates,[2] which gave her a maximum of one-third. That was reduced even more by the law giving her a mere life estate in his movable property which could be entirely defeated by a will.[3]

In addition to Parliament's efforts to reduce the widow's claims on her deceased husband's intestate estate, a husband could dramatically limit a wife's dower rights with effective estate planning by putting all of his property into trust, making it payable to children or others upon his own death, and a wife could not defeat her husband's trust through the equity courts.[4] And then, as well as today, many husbands pressured their wives to relinquish their dower interests altogether

---

1 Dower is different from a dowry. The former is a legal right in a husband's estate upon his death, where the latter is property that the wife's family usually pays to the groom upon their marriage. Not surprisingly, the law viewed dower as the wife's right to reacquire the property her family gave to the couple upon their marriage, and thus the values of dower and dowry were often similar. When land could not be transferred via a will before 1540, but had to pass by intestacy, dower could not be easily defeated except through a use (an early form of a trust).

2 22 & 23 Car.II c. 10.

3 See Amy Louise Erickson, Women and Property in Early Modern England (London: Routledge, 1993).

4 Trusts then, and today, have been used to defeat a widow's life estate in the property because the trust consists of an inter vivos transfer out to others. Thus, the property is not owned by the decedent husband at death and the surviving widow would have no claims on it. Wives generally could not defeat a surviving husband's life estate because married women could not own property in their own names, and therefore place it into trust, until the late nineteenth century with the passage of married women's property acts.

through what was called a strict settlement in favor of an annuity that would be a charge upon certain lands. These strict settlements, like the pre-nuptial agreements of today, asked wives to give up their legal entitlements in their husbands' estates in exchange for a set amount for her support until her own death, but virtually never gave her any ownership interest in any of the property itself. And if the property upon which the annuity was based was sold, she generally was out of luck.

In this country in the nineteenth century, most state laws followed the laws of England, including the use of trusts or wills to completely cut off a surviving widow's claims on her husband's property and the property they acquired during the marriage, leaving her only with the income from her dower lands for life. And he could often defeat even that meager right by the use of a trust. As Blackstone put it, under coverture, husband and wife are deemed one, and that one is the husband.[5] Because men and women started from very different positions when they entered marriage, and because the men took ownership of all marital wealth, including wealth acquired by their wives' labors, they were very differently situated at death. And although it may have seemed that a wife's dower interest was more generous than a husband's interests in his wife's estate at death, that difference was the result of very significant barriers to a woman's ability to own property during life and during marriage.

In the late twentieth century, however, it was deemed to be unconstitutional for wives' and husbands' rights in their deceased spouse's estates to be unequal, so most states passed statutes giving all surviving spouses an outright share of a decedent spouse's estate, or a life estate in a portion of a decedent's estate. *Curtesy*, which was the term for a husband's rights in his wife's real property, has largely disappeared, although you will often encounter the term *dower* in many state statutes even today. Those states that have retained dower continue to use that term, simply applying it equally to both husbands and wives. In addition, most states have abolished distinctions between real and personal property, treating a surviving spouse's right to a portion of a decedent spouse's estate as an across-the-board right, regardless of the nature of the property.

One of the most important changes of the twentieth century occurred in the treatment of the surviving spouse under intestacy laws. Because only blood kin were traditionally deemed to be an *heir*, the surviving spouse was entitled only to dower or curtesy, and to whatever additional property the decedent spouse devised by will, but was not entitled to inherit by intestacy as an heir. Following studies in the 1970s, most states amended their intestacy statutes to give the surviving spouse far more than the one-third that had been dictated by the early common law. Today, a spouse is likely to inherit 100% of a decedent spouse's estate if there are no children, and the UPC provides that the surviving spouse takes 100% even if there are children, so long as neither spouse has children by a prior relationship.

With the recognition that most people want their surviving spouse to take the majority of property, states also adopted more generous statutes to ensure that the surviving spouse receives a statutory minimum if the decedent makes a will and intentionally or inadvertently disinherits the surviving spouse. Forty states have adopted statutes that give a surviving spouse a minimum share of a deceased spouse's estate even if he makes a will leaving the property to others. Called a *forced* share or an *elective* share, this entitlement cannot be defeated by a will, and can only be avoided through a pre-nuptial or post-nuptial agreement whereby the surviving spouse consents to waive his or her elective share rights. In the absence of such an agreement, the surviving spouse may elect to take a statutory share of a deceased spouse's estate, or may agree to take however much the deceased spouse chooses to devise to the survivor, if the survivor is competent to make that election. If the deceased spouse devises less than the elective share amount to the surviving spouse, however, the survivor may be forced to take a full elective share if she has health care debts or the survivor is subject to a conservatorship. And if the surviving spouse elects a statutory share, doing so may

[5] William Blackstone, Commentaries, vol. I, Chap. 15. p. 430.

frustrate your client's well-developed estate plan. In the ebb and flow of survivor's rights, we are in a period in which the survivor is generally very well provided for, but with the increase in second and third marriages, marriages of short duration, and the myriad issues of blended families, we may see another period of reduction of the rights of surviving spouses in the next few decades.[6]

Also, the laws of homestead, family allowance, and exempt property in most states provide that the surviving spouse and/or minor children are entitled to receive a certain amount of property—perhaps the family home, perhaps only an allowance—from the decedent's estate before debts are paid and even before the statutory elective share. Unless Henry and Wanda live in a state like Florida or Texas, with very generous homestead protections, the amount granted to the surviving family for homestead, family allowance, and exempt property isn't going to require that you make major adjustments to your estate plan. But it is still important that you understand what these protections do, and that you account for them in your estate plan.

You will cover the family protections, intestacy, and the elective share more fully in your Trusts and Estates class, but you need to know enough about them to calculate the minimum of Henry's and Wanda's estates that must pass to each other so as not to trigger the right to take an elective share. So calculating the surviving spouse's statutory share is usually the first order of business. Of course, if the couple comes to your office and tells you that they want to leave all of their property to the survivor, and only upon the survivor's death will any property pass to descendants, then you don't need to calculate the elective share, although you may still have homestead issues. But you need to keep these statutory rights in mind whenever you are advising a married person as to his or her estate plan.

## FAMILY SET-ASIDES

### HOMESTEAD PROPERTY

Nearly all states have adopted laws that grant to surviving spouses, minor children, and sometimes all children regardless of age, certain property before anything else is taken out of an estate, including debts and filing fees. Many states allow the surviving spouse or minor children to reside in the family home until the spouse remarries, the children reach an age of majority, for life, or perhaps indefinitely. Homestead laws are quite complex, sometimes allowing a surviving spouse or children to take a certain allowance from the decedent's estate, or perhaps to sell the family home and receive a portion of the proceeds. Florida gives the surviving spouse a life estate in the homestead, with a vested remainder in the children, or the surviving spouse can elect to take a one-half interest in the homestead in fee simple absolute while the children take the other half, and the decedent is prohibited from devising the homestead away from the surviving spouse if she has minor children.[7] Minnesota gives the surviving spouse the entire homestead if there are no descendants, or a life estate with a remainder in the descendants.[8] If you are going to practice in a state with a generous homestead provision, you will want to address homestead rights expressly.

---

[6] Most elective share statutes gave the surviving spouse a percentage, usually between one-third and one-half of a decedent spouse's net probate estate. In the past thirty years, however, many states have changed their elective share statutes to give surviving spouses a percentage in all property the decedent spouse controlled at death, including property passing via will substitutes. This has made it very difficult to use estate planning to limit the spousal share for spouses of very short marriages or for spouses who actually have more wealth than the decedent spouse. As a result, the UPC has developed a more fine-tuned elective share statute that adjusts the spousal share downward if the marriage is of short duration, assuming that the spouse did not contribute greatly to the decedent spouse's accumulated wealth. The UPC also adjusts the elective share based on the amount of wealth the surviving spouse has, so that if the survivor is the wealthier of the couple, the survivor may not elect against the decedent spouse's estate. Some states have also reduced the intestate share of the surviving spouse, as Florida did in 2011. See Fl. Stat. § 732.102.

[7] See Fl.Stat. § 732.401 and Fla. Const. Art. X, § 4.

[8] See Minn. Stat. § 542.2–402.

There are three general types of homestead statutes:

i. The first type gives the surviving family members some interest in the actual real property owned by the decedent spouse, either outright ownership or a life estate or a right to reside in the home for a certain period, sometimes only until the children reach age of majority or the spouse remarries.

This type of homestead statute gives the survivor an actual interest in the real property itself if it is owned individually by a married person and the couple is residing in the home as their primary residence. Thus, in the case of Henry and Wanda, Henry owns the home individually (since Janet has relinquished her claims) and Wanda is likely to be entitled to a life estate or a homestead right to remain in the home at least until the minor children reach 18. Henry, of course, would not be entitled as a surviving spouse to any homestead because he already owns the primary residence. If Henry and Wanda owned the home as joint tenants with rights of survivorship, or tenants by the entirety, however, then the survivor would take sole ownership of the home and there would be no homestead right or limitation. This type of homestead statute dramatically limits the ability of the decedent to control the disposition of the family home upon death when it is owned by only one of the spouses.

ii. The second type of homestead statute protects the surviving spouse's right to a certain sum, or value, tied to particular real estate. For example, Missouri grants to the surviving spouse $15,000 of homestead, Wyoming protects $30,000, and New Hampshire $120,000.[9]

What these laws do is protect the home from forced sale if the home is valued at less than the statutory amount. If the home is worth more, and there are creditors of the estate, the creditors can force a sale of the home, but the surviving spouse is entitled to the proceeds up to the statutory amount. If a decedent spouse owns the family home in his own name, and it is worth $500,000 but it has a $250,000 mortgage on it, then he has $250,000 in equity in the home. If the state's homestead law protects $100,000, then upon a forced sale the mortgage company would receive the first $250,000 to repay the mortgage, the surviving spouse would receive the next $100,000 free and clear of any debts, and the remaining $150,000 would be included in the decedent's estate and would be available to pay other debts, like credit card debts or lingering medical bills. But even if the family home was the only significant asset, and the decedent had medical debts that would more than wipe out the value of the home, homestead protections will give to the surviving spouse the statutory amount before any non-home-related debts are to be paid.[10] This form of homestead appears to be the most common.

iii. The third type of homestead statute merely grants to the surviving spouse an allowance or a preset cash amount. The UPC currently provides the surviving spouse with $22,500 to be immediately available to help pay for rent, mortgage payments, or other housing needs.[11] If there is no surviving spouse, then the homestead is payable to minor children and any dependent children of the decedent.

This type of homestead law is not tied to any particular real property, thus protecting surviving spouses who rent their homes, or who live in mobile homes. But it is also rather stingy compared to the protections available under some of the other types of homestead laws. Florida and Texas protect the entire property, up to any value. Thus, the Palm Beach billionaire's home worth millions passes entirely to a surviving spouse or minor children and before the payment of other debts, regardless

[9] See Mo. St. Title xxxi, § 474.290; Wy. St. §§ 2–7–504 & 508; N.H. § 480:1.

[10] Homestead generally does not protect against the debts of the home, i.e., mortgages, property taxes, and mechanic's liens for work done on the home.

[11] UPC § 2–402.

of value, just as the poor man's bungalow does. But families that do not own their own homes receive no benefit in those states.

Homestead can be a complicated issue, especially in states that provide protections tied to the actual real property. In our example, the family home that is currently titled in Henry and Janet's names would be considered homestead, and Wanda and the minor children would likely have some right to continue to reside in the home, even if Henry's debts would otherwise eat up the value of the home. For our purposes, however, we would like for you to determine the value of homestead under the UPC and under the law of your state, because we cannot move on to calculating the intestate or elective shares until we know how much property will come off the top for homestead and the other family set-asides.

## FAMILY ALLOWANCE

Family allowance is usually an amount of cash that is provided to the surviving spouse and/or minor children to enable them to pay bills until the estate is probated and they acquire the decedent's property outright. The UPC allows for a "reasonable allowance" out of the estate up to a maximum of $27,000 for the surviving spouse and minor children or any other children the decedent was in fact supporting.[12] Usually family allowance is given in cash, or easily liquidated property, so that the family can pay its bills right away. States that allow a family allowance have widely divergent amounts. Oregon allows a court to assign any amount to the surviving spouse and dependent children up to the entire estate after debts are paid.[13] Indiana allows $25,000 for family allowance,[14] and Colorado allows a *reasonable* allowance for one year.[15] Although Wanda and Henry may seem to have enough property of their own that they don't need a family allowance, it is typically ordered whenever there is a surviving spouse and/or dependent children.

## EXEMPT PROPERTY

Many states also allow the surviving spouse, children, or both to receive certain items of personal property up to a certain value, like the decedent's automobile, tools of a trade, family mementos, or other items that are either important for the family's support or provide personal reminders of the decedent. For example, Ohio allows the surviving spouse to take one watercraft and one outboard motor,[16] Florida allows the family to retain two automobiles,[17] and New Jersey allows the family to retain the decedent's wearing apparel.[18] The UPC allows the surviving spouse to choose up to $15,000 worth of the decedent's household furniture, automobiles, furnishings, appliances, and personal effects.[19] If there is no surviving spouse, then all of the decedent's children, regardless of age or dependency, may share in the exempt property under the UPC.

Homestead, Family Allowance, and Exempt Property generally are given to the surviving spouse or, in the absence of a surviving spouse, to minor children directly. If there is no surviving spouse or minor children, adult children are usually entitled to the exempt property, but usually not family allowance. And homestead is so variable, that you will need to consult the laws of your state to determine if it inures to the benefit of adult children.

---

12 See UPC § 2–404.

13 Ore. Rev. Stat. § 114.085.

14 Ind. Code § 29–1–4–1.

15 Colo. Rev. Stat. § 15–11–404.

16 Ohio Rev. Code Ann. § 2106.18–19.

17 Fla.Stat. Ann. § 732.402.

18 N.J. Stat. Ann. § 3B:16–5.

19 UPC § 2–403.

### Exercise 1—UPC Homestead, Family Allowance, and Exempt Property Set-Asides

For our exercises here, assume that if Wanda survives Henry she will take all of the homestead, family allowance, and exempt property, and vice versa if Henry survives Wanda. Now calculate the amount of homestead, family allowance, and exempt property each would be entitled to from the other's estate, under the UPC and then do it under the laws of your own state.

#### *a. UPC Family Set-Asides*

Under the UPC, the surviving spouse is entitled to $22,500 homestead,[20] $27,000 family allowance,[21] and exempt property up to $15,000[22] for a total of $64,500 in family set-asides. Examine Henry's and Wanda's property that was itemized in Chapter 2 and identify where this money and property should come from for each spouse's estate. That is, if there isn't enough cash in the bank accounts, for instance, what property should be used to pay for these set-asides? In most instances, a surviving spouse may choose personal property in lieu of the family allowance, but may not choose cash in lieu of the exempt property.

Moreover, these amounts are deducted from the estate before any debts or other devises are satisfied, and they are usually paid out of the probate estate because they are payable only after the decedent has died.[23] All that non-probate property, like joint tenancies with rights of survivorship, or life estates and remainders, have already vested in the successors upon the death of the decedent. Even trust property will vest in the beneficiaries if explicit provisions are not made to reserve some property to pay final debts, the family set-asides, or other entitlements. This means that the only available property to pay these set-asides will be property left in the probate estate. Hence, you will need to ensure as part of your estate plans for Henry and Wanda that each has adequate property to satisfy these set-asides.

Once you have identified the amount of property to be deducted for the set-asides, go ahead and subtract their value from the respective property in our property chart. And while we are at it, let's deduct the debts as well. Normally, you wouldn't think too carefully about simple debts, like credit cards or a car loan, when you are making an estate plan. But it's always good to know if your client's debts are small, large, close to their total wealth, or are relatively insignificant.

**Calculating the Net Probate Estate Under the UPC**

| | | | |
|---|---|---|---|
| Henry's Probate Property | $ | Wanda's Probate Property | $ |
| Minus Homestead | –$ | Minus Homestead | –$ |
| Minus Family Allowance | –$ | Minus Family Allowance | –$ |
| Minus Exempt Property | –$ | Minus Exempt Property | –$ |
| Minus Probate Debts | –$ | Minus Probate Debts | –$ |
| **Henry's Net Probate Estate** | **$** | **Wanda's Net Probate Estate** | **$** |

Keep these numbers handy for the rest of this Chapter as we will be using Henry's and Wanda's net probate estates for calculating both their intestate shares and elective shares.

[20] UPC § 2–402.

[21] UPC § 2–404.

[22] UPC § 2–403.

[23] It is possible to direct that these set-asides be paid from trust property, but you will need to indicate that in any trust documents you create. Otherwise, the default rule that they will be paid from the probate estate will be assumed.

### b. *Set-Asides Under the Laws of Your State*

Now calculate the homestead, family allowance, and exempt property set-asides under the laws of your state and identify from what property they will be satisfied for both Henry's and Wanda's estates.

**Calculating the Net Probate Estate Under the Laws of Your State**

| | | | |
|---|---|---|---|
| Henry's Probate Property | $ | Wanda's Probate Property | $ |
| Minus Homestead | –$ | Minus Homestead | –$ |
| Minus Family Allowance | –$ | Minus Family Allowance | –$ |
| Minus Exempt Property | –$ | Minus Exempt Property | –$ |
| Minus Probate Debts | –$ | Minus Probate Debts | –$ |
| **Henry's Net Probate Estate** | **$** | **Wanda's Net Probate Estate** | **$** |

For simplicity's sake, we will continue to use the UPC value for these family set-asides as we continue to work through the calculations necessary for determining the intestate and elective shares.[24] But for added practice, you should continue to do the same calculations using the laws of your own state for the intestate share, the elective share and the set-asides. That way you will get to do all of these problems at least twice, once under the UPC and once under the laws of your own state. This is a case where practice makes perfect or, if not perfect, then significantly less likely to constitute malpractice.

### c. *Determining the Property Used to Satisfy the Set-Asides*

Except for the mortgage on their home, Henry's and Wanda's debts are quite small. Nevertheless, once we subtract the respective debts and set-asides, their net probate estates will consist primarily of fairly non-liquid assets. The personal property, clothes and jewelry are not likely to fetch much on the market if they had to be sold, and neither is likely to want to sell the house, the painting, or even a car. And even if they could sell the house, it would probably take six months to a year to do so, and there might be up-front costs associated with selling it, like updating the old wiring or fixing other defects. Wanda's private bank account won't cover everything, and Henry doesn't have a bank account without a POD designation, so his estate won't have any cash from which to pay the family allowance or homestead allowance. In many states, Wanda would be entitled to a family allowance in addition to the cash she receives from the joint tenancy in their joint bank accounts, although most courts that have the discretion will take into account cash the surviving spouse receives in joint bank accounts that was contributed by the decedent spouse to offset the family set-asides.

In Chapter Two you calculated the three categories of property each had currently established: probate property that would pass to will beneficiaries or intestate heirs, non-probate transfers to the surviving spouse, and non-probate transfers to others. In identifying that property, you should be starting to get a feel for an appropriate balance of the three types so as to further multiple goals of sound estate planning (probate avoidance, adequate provisions for the surviving spouse, flexibility and lifetime access to property, etc.). Now we need to think about management of the property and the ease of administration based on the kind of property each has in their estates. Remember, debts of the decedent's estate can be pushed out a bit, but immediate bills for the living need to be paid. And life insurance, while it's a great thing, doesn't cover many obligations of the

[24] For simplicity's sake, just use the $64,500 family set-asides for all the rest of the problems in this Chapter, even if you are calculating the elective share under a rule that is different from the UPC. Use the family set-asides of your own state, however, in calculating these if you prefer.

estate if it is payable to someone else, like Janet. So it's a good idea to look at how much of Henry's and Wanda's estates are liquid enough to pay bills and the set-asides in the first six months.

To do that, go through this chart and identify in the last column whether the assets are Liquid (L), Non-Liquid (NL), or Somewhat Liquid (SL). Somewhat liquid assets would include items like stock in the securities account that could be sold in an emergency, but which one would rather not have to sell if the market happens to be in a down period. Non-liquid assets would include any property that would take six months or longer to sell, or goods for which there is not likely to be a market.

| Property | Value | Ownership | Liquid/ Non-Liquid |
|---|---|---|---|
| House | $500,000 (–$300,000 mortgage) = $200,000 | Henry and Janet, but Janet waived all rights in the house in the divorce settlement | |
| Henry's 401(k) retirement account (he contributed all the money) | | Henry owns the account, but Wanda is the primary beneficiary, and the 4 kids are secondary beneficiaries for any amounts left at his death . | |
| Henry & Wanda's joint checking and savings accounts | | Joint Tenancy with Right of Survivorship | |
| Wanda's investment account | | Joint Tenancy with right of survivorship with her father, and each contributed half the funds. | |
| Henry's Ford Explorer | | Henry's name | |
| Wanda's VW Passat | | Henry's name | |
| Steve's 1984 Volvo 240 | | Henry and Steve's names | |
| Doris' 2022 BMW | | Henry and Doris' names | |
| Life insurance policy with Allstate on Henry's life | | Payable to four children | |
| Life insurance policy with Prudential on Henry's life | | Payable to Janet as primary, and Steve and Doris as secondary beneficiaries | |
| Wanda's jewelry and silverware | | Inherited from her relatives | |
| Wanda's father's Montana cabin | | Dad's name but with a POD designation for Wanda, it is controlled by her father and paid for entirely by her father | |
| Henry's IRA (he contributed all the money) | | Owned by Henry but he waived all rights to withdraw in the divorce agreement. It is held as a POD account with Janet as primary beneficiary, Steve and Doris as secondary beneficiaries | |
| Henry's private bank account | | Henry's name with POD beneficiary designation of his brother Bob | |
| Wanda's private bank account | | Wanda's name only | |
| Henry's 529 Plan for Steve | | Henry's name, POD Steve | |
| Henry's 529 Plan for Doris | | Henry's name, POD Doris | |
| Basquiat painting | | Life estate in Wanda's father and mother, remainder in Wanda | |
| Henry's personal property/clothes/ electronics, etc. | | Henry | |

| Property | Value | Ownership | Liquid/ Non-Liquid |
|---|---|---|---|
| Wanda's personal property/clothes/ jewelry, etc. | | Wanda | |
| Henry and Wanda's joint household furnishings | | Henry and Wanda as joint tenants with rights of survivorship | |
| Henry's mother's bank accounts | | Henry and his mother, but his mother contributed all the money | |
| Henry's mother's condominium in Des Moines | | Henry's mother, Henry, and his 3 siblings as joint tenants with rights of survivorship | |

What you should discover from this exercise is that much of Henry's and Wanda's property is not liquid, meaning that it can't be easily used to pay debts or the family set-asides. For instance, although the Basquiat painting is valuable, it would have to be sold if Henry needed cash to pay his bills. Similarly, the cars, Wanda's jewelry, all of their personal property and furnishings can't be immediately used to pay bills, although they could be sold if necessary. They are somewhat liquid but have to be converted to cash before they can be used to pay debts. Other property, like the IRA payable to Janet, is simply not available at all to pay set-asides or debts because, upon Henry's death, Janet immediately owns the account. The same is true of Steve's and Doris's cars and Wanda's investment account held in joint tenancy. These are non-liquid assets. The cash in the bank accounts are the only truly liquid assets. Securities accounts can often be cashed in fairly easily if they are established with post-tax investments. But if they were financed with pre-tax money (i.e., are tax-deferred investments which characterizes most retirement account plans like Henry's IRA and 401(k)) there will be penalties for early withdrawal that makes cashing them in less advantageous.[25] A good estate plan will ensure that there are adequate liquid assets (cash in the bank or securities that can be easily converted to cash) to pay the estate's set-asides and debts. Financial planners will generally advise that one should have enough cash on hand, easily accessible, to cover three to six months' of living expenses in case the primary bread-winner loses her job or dies. Do Henry and Wanda meet this recommendation?

## THE LAW OF INTESTACY AND CALCULATING THE SURVIVING SPOUSE'S INTESTATE SHARE

As mentioned at the beginning of this Chapter, the surviving spouse did not qualify as a legal heir under the early common law. Rather, the surviving spouse received a dower interest or other statutorily protected amount of property, but heirs were defined as lineal descendants or collateral relatives by blood. With changes to the laws of intestacy, the surviving spouse has become the principal heir in virtually all states,[26] entitled to half or all of a decedent spouse's estate if the decedent dies intestate. Many states have followed the lead of the UPC, however, and made the intestacy calculation a bit more tricky by accounting for the ubiquitous blended family.[27] Where a husband and wife have been married for decades, have no prior marriages, and all the children are

[25] We don't have time to go into any detail here about the tax implications of retirement plans and their benefits. Suffice it to say that there are potential tax consequences that even modest estate plans need to consider.

[26] This is not so in Arkansas and Kentucky, which distribute intestate estates to lineal descendants before surviving spouses. See Ark. Code § 28–9–204; Ky. Code § 391.010.

[27] We will not discuss the 2019 UPC changes to intestacy distributions.

the children of both, the intestacy calculation is quite simple. But with blended families and step-children, the calculation can be a bit trickier.

The UPC provides that, after the deduction of the family set-asides and debts, the surviving spouse is entitled to 100% of a decedent's net probate estate if there are no children, or all children belong to both spouses. That is not the case with Henry and Wanda, however. Study the UPC provision below and calculate what Henry and Wanda would take as intestate shares in the other's net probate estate if either died intestate.

**UPC § 2-102. SHARE OF SPOUSE.**

The intestate share of a decedent's surviving spouse is:

(1) the entire intestate estate if:

(A) no descendant or parent of the decedent survives the decedent; or

(B) all of the decedent's surviving descendants are also descendants of the surviving spouse and there is no other descendant of the surviving spouse who survives the decedent;

(2) the first [$300,000], plus three-fourths of any balance of the intestate estate, if no descendant of the decedent survives the decedent, but a parent of the decedent survives the decedent;

(3) the first [$225,000], plus one-half of any balance of the intestate estate, if all of the decedent's surviving descendants are also descendants of the surviving spouse and the surviving spouse has one or more surviving descendants who are not descendants of the decedent;

(4) the first [$150,000], plus one-half of any balance of the intestate estate, if one or more of the decedent's surviving descendants are not descendants of the surviving spouse.

## Exercise 2—Calculating the Intestate Shares

Calculate what Henry's intestate share of Wanda's estate would be, and what Wanda's intestate share of Henry's estate would be under the UPC using the value of their net probate estates calculated in Exercise 1 of this Chapter.

| | |
|---|---|
| Henry's Intestate Share of Wanda's Estate under the UPC | $ |
| Wanda's Intestate Share of Henry's Estate under the UPC | $ |

Now calculate them under the laws of your state.

| | |
|---|---|
| Henry's Intestate Share of Wanda's Estate under your state's laws | $ |
| Wanda's Intestate Share of Henry's Estate under your state's laws | $ |

Assuming that there is something left in either of their net probate estates after the surviving spouse's share is taken out, calculate the shares to which the children would be entitled under the UPC and your state's intestacy provisions.

**SECTION 2–103. SHARE OF HEIRS OTHER THAN SURVIVING SPOUSE.**

(a) Any part of the intestate estate not passing to a decedent's surviving spouse under Section 2–102, or the entire intestate estate if there is no surviving spouse, passes in the following order to the individuals who survive the decedent:

(1) to the decedent's descendants by representation;

(2) . . . .

### Children's Shares Under the UPC

| Residue of Henry's NPE[28] | $ | | Residue of Wanda's NPE[29] | $ | |
|---|---|---|---|---|---|
| | % per child | Dollar amount | | % per child | Dollar amount |
| Steve | | | Steve | | |
| Doris | | | Doris | | |
| Gillian | | | Gillian | | |
| Benjamin | | | Benjamin | | |

Now calculate the intestate shares of the surviving children under the laws of your own state.

### Children's Shares Under the Laws of Your State

| Residue of Henry's NPE minus surviving spouse's share | $ | | Residue of Wanda's NPE minus surviving spouse's share | $ | |
|---|---|---|---|---|---|
| | % per child | Dollar amount | | % per child | Dollar amount |
| Steve | | | Steve | | |
| Doris | | | Doris | | |
| Gillian | | | Gillian | | |
| Benjamin | | | Benjamin | | |

Although you are unlikely to need to know exactly how much property would pass to each beneficiary under intestacy if your clients are in your office asking for an estate plan, including a will and perhaps a trust, it is good to have a basic feel for how the property would pass if your client did nothing. This is, essentially, the status quo—where they likely would be if they hadn't come to your office.[30] It's your starting point in devising an estate plan. Now you can go forward with a good understanding of what property distribution the default rules would provide. All non-probate transfers to each other, and non-probate transfers to others would pass according to the property rights already established in these instruments and accounts. Only the probate property would be used for the family set-asides and intestate shares. Henry and Wanda may be happy with the statutory default distributions, in which case you have helped them to understand where they stand

[28] This is what is left in Henry's NPE after Wanda's intestate share is deducted.

[29] This is what is left in Wanda's NPE after Henry's intestate share is deducted.

[30] In our case Henry has a prior will but it was executed before he married Wanda. As a pre-marital will, it will be valid only in part, because Wanda would be entitled to a share as a pretermitted spouse, and Benjamin and Gillian would each be entitled to shares as pretermitted children.

now. More likely, however, you have spotted some issues they need to work on, and they may have a new or different idea of how they want their property distributed at their death.

Before we go on to start building their estate plan, however, we need to do one more calculation: calculate the elective share. Even if you draft a sound estate plan for Henry and Wanda, you need to understand how the elective share may limit what you can do and what you can't do. So let's turn to the elective share for our next exercise.

## THE LAW OF ELECTIVE SHARES AND COMMUNITY PROPERTY

As we mentioned above, there are 40 states that require that a decedent spouse provide a minimum share of his estate to a surviving spouse. In addition, nine states are community property states, which means that the surviving spouse will own, in her own right, half of all marital/community property. Only one state, Georgia, has no elective share provision for a surviving spouse, although Georgia does allocate to a surviving spouse enough property to provide support for one year. In those 40 states that have an elective share, the amount to which the surviving spouse is entitled is usually between one-third and one-half of the decedent spouse's *relevant* estate (generally called the *elective estate*). Figuring out the percentage is the easy part. The difficult part comes in identifying the relevant estate, i.e., what property goes into the elective estate from which the elective share is drawn. Calculating the elective estate, therefore, is going to be our focus for the remainder of the Chapter.

It should also be noted that as some states have modified their elective share statutes, they permit a surviving spouse to take their statutorily defined share regardless of whether the decedent spouse dies testate or intestate. In other words, in some states a surviving spouse may be able to take an elective share, even if they are also entitled to an intestate share. Originally, the elective share was only to be taken if the decedent died testate. But many of today's elective share statutes do not preclude an election if the decedent died intestate, including the UPC. This does not mean the surviving spouse gets both an elective share and an intestate share, but he or she may be entitled to choose whichever share is greater.

## MODELS FOR CALCULATING THE ELECTIVE ESTATE

There are three basic models for calculating the elective estate and the surviving spouse's share, although specific differences within each model can be quite significant. The primary distinction lies in the category of property against which the elective share is calculated.[31]

i. *Percentage of Net Probate Estate*—Nearly half the states, like Rhode Island, Massachusetts, New York, Indiana, and South Dakota, give the surviving spouse a set percentage of the decedent spouse's *net probate estate.*

Remember, the net probate estate is all property owned outright at death by the decedent, that does not pass by a will substitute automatically at death, and is calculated after homestead, family allowance, exempt property, and debts are taken out of the decedent spouse's estate. Property held in a revocable trust, in joint tenancies, or in accounts with POD designations pass outside the probate estate and are therefore not considered part of the elective estate in those 18 states plus the District of Columbia that base the elective share on the net probate estate.[32] Some of these states vary the percentages of the surviving spouse's share based on the presence or absence of children, whether they are minors, and whether the surviving spouse is a first or later spouse. So you will

---

[31] See ACTEC Survey on elective share statutes in different states: https://www.actec.org/assets/1/6/Surviving_Spouse%E2%80%99s_Rights_to_Share_in_Deceased_Spouse%E2%80%99s_Estate.pdf?hssc=1.

[32] At time of publication, these were: Alabama, Arkansas, Connecticut, Illinois, Indiana, Iowa, Kentucky, Massachusetts, Michigan, Mississippi, New Hampshire, Ohio, Oklahoma, Rhode Island, South Carolina, Tennessee, Vermont, Wyoming, and the District of Columbia.

need to study carefully the nuances of your state's elective share law. And in states that use the net probate estate, the surviving spouse cannot take both an intestate share and an elective share. The survivor takes an intestate share if the decedent spouse left no will, and an elective share if the decedent spouse died with a will that does not leave at least the statutory minimum to the survivor.

But the easy part is that the elective share is based solely on the probate property. And all that is required in the planning stage is to ensure that the decedent devises an appropriate amount of property in the will to the surviving spouse to cover the elective share. If the decedent does not do so, the surviving spouse may "elect against" the will, thereby taking a larger statutory share and proportionately reducing all the other bequests. That is sure to generate tension among the survivors and will beneficiaries. Thus, ensuring that, at minimum, the statutory share is made to the surviving spouse reduces friction and prevents an election from reducing everyone's shares proportionately, which can cause real headaches in the administration of the estate if some property is more easily liquidated than others.

In the case of Henry and Wanda, you know what their net probate estates are after payment of debts and the family set-asides.

ii. *Percentage of the Augmented Estate*—The second model for calculating the elective estate is to give the survivor an amount of property equal to a percentage of *all* (or nearly all) of a decedent spouse's property, including property that passes outside probate via a will-substitute. These states recognize that a spouse can completely defeat a surviving spouse's elective share by simply putting all of his or her property into a revocable trust or a joint tenancy, so that there is nothing left to probate. In these states, the elective estate is based on what is called an *augmented estate*, i.e., usually the decedent's entire estate, or all property the decedent owned, controlled, or benefitted from in some way during life. In some states the augmented estate is identical to the gross taxable estate as determined by the Internal Revenue Code, but many states deviate from the IRC's taxable estate categories, requiring that you undertake a variety of different computations for the different estates.[33]

In the case of Henry and Wanda, the augmented estate will consist of each one's net probate estate, their non-probate transfers to each other, and their non-probate transfers to others. Again, some states make some adjustments for certain kinds of property, like life insurance or property over which the decedent has a power of appointment. But the general rule of thumb is that we need to capture all of the decedent's property to calculate the elective share.

In states that use the augmented estate model, once we have calculated the decedent's augmented estate, and then determined the percentage of that estate to which the surviving spouse is entitled, we then have to determine the property from which the elective share will be payable, crediting against the elective share property that is already set to pass to the surviving spouse. For instance, Henry is already passing $1,342,000 to Wanda in non-probate transfers. That property will be offset against Wanda's elective share in the augmented estate states, but often not in the net probate estate states. But if Wanda is entitled to $500,000 for her elective share and she was only receiving $300,000, we would need to plan Henry's estate a bit more carefully. The difference can come from the probate property by devising Wanda an adequate amount in the will. Or, property currently set to pass to others outside probate could be changed to pass to Wanda. If adequate property is not set to pass to the surviving spouse, however, he or she can elect against the estate and take the entire probate estate, and if that still isn't enough, some of the non-probate transfers to others may have to be voided or reduced.

[33] The states using some form of an augmented estate are Alaska, Delaware, Florida, Idaho, Maryland, Montana, New Jersey, New York, North Carolina, Oregon, and Pennsylvania.

The use of the augmented estate makes it difficult for a decedent spouse to intentionally or unintentionally disinherit a surviving spouse, and states that use the augmented estate make it very difficult for a decedent spouse to provide less than the statutory share unless the surviving spouse waives her right to these statutory entitlements through a pre- or post-nuptial agreement. This means that a spouse who was married only a few years, or even a few weeks, will be entitled to the same mandatory statutory share that a spouse of 50 years will receive. And it also means that a surviving spouse who has more wealth than the decedent spouse can still take an elective share, reducing or perhaps cutting off the inheritances of children or other testate beneficiaries.

iii. *Percentage of Graduated Super-Augmented Estate*—The third model for calculating an elective share arose from the UPC drafters' decision that it was unfair for spouses of short marriages to receive the same percentage of a decedent spouse's estate as spouses of long marriages, and that the wealthier spouse should receive an elective share at all. Thus, the UPC model begins with the decedent spouse's *augmented* estate, but then calculates the *elective* estate by pro-rating the estate based on length of marriage. It also adds into the calculation the surviving spouse's own property to exclude any spouse that is wealthier than the decedent from taking an elective share. We call this the *graduated super-augmented estate.*[34]

It is *graduated* because the elective estate increases from 3% of a decedent spouse's estate to 100% of the estate, based on length of marriage to recognize that the longer the marriage, more of a decedent's wealth was acquired with the contribution of the other spouse. And it is a *super-augmented* estate because the calculation includes all of the surviving spouse's property in calculating the elective share estate. But the calculation then credits the surviving spouse's own property back in such a way as to prevent an election if the survivor owns more than half of the property in the super-augmented estate. The UPC calculation may seem particularly difficult, but it makes a lot of sense. The UPC is using the elective share to replicate as accurately as possible the property distribution of a community property state in which half of all property acquired during the marriage by the joint efforts of both parties will belong to each spouse.[35] But the UPC does not ultimately correct the imbalance of winning the lottery if the poorer spouse dies first.

---

[34] States that have adopted the UPC model are Colorado, Hawaii, Kansas, Maine, Minnesota, Montana, Nebraska, North Dakota, South Dakota, Utah, Virginia, and West Virginia.

[35] In a community property state, each spouse owns one-half of all property acquired during the marriage as community property and can devise his or her share as they please when each dies. In a common law state, however, the surviving spouse takes a share of the decedent spouse's estate, but the decedent spouse does not get a share of the surviving spouse's estate. It would seem odd to allow a decedent spouse to devise half of the surviving spouse's property while the surviving spouse is still alive. The UPC, therefore, reduces the elective share down to zero if the surviving spouse has more wealth and, presumably, benefitted proportionately more as a result of the decedent spouse's labor during the marriage than the decedent spouse benefitted from the surviving spouse's labor during the marriage. But it doesn't give the decedent spouse any interest in the surviving spouse's property.

To see why this isn't an exact reproduction of the effects of a community property state, consider a husband and wife who marry right out of college with virtually no assets. Over a 50 year marriage, they work together, raise children, and amass a collective net worth of $2 million. If $1.4 million is titled in the husband's name and $.6 million is titled in the wife's name, they would each get half if they lived in a community property state. The wife would own half of the husbands $1.4 million which he could not devise, and the husband would own half of the wife's $.6 million which she could not devise, and it wouldn't matter which spouse predeceased the other, as each would have $1 million in property to dispose of. In a common law state, however, if the husband died first, the wife would get an elective share of, let's say, 1/3 of her husband's estate to augment her $.6 million, leaving him to dispose of $.93 million while she gets $1.07 million (her $.6 million plus the $.47 million that she got from her husband's estate as elective share). That would work out to pretty close to a 50–50 split. But what if she died first and he gets an elective share of 1/3 of her estate? He would get $1.6 million in total wealth to dispose of as he chooses (his $1.4 million plus 1/3 of her $.6 million), while she would only get $.4 million. Thus, in the case of a distribution between husband and wife that is already unequal, the inequality is increased if the poorer spouse dies first.

Now under the UPC, in our hypothetical, the husband would be precluded from electing simply because his share of the couple's wealth is greater than hers, but she would be able to elect. So the UPC helps prevent the asset inequality from getting worse. And if she is able to elect, she will get ultimate control of 50% of the couple's total wealth. You will see how that calculation works out in the exercises in this Chapter. But if she dies first, she only gets to dispose of her $.6 million and he gets to keep his $1.4 million. And if the asset distribution is even more unequal, let's say $1.8 million of the couple's assets are titled solely in the husband's name and only $.2 million in the wife's name, being the survivor is like winning the lottery. In that case, again, the husband would

Furthermore, the surviving spouse is entitled only to property *equal in value* to the relevant percentage of the decedent spouse's estate. But in the case of the UPC's graduated super-augmented estate, we not only offset probate and non-probate transfers to the surviving spouse to determine if an election is possible, we also offset an equal portion of the spouse's own property. If the surviving spouse is the wealthier of the two, the survivor won't be able to elect at all, because the offset for her own property will be greater than her elective share. You will see how this works in the exercise below, and you are likely to have worked through this in your course on Trusts and Estates. Although it may seem like a very convoluted set of calculations, the theory behind the UPC rules are quite simple: take account of all of the couple's property (including non-probate transfers), determine the share based on length of marriage (to account for the spouse's likely role in the accumulation of that property), offset all transfers to the spouse (both probate and non-probate), and then offset also a proportionate share of the surviving spouse's property (to prevent the wealthier spouse from taking an elective share of the poorer spouse's estate). What is left, if anything, is the statutory minimum the decedent spouse must give to the surviving spouse in her estate plan.

## COMMUNITY PROPERTY STATES

In those states that have community property,[36] be aware that the decedent spouse may devise only half of the community property. The rest belongs to the surviving spouse. And although most community property states give all of the community property to the survivor by intestacy if the decedent spouse fails to execute a will, a decedent spouse is entitled to devise half of the community property entirely away from the surviving spouse. Because community property is identified as that property which was acquired by the couple during the marriage, and does not include separate property brought to the marriage and not comingled, and separate inheritances during the marriage, community property states naturally protect the spouse of a long-term marriage with a greater share than the spouse of a short-term marriage. Thus, you don't have to do the complex calculations of elective shares like those of the UPC if you are practicing in a community property state. In fact, the UPC was designed to replicate, as closely as possible, the outcome that would result under a community property regime. The UPC's calculation is so complicated, however, because the parties don't start out with equal, freely alienable shares as they do under community property laws.

### Exercise 3—Elective Share Calculations

Now let's calculate how much Henry would be entitled to of Wanda's estate under each of the three models, and how much Wanda would be entitled to of Henry's estate under each of the three models, using the basic one-third percentage for the elective share in the first two models. The third UPC model uses 50% of a portion of the couple's total wealth based on Henry's and Wanda's length of marriage. So, go back to the chart you completed in Chapter 2, and the net probate estate calculations you did in Exercise 1 of this Chapter where we deducted the set-asides and debts, and then identify how much of Henry's and Wanda's property will comprise the various elective estates. The elective estate might be the net probate estate, the augmented estate, or the graduated super-augmented estate, depending on the laws of your state. Then the elective share will be one-third of the elective estate (or one-half under the UPC).

---

not be able to elect if the wife dies first, but she only gets to dispose of her \$.2 million or 10% of the couple's total wealth. If he dies first, she would take her elective share, which under the UPC would entitle her to 50% of the couple's combined wealth, minus her assets, for an elective share of \$.8 million of his estate. Thus, the UPC corrects the imbalance when the wealthier spouse dies first, but does not give the poorer spouse any part of the wealthier spouse's estate when the poorer spouse dies first. In a community property state, it doesn't matter which spouse dies first, as each has ultimate control over one-half of all the community property.

[36] These are Arizona, California, Louisiana, Nevada, New Mexico, Texas, Washington, and Wisconsin. Idaho is a blended community property/augmented estate state.

To fill in the chart below, you will need to determine Henry's and Wanda's net-probate estates (HNPE and WNPE), how much each currently has passing outside probate to the survivor (H2WNP and W2HNP), and how much each currently has passing outside probate to others (H2ONP and W2ONP). The augmented estate will consist of each one's HNPE + H2WNP + H2ONP = augmented estate. The graduated super-augmented estate consists of the couple's total wealth, or Henry's and Wanda's combined augmented estates.

But there is a small glitch you will need to account for in the UPC calculation. We have calculated Henry's and Wanda's net probate estates by deducting the set-asides and the debts for each. But in calculating the graduated super augmented estate, we only reduce the total marital estate by one set of set-asides, although we take both spouses' debts out. Thus, in calculating Wanda's elective share of Henry's estate, we would add Henry's probate estate (which was reduced by the set-asides and his debts), his non-probate transfers to Wanda and to others, and Wanda's total property. Her total property includes her probate property, her non-probate transfers to Henry and to others, and her debts are taken out. But since we are imagining that Henry will die first, we don't also need to take out of Wanda's property any set-asides for Henry because he would not be entitled to them since he is deemed to predecease her.[37] To make our calculations easier, we are just going to add back in one set of family set-asides in calculating the graduated super-augmented estate rather than adjusting each one's net probate estates.

| | Henry | Value of Property | Wanda | Value of Property |
|---|---|---|---|---|
| A. | Net Probate Estate Value (HNPE)(minus debts and set-asides) | $ | Net Probate Estate Value (WNPE) (minus debts and set-asides) | $ |
| B. | Non-Probate X-fers to Wanda (H2WNP)(minus debts associated with H2WNP property) | $ | Non-Probate X-fers to Henry (W2HNP) (minus debts associated with W2HNP property) | $ |
| C. | Non-Probate X-fers to others (H2ONP) (minus debts associated with H2ONP property) | $ | Non-Probate X-fers to others (W2ONP) (minus debts associated with W2ONP property) | $ |
| D. | Augmented Estate Value = H's A+B+C | $ | Augmented Estate Value = W's A+B+C | $ |
| E. | Add one set of family set-asides back in | $ 64,500 | Add one set of family set-asides back in | $ 64,500 |
| F. | Graduated Super-Augmented Estate Value = H's (D + E) + W's D | $ | Graduated Super-Augmented Estate Value = W's (D + E) + H's D | $ |

Now that you know the value of each of these types of property, you can calculate the elective shares under each of the three models.

37 Of course, there might be exempt property, homestead, or family allowance payable from the surviving spouse's estate to minor children, but until we know when the surviving spouse will die and whether there even will be minor or dependent children, or perhaps a new surviving spouse, we don't take into account the second set of family set-asides.

### a. *Elective Share of the Net Probate Estate*

To calculate the elective share based only on the net probate estate, we will use only the property listed in category A on the chart, which includes only their probate property passing through their probate estate, minus probate debts and family set-asides.

1. Calculate Wanda's elective share of Henry's estate where the state's law allows a surviving spouse to elect one-third of the decedent spouse's net probate estate. (1/3 x HNPE)

Wanda's Elective Share = $_______________

2. Calculate Henry's elective share of Wanda's estate where the state's law allows a surviving spouse to elect one-third of the decedent spouse's net probate estate. (1/3 x WNPE)

Henry's Elective Share = $_______________

As you can see from these calculations, a spouse will always be entitled to receive at least a portion of a decedent spouse's estate if that spouse executes a will. For spouses who leave each other their entire estates, the elective share is not a concern. But if a spouse is providing for the survivor through non-probate property, like life insurance or proceeds from a trust, the decedent spouse may still be required to leave a portion of the probate estate to the survivor as well. Once we have calculated the amount of the elective share, we need to determine if the decedent spouse has satisfied that amount. In some states, non-probate transfers of property will be used to off-set the elective share. Thus, if a large life insurance payment is made to the surviving spouse that more than covers the elective share, then the entire probate estate may be freed up to pass however the decedent wishes. But other states do not look at non-probate transfers, in which case the decedent MUST devise at least the requisite percentage of probate property to the surviving spouse, regardless of the quantity of non-probate property that is set to pass to the surviving spouse.

### b. *Elective Share of the Augmented Estate*

To calculate the elective share based on the deceased spouse's augmented estate, we will use only the property listed in categories A, B and C on the chart for each spouse, which includes their probate property passing through their probate estate, minus probate debts and family set-asides, their non-probate transfers to their surviving spouse and their non-probate transfers to others, minus any related debts. Importantly, we only use Henry's property to determine his augmented estate and we only use Wanda's property to determine her augmented estate.

1. Calculate Wanda's elective share of Henry's estate where the state's law allows a surviving spouse to elect one-third of the decedent spouse's augmented estate. [1/3 x (HNPE + H2WNP + H2ONP)]

Wanda's Elective Share = $_______________

2. Calculate Henry's elective share of Wanda's estate where the state's law allows a surviving spouse to elect one-third of the decedent spouse's augmented estate. [1/3 x (WNPE + W2HNP + W2ONP)]

Henry's Elective Share = $_______________

As you can see, Henry's and Wanda's elective shares would be much larger if you are in a state that uses the augmented estate. However, all of these states offset the elective share by subtracting *all* probate and non-probate transfers to the surviving spouse. Thus, Henry is already passing $1,342,000 to Wanda, and Wanda is already set to pass $117,000 to Henry outside probate. If these amounts are greater than the elective share, then the surviving spouse may not elect against the decedent spouse's estate. If there is not enough property already passing to the surviving spouse, you will need to plan some more, either through the probate estate or through additional non-probate transfers. And note too that if Wanda dies first, Henry will still be entitled to one-third of her entire property, regardless of the fact that he possesses more wealth than she does.

### c. *Elective Share Under the UPC*

The UPC calculation of the elective share is far more complicated than using either the augmented estate or the net probate estate. So we'll go through this exercise more slowly. There are four steps involved:

1. *Calculate the super-augmented estate*, which consists of the total wealth of both spouses, minus both their debts, and minus one set of family set-asides (FSA). To get this number we add up all of Henry's category A, B and C property as well as Wanda's category A, B and C property. Then we add back in one set of family set asides because we have reduced it from both net probate estates.
2. *Determine the marital property portion* (multiply the super-augmented estate by a percentage to reflect length of marriage).
3. *Multiply by the elective share percentage (50%).*
4. *Offset the elective share* by a percentage of the surviving spouse's wealth and then deduct all property transfers from the decedent spouse to the surviving spouse to see if the survivor is entitled to elect.

#### i. *Calculation of the Super-Augmented Estate*

The super-augmented estate consists of the total wealth of both spouses. In Henry and Wanda's cases you need to add all six amounts of property: HNPE + WNPE + H2WNP + W2HNP + H2ONP + W2ONP + FSA = Super-augmented estate (be sure that all debts have been deducted either in a lump sum or by deducting them from each type of property).

**UPC § 2–203. Composition of the Augmented Estate; Marital-Property Portion.**

(a) . . . the value of the augmented estate, . . . consists of the sum of the values of all property, whether real or personal, movable or immovable, tangible or intangible, wherever situated, that constitute:

(1) the **decedent's net probate estate**;

(2) the **decedent's nonprobate transfers to others**;

(3) the **decedent's nonprobate transfers to the surviving spouse**; and

(4) the **surviving spouse's property and nonprobate transfers to others.**

From the chart above on page 63 you should add Henry's A, B, and C and Wanda's A, B, and C plus $64,500 to get a total of their super-augmented estate of:

Total = $______________

About the only thing easy with the UPC calculation is that the super-augmented estate is the same for both Henry and Wanda. So the total number will be our starting point for each of them.

#### ii. *Calculation of the Marital Property Portion of the Super-Augmented Estate*

This entails multiplying the super-augmented estate by a percentage based on length of marriage. The UPC § 2–203 provides as follows:

**UPC § 2–203. Composition of the Augmented Estate; Marital-Property Portion.**

(a) . . .

(b) The value of the marital-property portion of the augmented estate consists of the sum of the values of the four components of the augmented estate as determined under subsection (a) multiplied by the following percentage:

| **If the decedent and the spouse were married to each other:** | **The percentage is:** |
|---|---|
| Less than 1 year | 3% |
| 1 year but less than 2 years | 6% |
| 2 years but less than 3 years | 12% |
| 3 years but less than 4 years | 18% |
| 4 years but less than 5 years | 24% |
| 5 years but less than 6 years | 30% |
| 6 years but less than 7 years | 36% |
| 7 years but less than 8 years | 42% |
| 8 years but less than 9 years | 48% |
| 9 years but less than 10 years | 54% |
| 10 years but less than 11 years | 60% |
| 11 years but less than 12 years | 68% |
| 12 years but less than 13 years | 76% |
| 13 years but less than 14 years | 84% |
| 14 years but less than 15 years | 92% |
| 15 years or more | 100% |

Henry and Wanda have lived together for many years, but they have been married only since 2021. This is one of those many situations in which the actual date on which their marriage became legal matters for significant economic rights. Although they may have had a functional marriage earlier, the probate court will consider only the number of years they have been legally married. So now, multiply their super-augmented estate by the relevant percentage to get the value of the marital property portion of the augmented estate (this is what we call the *graduated super-augmented estate*).

| | | |
|---|---|---|
| Super-Augmented estate | | $__________ |
| Relevant percentage (Determined by marriage length) | x | __________% |
| Elective estate (marital property portion of the augmented estate) | = | $__________ |

*iii. Calculation of the Elective Share*

Once we know the value of the elective estate, we take one-half that amount to determine the elective share that each may be entitled to receive in the estate of the other.

> **UPC § 2–202. ELECTIVE SHARE.**
>
> (a) [Elective-Share Amount.] The surviving spouse of a decedent who dies domiciled in this state has a right of election, under the limitations and conditions stated in this [part], to take an elective-share amount equal to 50 percent of the value of the marital-property portion of the augmented estate.
>
> (b) . . .

So now divide the elective estate in half and you will have the elective share to which Henry and Wanda are each entitled.

| | | |
|---|---|---|
| Elective Estate | | $__________ |
| Divide in half | | x .5________ |
| Elective Share | = | $__________ |

This number represents one-half of the couple's total property, regardless of its origin, in whose name it is titled, or how long it has been owned. The Basquiat painting and Steve's car are all mixed together, including the IRA and life insurance payable to Janet and the older kids that Henry acquired before he met Wanda.

*iv. Offsetting the Elective Share Percentage*

Once we know the value of the elective share, we know how much each spouse would be entitled to at the death of the other. But, of course, it doesn't seem fair to add the surviving spouse's own wealth into the equation to get an elective share if the surviving spouse keeps her own wealth *and* takes a share of the decedent spouse's estate as well. The reason for adding the surviving spouse's own wealth into the equation is to adjust the elective share so that the wealthier spouse won't be entitled to an elective share in the poorer spouse's estate, while the poorer spouse may be entitled to an elective share in the wealthier spouse's estate. How do we do that? Well, now that we have an amount that each spouse is entitled to from the couple's total combined marital property, we offset against that amount three classes of property:

1. Amounts which pass to the surviving spouse by a will or intestate succession (UPC § 2–204),
2. Amounts which pass to the surviving spouse from the decedent spouse via will-substitute (UPC § 2–206), and
3. The marital property portion of amounts included in the augmented estate attributable to the surviving spouse (UPC § 2–207).

At this point, neither Henry nor Wanda has made a will, so we don't have any category 1 property and neither is planning on having any intestate property. We do, however, know how much property each is currently set to have pass to the other through non-probate transfers, i.e., the category 2 property. We can also easily determine the category 3 property by multiplying the amount of Henry's augmented estate by the relevant percentage for length of marriage and crediting it against his elective share. And we can do the same for Wanda.

So let's see if Henry would be able to elect against Wanda's estate, and vice versa. Just looking at the way Henry and Wanda currently hold their property, we can calculate the offsets for each one's elective share by identifying the property in category 2 (non-probate transfers to the surviving spouse) and category 3 (the marital property portion attributable to the surviving spouse).

| | | | | |
|---|---|---|---|---|
| A. | Henry's Elective Share Amount | $ | Wanda's Elective Share Amount | $ |
| B. | Amounts Henry receives from Wanda as non-probate transfers (W2HNP) | –$ | Amounts Wanda receives from Henry as non-probate transfers (H2WNP) | –$ |
| C. | Marital Property Portion of Henry's Estate (H's augmented estate x % for length of marriage)[38] | –$ | Marital Property Portion of Wanda's Estate (W's augmented estate x % for length of marriage) | –$ |
| D. | Total that H would be entitled to | $ | Total that W would be entitled to | $ |
| | May Henry Elect? | | May Wanda Elect? | |

Note that Henry may not elect if Wanda dies first because his marital property portion is greater than the elective share to which he is entitled (C>A). But Wanda might be able to elect as the poorer spouse if Henry dies first. As their marriage continues and the percentage of the total estate that is included in the elective estate increases, she may be able to elect. To see how that might happen, recalculate the elective shares assuming that Henry and Wanda have been married 15 years or more and the relevant percentage is 100%. How does that change the situation?

| | |
|---|---|
| Super-Augmented estate | $__________ |
| Relevant percentage (Determined by marriage length) | × 100 % |
| Elective estate | =$__________ |

Then take 1/2 of that.

| | |
|---|---|
| Elective Estate | $__________ |
| Divide in half | × .5__________ |
| Elective Share | =$__________ |

Now do the appropriate offsets attributing 100% of Henry's and Wanda's augmented estates as category 3 property (the marital property portion of the surviving spouse).

| | | | | |
|---|---|---|---|---|
| A. | Henry's Elective Share Amount | $ | Wanda's Elective Share Amount | $ |
| B. | Amounts Henry receives from Wanda as non-probate transfers (W2HNP) | –$ | Amounts Wanda receives from Henry as non-probate transfers (H2WNP) | –$ |
| C. | Marital Property Portion of Henry's Estate (H's augmented estate x % for length of marriage) | –$ | Marital Property Portion of Wanda's Estate (W's augmented estate x % for length of marriage) | –$ |
| D. | Total that H would be entitled to | $ | Total that W would be entitled to | $ |
| | May Henry Elect? | | May Wanda Elect? | |

Note, Henry still cannot elect. But Wanda can. Why?

---

38 The offset amount for Henry's own property consists of his augmented estate multiplied by the same percentage by which we multiplied the couple's total property in step ii above. And we do the same for Wanda's own property. Remember, this is property that the survivor keeps and can freely dispose of at his or her death because the decedent spouse will not have a claim on the survivor's estate.

Did you notice how, by adding in both spouse's total property (their individual augmented estates), and then offsetting the elective share with the same percentage of the surviving spouse's property, the UPC guarantees that whichever spouse has more than half the total wealth of the couple will never be entitled to an elective share. We can see this by looking at the basic equation:

$[\frac{1}{2} \times X\%(\text{H's total wealth} + \text{W's total wealth})] \geq X\%(\text{surviving spouse's total wealth})$

If the left side of the equation is greater than the right side, the spouse may be able to elect, but not if the left side is less than the right side.

For those of you who went to law school because you hated math, I promise that this is probably the most complicated calculation you'll be required to do, and not all states do it this way. But the UPC's elective share calculation makes a lot of sense. It only allows the spouse with less than half of the couple's total wealth to elect, which makes sense because the wealthier spouse doesn't need a share from the poorer spouse's estate, having already received more than one-half of the marital property.

And second, the UPC calculation gradually increases the amount of the elective share from half of 3% to half of 100% of the couple's total wealth based on length of marriage. Thus, if we assume that most couples work together to amass wealth during their marriages, spouses of long marriages will have contributed significantly to each other's total wealth, while spouses of short marriages will have contributed far less. The UPC's graduated super-augmented estate therefore reduces the amount of elective share wealthier spouses and those of short marriages can take, leaving the residue of the decedent spouse's estate to pass freely to children by other marriages, or to other beneficiaries. The UPC ultimately attempts to recreate at death the effects that would be obtained in a community property state, giving each spouse an entitlement to 50% of the couple's total wealth that was reasonably attributed to the marriage.

And just in case the calculations made your head hurt, or you didn't come to the correct amount, here is a different way of representing the calculations.

You first determine the elective share each is entitled to:

| | | | | | | | | | | |
|---|---|---|---|---|---|---|---|---|---|---|
| 1/2 | × | __ | % | (__________ | + | __________ | + | $64,500) | = | __________ |
| | | ?[39] | % | (H's augmented estate) | | (W's augmented estate) | | (FSA) | | (elective share) |

Once you have their elective share amounts, we need to subtract against that number all property passing to the surviving spouse, plus an offset for each one's total wealth.

1. Whether Henry can elect against Wanda's estate, you must calculate:

| | | | | | | | |
|---|---|---|---|---|---|---|---|
| __________ | – | __________ | – | __ | %(__________________) | = | __________ |
| (Elective Share) | – | (W2HNP) | | ? | %(Henry's augmented estate) | = | |

If that number is 0 or less, then Henry may not elect.

2. Whether Wanda can elect against Henry's estate, you must calculate:

| | | | | | | | |
|---|---|---|---|---|---|---|---|
| __________ | – | __________ | – | __ | %(__________________) | = | __________ |
| (Elective Share) | – | (H2WNP) | – | ? | %(Wanda's augmented estate) | = | |

[39] This is the percent based on length of marriage from the chart.

If that number is 0 or less, then Wanda may not elect.

---

## Lessons Learned

*i. Planning with the Net Probate Estate Model*

Now that you know how much each spouse would be entitled to from the probate estate of the other (in a state that bases the elective share on the net probate estate), you know that whatever estate plan you devise will need to ensure that the surviving spouse will receive property valued at least this much in the will itself, or by intestacy. If either Henry or Wanda dies intestate, however, the intestate share is likely to be more than the elective share, anywhere between 50% and 100% of the net probate estate. However, assuming that Henry and Wanda want wills, which is why they are in your office in the first place, you have two choices. You can either make sure that you draft wills so that each gives to the other at least the required percentage under your state's law of the net probate estate. Or, second, you can ensure that there is no probate estate against which the surviving spouse can elect a share by placing all their property in a trust or other form so that there is no property left to pass by probate.

The second option is a bit more difficult, in large part because it's hard to make sure that all property is held in trust (what about their socks and underwear?). Most decedents will die with at least some property owned outright that passes under a will or by intestacy. Although most states have statutes allowing for summary administration when the estates are small, and there is no real property in the estate, a pretty small estate can easily be swallowed up by the family set-asides. Thus, if Henry or Wanda really wanted to minimize the elective share, they should plan to die owning outright less than the family set-asides. The rest of their estates, like the home, Wanda's jewelry, the painting, and other big ticket items could be placed in trust to pass according to the trust terms, thus avoiding any elective share issues.

Most spouses, however, don't want to disinherit their surviving spouse. Most want their surviving spouse to take a significant portion of their estates, unless they are in a second or third marriage of short duration and their surviving spouse has plenty of her own property. Does Wanda likely want Henry taking a sizable amount of her estate which he could ultimately pass on to a third wife, or would she rather have it pass to her children? In her situation, many testators would want their children to take the majority of their property. Thus, you will need to discuss with your clients how much property each has, how much each wants the other to receive, and whether property they are already passing to their surviving spouse should count toward the statutory minimum. It would make little sense to allow Wanda to elect against Henry's will if she is already receiving significant property via a will-substitute. And Henry doesn't really need any property from Wanda, at least not much over what he is already getting via non-probate transfers.

Some states quite logically determine whether the spouse is entitled to elect based on property passing to the surviving spouse both via a will and outside probate via a will substitute. Thus, if Henry's probate estate were only $100,000, and Wanda was entitled to $33,000 as her elective share, she would not be able to elect if, for instance, Henry had a life insurance policy for $500,000 naming Wanda the primary beneficiary. If she is already receiving more than her elective share outside probate, through non-probate transfers at death, many states will not allow her to also elect against the probate estate. But, not all states do this, so you must carefully study your own state's elective share statutes to determine whether your client will need to devise adequate property to the surviving spouse in a will, or whether non-probate transfers will be sufficient.

### *ii. Planning with the Augmented Estate Model*

When you are calculating the elective share in a state that uses the augmented estate, you will see that each spouse is likely to be entitled to quite a bit more as a statutory minimum than in the net probate estate states, especially in states where the amount is not reduced for length of marriage. The good news is that all non-probate transfers to the surviving spouse will be taken into account in determining whether the spouse can elect. This means that you will need to determine whether each has already provided a sufficient amount of property to the other through non-probate transfers to equal the elective share. To do this, you need to compare the amount that each is already set to give to the other (H2WNP and W2HNP) to the amount to which each is entitled. If the non-probate transfers to the surviving spouse are not enough to equal the elective share minimum, then you will need to advise your client to make up the difference either through additional non-probate transfers, or by making adequate bequests to the surviving spouse in the will.

In states that use the augmented estate model, it is very difficult to reduce the size of the elective estate and thereby reduce the elective share by judicious use of joint tenancies, inter vivos transfers, or revocable trusts. All that property that passes outside of probate, via beneficiary designations or joint tenancies, will be included in the augmented elective estate and, if the surviving spouse is not adequately provided for, there can be quite an upset to an estate plan. You can easily see that Henry has provided enough property for Wanda through non-probate transfers to equal the amount of her elective share if the elective share percentage is less than 40%, but if the percentage is greater, then Henry has not provided enough for Wanda because he has such large gifts going to others outside probate. The question for Henry, therefore, is whether he wants to redirect to Wanda some of the property he already has established (like the life insurance payable to the 4 kids or the house which he could put into joint tenancy and avoid having it count as probate property) or whether he wants to acquire some additional property to give to Wanda (another $500,000 life insurance policy should take care of it).

Wanda is in a slightly different position. She has a very large probate estate and is making a fairly small gift to Henry as a non-probate transfer. Of her nearly $900,000 estate she is only giving him $117,000, which is less than one-sixth. But she currently has a large probate estate and could easily give him a larger portion of that in her will to make up for the difference. But what is going to happen if Wanda does in fact inherit the Montana property from her father or more property from her father's estate if he dies before she does? Suddenly the $117,000 non-probate transfers to Henry and the will bequests won't come anywhere near providing for his elective share. If she inherits a few million dollars' worth of property from her father, Henry will be entitled to one-third of that! So how should Wanda's estate be set up to be ready to deal with that contingency? In such a case, a $1,000,000 life insurance policy payable to Henry on Wanda's life would free up all of her father's property to pass to their children and not to Henry or his possible third wife. This is also a good time for Wanda to point out to her father that he could do some judicious estate planning to prevent Wanda from getting the property outright, and therefore prevent Henry from being able to take an elective share on that property if she predeceases him by perhaps passing it directly to the grandchildren. Although these considerations are going beyond the scope of our fairly simple exercise, you should be able to see how the elective share, especially one using the augmented estate, can really influence an estate plan.

### *iii. Planning with the Graduated Super-Augmented Estate Model*

The graduated super-augmented estate model is likely to throw less of a wrench into an estate plan in the sense that shorter second and third marriages will require a smaller elective share. But Henry and Wanda are likely to have a lengthy marriage. They have already been together nearly 10 years, and the next 10 years are likely to fly by fairly quickly. This means that each will likely to be entitled to a sizable share of the other's estate, except that whichever spouse is wealthier will not be able to elect. Thus, if Wanda dies before Henry, he probably won't be able to take an elective share of her estate, unless Wanda's father dies and she inherits a sizable amount of property from him, at which point her estate will be larger than Henry's. (This should tell you something about the advice you might want to give Wanda's father if you were his estates attorney.) If she is wealthier, he will likely be able to elect against her estate. If Henry dies first, Wanda will be able to elect, especially so if Henry's mother dies and he inherits her modest property. But if Wanda's father dies before Henry leaving her significant property, then she won't be able to elect.

In the early stages of their marriage the elective share is such a small proportion of either one's estate, that each is already likely to be giving property to the other sufficient to satisfy the elective share. But as time goes on, the elective share percentages under the UPC will increase, and their wealth is likely to grow through inheritances from parents, which will need to be taken into account in both of their estate plans. You should remember that inheritances generally are not treated as community property, but they are included in the elective estate in many common law states. Should a surviving spouse have an elective share in property the decedent spouse inherited from his family? Should you recommend that Henry waive any interest in Wanda's father's property should it pass to Wanda?[40] Would you be in a conflict situation if you recommended that he waive his property interest? How do you point it out without potentially breaching your duty to one or the other?

Although you may be working all these calculations in the privacy of your office outside of the presence of your clients, you will need to have a conversation with Henry and Wanda about the elective share. Although most people know that they cannot disinherit their surviving spouses, they rarely know the details of exactly how much of the other's estate each is entitled to and that steps can be taken to reduce or increase those amounts. You may have a sense of how best to handle the elective share (perhaps Wanda should get a larger amount of Henry's estate than he takes of hers, or he should not get an increased amount if Wanda's father dies and she acquires his property outright). But they may have very different ideas. It is terribly important, therefore, that you have a conversation with Henry and Wanda about their preferences, expectations, and understanding of how the elective share works. If they can talk openly about each one's entitlements, and whether to take them or not, then you and they have a good relationship. But if they start bristling, you might need to polish up that letter recommending sole representation.

Remember too, when your clients walk out your door with their nifty estate planning documents all up to date and neatly executed, they are perfectly positioned to be hit by a bus on the way home. But that rarely happens. So the estate plan you create for them should be flexible enough to grow and change as their lives progress. Of course, you will find that certain changes simply cannot be anticipated, and you will instruct them to come back to you for modifications if either parent dies, they divorce, or one of them wins the lottery. Chances are they won't do it right away. So you should be looking at their estates with an eye toward drafting as much flexibility as possible to accommodate the changes that are likely to happen to them. How you do that, however, is next.

## *PRACTICE PROBLEMS*

We realize that calculating the elective share may seem like a mathematical nightmare, but it is incredibly important. As a good rule of thumb, you will generally want to ensure that any married client is providing a minimum of one-third to one-half of his or her estate to the surviving spouse, either through the will or through will-substitutes. Life insurance is a very effective way to ensure that the surviving spouse has adequate property from the decedent spouse's estate. If Wanda and Henry each had a $500,000 life insurance policy payable to the other, they would be well on the way

[40] Remember that if Wanda's father's property passes to Wanda it will likely only go to Gillian and Benjamin if Wanda outlives Henry. But if Wanda predeceases Henry and he is entitled to an elective share in her estate, he might take some of that property where it will ultimately pass to Steve and Doris. What would Wanda's father think about that?

to providing adequate property to cover each other's elective share. Although you generally don't have to calculate the elective share when you are drafting the estate documents, because you won't have the exact numbers of each person's total wealth, you will need to keep in mind how much property needs to pass to the surviving spouse, through one mechanism or another, to satisfy the statutory minimum under the laws of your state.

For practice, therefore, calculate the elective shares of Henry's and Wanda's property, using the property chart (and taking into account debts and family set-asides), but with these additional items. Calculate the elective shares under all three models as well as the law of your own state.

1. Wanda's father dies, leaving his entire estate to Wanda outright, including the vacation home, valued at a total of $3,000,000.
2. Wanda's father is still alive, but Henry's brother dies and Henry inherits his brother's business which is worth $2,000,000.
3. Wanda's father and Henry's brother are still alive, but now Henry's mother dies, leaving Henry the money in the bank accounts and Henry's 1/4 share of the condo in Des Moines.

| | **Net Probate Estate Model of 1/3** | **Augmented Estate Model of 1/3** | **UPC Model** | **Your State** |
|---|---|---|---|---|
| 1. Wanda's father dies, leaving his entire estate to Wanda outright, including the vacation home. | Wanda:<br><br>Henry: | Wanda:<br><br>Henry: | Wanda:<br><br>Henry: | Wanda:<br><br>Henry: |
| 2. Wanda's father is still alive, but Henry's brother dies and Henry inherits his brother's business. | Wanda:<br><br>Henry: | Wanda:<br><br>Henry: | Wanda:<br><br>Henry: | Wanda:<br><br>Henry: |
| 3. Wanda's father and Henry's brother are still alive, but now Henry's mother dies, leaving Henry the money in the bank accounts and Henry's ¼ share of the condo in Des Moines. | Wanda:<br><br>Henry: | Wanda:<br><br>Henry: | Wanda:<br><br>Henry: | Wanda:<br><br>Henry: |

Don't forget to fill out your time sheet, although you may want to reduce the hours a bit if you took a long time figuring out these calculations. And although many lawyers might give these figures to the firm's accountant, that person's time will need to be factored in to your client's bills, so either way keep track of it all.

# CHAPTER 4

# PLANNING FOR INCAPACITY

Estate planning for most clients will include more than simply creating the appropriate documents for the *property* to pass at your client's death. Your client may need some help arranging how she will hold her property during her life, as well as arranging to have it pass to her preferred beneficiaries at her death. But what is going to happen during that period prior to death, when many people are unable to manage their property, and perhaps are unable to make health care decisions for themselves, but have not yet died? Few die in the bloom of youth from a freak accident. The vast majority of people will die after a period of some incapacity. If that period is short, a few weeks or maybe even a month or two, the property can probably be safely ignored. But if that period extends much longer or, as in the case of some people, for years, then arrangements need to be made to manage your client's property and assist your client in making health care decisions while still alive.

When we think of providing a thorough estate plan, there are four basic matters that need to be dealt with:

1. Management of the client's health care decisions during the period of incapacity, before the client has died.
2. Decisions regarding termination of life-sustaining care and funeral directions, or disposition of the body.
3. Management of property during the period of incapacity, before the client has died.
4. Disposition of the property after the client has died.

Prior to any incapacity, your client is fully capable of making health care decisions and management decisions regarding property. But once incapacity strikes, someone needs to be prepared to step in and make decisions in the best interests of the client. Having this conversation with your client about who should make health care decisions, or who should manage the property during incapacity, is one of the most important conversations you will have. In this Chapter, you will prepare incapacity documents for Henry and Wanda to deal with both their health care and their property in case they become incapacitated.

You will also draft a living will and funeral directions. Funeral directions are often included as part of a will, but in many instances the will might not be found, and it certainly won't have been probated yet when decisions about disposition of the body need to be made. The preferred way to direct the disposition of one's body is through a separate document outlining funeral directions. This can include whether one wants one's tattoos removed, dried, and mounted into wall art or one's skull bleached and dried and mounted on a boyfriend's car hood,[1] or something as mundane as cremation and the ashes scattered at sea. In this Chapter we are going to prepare documents for 1–3 above. The fourth item we will take up in the next two Chapters.

## HEALTH CARE DECISIONS

There are three basic documents that should be drafted to cover health care decision-making and disposition of the body at death. The first is a *health care proxy*, or *durable power of attorney*

---

[1] See http://metro.co.uk/2013/07/07/johnny-depp-reveals-he-wants-his-tattoos-taken-off-and-framed-after-his-death-3872239/.

*for health care.* The health care proxy identifies an agent to make health care decisions at any time when the person is unable to do so. If a patient is undergoing a simple surgery and the surgeon discovers a tumor and wants authority to remove it while the patient is still under anesthesia, the health care agent can make that decision. An hour later when the patient wakes up, he or she can resume the power to make her own individual health care decisions. Most hospitals will require that a health care proxy be identified prior to undergoing any surgery, but in the absence of written instructions a spouse, parent, or child will be called upon to exercise that authority. For simple health care decisions, the patient may simply want whoever is handy to make decisions that might arise during a simple procedure if they are unable to do so. But it is usually better to have the paperwork in place to identify who should make these decisions, especially when there are ongoing health issues and decisions that, unlike the emergency tumor decision, don't have to be made on the spot.

The health care proxy identifies a primary and at least one alternate agent for health care decisions, and the proxy may limit the decision making to certain kinds of situations (the patient is in a coma or under anesthesia) or certain kinds of considerations (no blood transfusions, chemotherapy, or respirator). If the patient wants to eschew traditional medicine or wants to specify that certain treatments for certain disorders are preferred, the patient can articulate those preferences in writing well in advance.

The second document is a *living will,* also called an *advance directive,* which instructs the agent and medical care-givers as to the patient's preferences regarding termination of life-support. These documents are an attempt to prevent the situations that Terri Schiavo and Nancy Cruzan[2] faced of living in a persistent vegetative state for years connected to life-support but with no chance of recovery. A living will tells the doctors when not to connect life-support, to withdraw life-support, or to use all efforts possible to sustain life if the patient is unable to resume consciousness and make such decisions herself. Do not resuscitate orders (DNRs) can be placed in a patient's medical records to comply with a living will. And if a patient has executed a living will, hopefully there won't be a battle between family members about whether or not to disconnect the life-support because the patient's wishes will be known and respected. As an attorney, your role in having a client execute an advance directive can become tricky. Although these documents are regularly executed with an attorney, it is unlikely that you or your law partners will be particularly well informed as to the medical consequences of any particular instructions. For instance, what is the result of withholding nutrition, hydration, or both from a terminally ill person? Do you feel comfortable advising someone on these matters?

The third document either nominates a particular person to make decisions about one's funeral and disposition of one's body after death (an *authorization for disposition of remains*), or spells out funeral instructions that the decedent would like to have followed. State law may not allow certain dispositions of human remains that raise health and safety issues, and one's body is not one's property after death to be disposed of according to a will. So funeral instructions or an authorization to an agent to make funeral decisions will not be legally binding, but most people will follow the wishes of the decedent so long as they are reasonable. Asking that one's spouse have one's tattoos dried and mounted on the wall may be asking a bit too much. But some spouses may be pleased at the idea, although if the spouse isn't pleased, it is unlikely that he or she is going to follow through with such instructions, even though they are clearly spelled out.

All three of these documents should be prepared in advance and executed according to state law well before they are needed, and they should be given to the relevant agents in advance as well. The more people who know of one's desire to have the plug pulled if one is in a persistent vegetative

---

[2] *Cruzan v. Director, Missouri Dept. of Health,* 497 U.S. 261 (1990); *Schiavo ex rel. Schindler v. Schiavo,* 403 F.3d 1223 (11th Cir. 2005).

state, the less likely there is to be litigation. The same is true of funeral directions. While everyone is mourning grandpa's passing and deciding on cremation over burial, it's better that they have clear instructions from grandpa that aren't memorialized in the will that just disinherited someone or left half his estate to his unknown mistress.

## Exercise 1—Health Care Proxy/Living Will/Authorization for Disposition of Remains

In this exercise, we want you to draft these three documents for either Henry or Wanda, after discussing with your client who they would like to have make these decisions. Considerations you might want to discuss with them may be:

- Does the client have existing health care concerns and are there family health issues likely to arise?
- Who is most likely to be readily available if a health care emergency arises?
- Who is most likely to make decisions of which the principal would approve?
- Who is likely to be upset if they aren't appointed to make these decisions?
- Whose judgment is likely to most conform to your client's wishes and whose judgments are likely to deviate from what your client would prefer?
- Where would assets come from to pay for health care if the client were in a persistent vegetative state?
- Would the client want life support terminated in all circumstances or only in some circumstances?
- Does the client want a big funeral, a military funeral, a wake, a party, or simple spreading of ashes at sea?
- Has the client made arrangements to buy a cemetery plot or is there a family crypt?
- Does the client want to be buried in particular clothes, with particular jewelry, or with the ashes of the family dog?
- Does your client want to pre-write his obituary or plan her memorial service in advance?

You can imagine that having this conversation with a person who is inches away from death would be quite difficult. But it can be very easy with a healthy person who can think about these tough issues without facing her own mortality. And although the documents that reflect these wishes can be easily changed, it usually gives everyone a sense of having accomplished something difficult when they are in place and taken care of.

Many lawyers may recommend to their clients that they complete these forms in consultation with their doctors or family members, rather than in the lawyer's office, and simply send them home with blank forms. That makes sense, especially if the client needs time to think about these decisions, or would benefit from a discussion with a doctor. But if your client is like many clients, they are likely to leave your office with every intention of executing the forms as soon as they get home, and then it just never seems to get done. Because these documents can be easily changed, it's not a bad idea to go ahead and have them executed during the execution ceremony for the will and/or trust, but also send them home with some blank forms in case they want to make changes later. And since you will be rounding up at least two witnesses and a notary for the will execution, it makes sense to have them help with executing these forms as well.

So let's begin. Reproduced below are four documents, a form health care proxy, a form living will, an authorization for disposition of remains, and a blended document that includes all three functions. Work together in pairs to draft these documents for Henry or Wanda appointing at least one alternate agent or, better yet, two alternate agents for each proxy. Then, draft an authorization for disposition of remains, using the sample reproduced below as a guide, but determine from your clients how they want their bodies disposed of. If you prefer, you can draft a single document that does all three functions, but you may find that your clients have disagreements as to one or all of these instruments and their designated agents and they may prefer to execute separate instruments.

Be sensitive to the fact that the laws in each state differ with regard to these instruments, so you should begin by looking up the advance directive laws for your state. Another valuable resources is Caring Connections, a program of the National Hospice and Palliative Care Organization, which provides documents for each state on its website at: https://www.caringinfo.org/planning/advance-directives/by-state/.

Consider why a single document for each function might be preferable and why separate documents might be preferable. Is it likely to be more efficient to have separate instruments if your client is going to appoint different agents to serve in the different capacities? Does your client want the surgeon who is removing her wisdom teeth to receive a document that spells out how she wants her remains disposed of? What do Henry and Wanda want? As you go over these documents with Henry or Wanda, be sure the client understands what each one will do. Be sure you do too!

### Health Care Proxy[3]

**(1) I,** ______________________________________________

hereby appoint ______________________________________________

*(name, home address and telephone number)*

*as my health care agent to make any and all health care de*cisions for me, except to the extent that I state otherwise. This proxy shall take effect only when and if I become unable to make my own health care decisions.

**(2) Optional: Alternate Agent**

If the person I appoint is unable, unwilling or unavailable to act as my health care agent, I hereby appoint ______________________________________________

*(name, home address and telephone number)*

as my health care agent to make any and all health care decisions for me, except to the extent that I state otherwise.

**(3)** Unless I revoke it or state an expiration date or circumstances under which it will expire, this proxy shall remain in effect indefinitely. *(Optional: If you want this proxy to expire, state the date or conditions here.)* This proxy shall expire *(specify date or conditions)*: ______________________________________________

**(4) Optional:** I direct my health care agent to make health care decisions according to my wishes and limitations, as he or she knows or as stated below. *(If you want to limit your agent's authority to make health care decisions for you or to give specific instructions, you may state your wishes or limitations here.)* I direct my health care agent to make health care decisions in accordance with the following limitations and/or instructions *(attach additional pages as necessary)*:

______________________________________________

In order for your agent to make health care decisions for you about artificial nutrition and hydration *(nourishment and water provided by feeding tube and intravenous line)*, your agent must reasonably know your wishes. You can either tell your agent what your wishes are or include them in this section. See instructions for sample language that you could use if you choose to include your wishes on this form, including your wishes about artificial nutrition and hydration.

**(5) Your Identification** *(please print)*

Your Name ______________________________________________

Your Signature ______________________________________________

Date ____________________ Your Address______________________________

**(6) Optional: Organ and/or Tissue Donation**

I hereby make an anatomical gift, to be effective upon my death, of: (check any that apply)

- ■ Any needed organs and/or tissues
- ■ The following organs and/or tissues ______________________________
- ■ Limitations ______________________________________________

If you do not state your wishes or instructions about organ and/or tissue donation on this form, it will not be taken to mean that you do not wish to make a donation or prevent a person, who is otherwise authorized by law, to consent to a donation on your behalf.

---

[3] Sample provided by the New York State Department of Health, available at: https://www.health.ny.gov/publications/1430.pdf.

Your Signature ____________________________ Date________________________

**(7) Statement by Witnesses** *(Witnesses must be 18 years of age or older and cannot be the health care agent or alternate.)*

I declare that the person who signed this document is personally known to me and appears to be of sound mind and acting of his or her own free will. He or she signed (or asked another to sign for him or her) this document in my presence.

Name of Witness 1 *(print)*_____________________________________

Signature ______________________________________________

Address _______________________________________________

Date__________________________________________________

Name of Witness 2 *(print)* ____________________________________

Signature ______________________________________________

Address _______________________________________________

Date__________________________________________________

## LIVING WILL[4]

I, MARY A. DOE, to my family, physician, attorney, clergyman, any medical facility where I may be a patient, and any person who may be responsible for my health, welfare, or care; when I am unable to participate in my medical treatment decisions, this Will shall stand as an expression of my wishes and directions.

I wish to live and enjoy life as long as possible. I have a right to make my own decisions concerning treatment that might unduly prolong the dying process. However, I do not wish to receive medical treatment which will only postpone the moment of my death from an incurable and terminal condition or prolong an irreversible coma. For purposes of this Declaration, 1) "irreversible coma" shall mean a permanent loss of consciousness from which there is no reasonable possibility that I may return to a cognitive and sapient life, and shall include but not be limited to a persistent vegetative state and 2) "terminal condition" means a condition that is reasonably expected to result in my death in a relatively short time regardless of the treatment that I may receive.

Therefore, if I am unable to participate in my medical treatment decisions, and my condition is terminal as defined above or if I have been in a coma for at least 60 days and that coma is irreversible as defined above, then I direct that:

1. Procedures other than manual feeding used to provide me with nourishment and hydration not be instituted or, if previously instituted, that they be discontinued.

2. Treatment or procedures which will only postpone the moment of my death or prolong an irreversible coma not be instituted or, if previously instituted, that they be discontinued.

3. My physician administer whatever is appropriate to keep me as comfortable and free of pain as is reasonably possible, including the administration of pain relieving drugs of any kind or other surgical or medical procedures calculated to relieve pain, even though such drugs or procedures may lead to permanent physical damage, addiction or hasten the moment of (but not actually cause) my death.

I acknowledge that if medical treatment or procedures are withheld or withdrawn that such a decision could or would allow my death. I desire that my wishes as expressed herein be carried out despite any contrary feelings, beliefs or opinions of my family, relatives, friends, conservator, or guardian. Any person or institution acting pursuant to this declaration shall be released from any liability for any damages incurred as a result of so acting.

I have designated as my agent, my spouse, John H. Doe, and his successors under my patient advocate designation, executed by me to make care, custody and medical treatment decisions for me in the event of my disability. I have discussed my wishes concerning terminal care with my agent, and I trust his judgment on my behalf.

I understand the meaning of this Declaration, and I am emotionally and mentally competent to make it.

IN WITNESS WHEREOF, I hereby set my hand this ___day of ________, 20__.

______________________________________

Mary A. Doe

We know the declarant and believe the declarant is of sound mind and is not acting under duress, fraud or undue influence. Witnesses:

On this ____day of ___________, 20__, MARY A. DOE appeared before us, and signed and acknowledged this Declaration as her free act and deed.

______________________________________

Witness 1

______________________________________

Witness 2

[Insert standard notary provision if required by law.]

---

[4] West Family 2 Family Estate Planning Guide, Appendix 26. Westlaw. © 2023 Thomson Reuters. No Claim to Orig. U.S. Govt. Works.

## AUTHORIZATION FOR FINAL DISPOSITION OF MY BODY

**State of Wisconsin**[5]

I, (print name and address), ______________________________

______________________, being of sound mind, willfully and voluntarily make known by this document my desire that, upon my death, the final disposition of my remains be under the control of my representative under the requirements of section 154.30, Wisconsin statutes, and, with respect to that final disposition only, I hereby appoint the representative and any successor representative named in this document.

All decisions made by my representative or any successor representative with respect to the final disposition of my remains are binding.

**Name of representative:** ______________________________

Address ______________________________

Telephone number ______________________________

(OPTIONAL) If my representative dies, becomes incapacitated, resigns, refuses to act, ceases to be qualified, or cannot be located within the time necessary to control the final disposition of my remains, I hereby appoint the following individuals, each to act alone and successively, in the order specified, to serve as my successor representative:

**1. Name of first successor representative** ______________________

Address ______________________________

Telephone number ______________________________

**SPECIAL DIRECTIONS**—You may write down your wishes concerning the type of funeral, burial, cremation, or anatomical donation of your body. This is the place to give guidance on whether you want or do not want services such as embalming, public or private viewing of your body, cremation or whole body burial, and other practical matters.

INSTRUCTIONS FOR RELIGIOUS, SECULAR, OR OTHER MEMORIAL OBSERVANCES:

SUGGESTED SOURCE OF FUNDS FOR IMPLEMENTING FINAL DISPOSITION DIRECTIONS AND INSTRUCTIONS

______________________________________________________________

______

This authorization becomes effective upon my death. I hereby revoke any prior authorization for final disposition that I may have signed before the date that this document is signed. I hereby agree that any funeral director, crematory authority, or cemetery authority that receives a copy of this document may act under it. Any modification or revocation of this document is not effective as to a funeral director, crematory authority, or cemetery authority until the funeral director, crematory authority, or cemetery authority receives actual notice of the modification or revocation. No funeral director, crematory authority, or cemetery authority may be liable because of reliance on a copy of this document. The representative and any successor representative, by accepting appointment under this document, assume the powers and duties specified for a representative under section 154.30, Wisconsin statutes.

Signed this ______ day of ______________________________

Signature of declarant ______________________________

**I hereby accept** appointment as representative for the control of final disposition of the declarant's remains.

5 Here is a Wisconsin Authorization. An internet-friendly fill-in-the-blank form is available at: https://www.dhs.wisconsin.gov/forms/advdirectives/f00086.pdf.

Signed this ______ day of ________________________________________

Signature of representative ________________________________________

**I hereby accept** appointment as successor representative for the control of final disposition of the declarant's remains.

Signed this ______ day of ________________________________________

Signature of first successor representative ____________________________

I attest that the declarant signed or acknowledged this authorization for final disposition in my presence and that the declarant appears to be of sound mind and not subject to duress, fraud, or undue influence. I further attest that I am not the representative or the successor representative appointed under this document, that I am aged at least 18, and that I am not related to the declarant by blood, marriage, or adoption.

**Witness 1** (print name)______________________________________________

Signature ________________________________________________________

Address _________________________________________________________

Date ___________________________________________________

**Witness 2** (print name)______________________________________________

Signature ________________________________________________________

Address _________________________________________________________

Date ___________________________________________________

**(OR)**

State of Wisconsin

County of ________________________________________

On (date)__________________________, before me personally appeared ________________________, known to me or satisfactorily proven to be the individual whose name is specified in this document as the declarant and who has acknowledged that he or she executed the document for the purposes expressed in it. I attest that the declarant appears to be of sound mind and not subject to duress, fraud, or undue influence.

Notary public ______________________________________________________

My commission expires ____________________________________________

## NEW YORK HEALTH CARE PROXY AND LIVING WILL[6]

Part I. Health Care Proxy

I, ____________________________________, hereby appoint:

____________________________________________________

(name, home address and telephone number of agent)

____________________________________________________

as my health care agent.

In the event that the person I name above is unable, unwilling, or reasonably unavailable to act as my agent, I hereby appoint

____________________________________________________

(name, home address and telephone number of agent)

____________________________________________________

as my health care agent.

This health care proxy shall take effect in the event I become unable to make my own health care decisions.

My agent has the authority to make any and all health care decisions for me, except to the extent that I state otherwise here:

____________________________________________________

____________________________________________________

____________________________________________________

____________________________________________________

____________________________________________________

____________________________________________________

Unless I revoke it, this proxy shall remain in effect indefinitely, or until the date or condition I have stated below. This proxy shall expire (specific date or conditions, if desired):

____________________________________________________

____________________________________________________

____________________________________________________

When making health-care decisions for me, my agent should think about what action would be consistent with past conversations we have had, my treatment preferences as expressed in this or any other document, my religious and other beliefs and values, and how I have handled medical and other important issues in the past. If what I would

[6] This is a copy of a New York Health Care Proxy and Living Will available at: https://www.caringinfo.org/wp-content/uploads/New_York.pdf. It is reproduced with the permission of Caring Connections at www.caringinfo.org. This website has sample documents for all states.

decide is still unclear, then my agent should make decisions for me that my agent believes are in my best interest, considering the benefits, burdens, and risks of my current circumstances and treatment options.

My agent should also consider the following instructions when making health care decisions for me:

____________________________________________________________

____________________________________________________________

____________________________________________________________

____________________________________________________________

____________________________________________________________

____________________________________________________________

____________________________________________________________

____________________________________________________________

____________________________________________________________

(Attach additional pages if needed)

**Part II. Living Will**

This Living Will has been prepared to conform to the law in the State of New York, and is intended to be "clear and convincing" evidence of my wishes regarding the health care decisions I have indicated below.

I, ____________________________________________, being of sound mind, make this statement as a directive to be followed if I become unable to participate in decisions regarding my medical care. These instructions reflect my firm and settled commitment to regarding health care under the circumstances indicated below:

LIFE-SUSTAINING TREATMENTS

I direct that my health care providers and others involved in my care provide, withhold, or withdraw treatment in accordance with the choice I have marked below: **(Initial only one box)**

[ ] (a) **Choice NOT To Prolong Life**

I do not want my life to be prolonged if I should be in an incurable or irreversible mental or physical condition with no reasonable expectation of recovery, including but not limited to: (a) a terminal condition; (b) a permanently unconscious condition; or (c) a minimally conscious condition in which I am permanently unable to make decisions or express my wishes. While I understand that I am not legally required to be specific about future treatments if I am in the condition(s) described above I feel especially strongly about the following forms of treatment:

[ ] I do not want cardiac resuscitation.

[ ] I do not want mechanical respiration.

[ ] I do not want artificial nutrition and hydration.

[ ] I do not want antibiotics.

OR

[ ] (b) **Choice To Prolong Life**

I want my life to be prolonged as long as possible within the limits of generally accepted health care standards.

RELIEF FROM PAIN:

Except as I state in the following space, I direct that treatment for alleviation of pain or discomfort should be provided at all times even if it hastens my death:

____________________________________________

____________________________________________

____________________________________________

____________________________________________

OTHER WISHES:

(If you do not agree with any of the optional choices above and wish to write your own, or if you wish to add to the instructions you have given above, you may do so here.) I direct that:

____________________________________________

____________________________________________

____________________________________________

____________________________________________

____________________________________________

____________________________________________

These directions express my legal right to refuse treatment, under the law of New York. I intend my instructions to be carried out unless I have rescinded them in a new writing or by clearly indicating that I have changed my mind.

My agent, if I have appointed one in Part I or elsewhere, has full authority to resolve any question regarding my health care decisions, as recorded in this document or otherwise, and what my choices may be.

OPTIONAL ORGAN DONATION:

Upon my death: (initial only one applicable box)

[ ] (a) I do not give any of my organs, tissues, or parts and do not want my agent, guardian, or family to make a donation on my behalf;

[ ] (b) I give any needed organs, tissues, or parts; OR

[ ] (c) I give the following organs, tissues, or parts only:

My gift, if I have made one, is for the following purposes: (strike any of the following you do not want)

(1) Transplant

(2) Therapy

(3) Research

(4) Education

**Part III. Execution**

Signed ______________________________ Date__________

Print Name

Address ______________________________

______________________________

I declare that the person who signed this document appeared to execute the living will willingly and free from duress. He or she signed (or asked another to sign for him or her) this document in my presence.

**Witness 1**

Signed ______________________________ Date__________

Print Name

Address ______________________________________________

______________________________________________________

**Witness 2**

Signed ___________________________________Date__________

Print Name

Address ______________________________________________

APPOINTMENT OF AGENT TO CONTROL DISPOSITION OF REMAINS[7]

I, ______________________________________________________________

(Your name and address)

being of sound mind, willfully and voluntarily make known my desire that, upon my death, the disposition of my remains shall be controlled by ______________________________________________________________
.

(name of agent)

With respect to that subject only, I hereby appoint such person as my agent with respect to the disposition of my remains.

SPECIAL DIRECTIONS:

Set forth below are any special directions limiting the power granted to my agent as well as any instructions or wishes desired to be followed in the disposition of my remains:

______________________________________________________________

______________________________________________________________

______________________________________________________________

______________________________________________________________

______________________________________________________________

Indicate below if you have entered into a pre-funded pre-need agreement subject to section four hundred fifty-three of the general business law for funeral merchandise or service in advance of need:

[ ] No, I have not entered into a pre-funded pre-need agreement subject to section four hundred fifty-three of the general business law.

[ ] Yes, I have entered into a pre-funded pre-need agreement subject to section four hundred fifty-three of the general business law.

______________________________________________________________

(Name of funeral firm with which you entered into a pre-funded pre-need funeral agreement to provide merchandise and/or services)

Statement by witness (must be 18 or older)

I declare that the person who executed this document is personally known to me and appears to be of sound mind and acting of his or her free will. He or she signed (or asked another to sign for him or her) this document in my presence.

Witness 1: ______________________________

(signature)

Address: ______________________________

Witness 2: ______________________________

(signature)

Address: ______________________________

ACCEPTANCE AND ASSUMPTION BY AGENT:

7 Prepared by the New York State Department of Health and is available at: https://www.health.ny.gov/forms/doh-5211.pdf.

1. I have no reason to believe there has been a revocation of this appointment to control disposition of remains.
2. I hereby accept this appointment.

Signed this __________day of ___________________________, 20__

___________________________

(Signature of agent)

After you have determined who your clients would like to appoint as agents to make health care decisions, whether they want to provide an advance directive or living will, and have decided on who should take care of the final disposition of their remains, now ask your clients to prepare a short (1/2 page) letter to family identifying how they would like their remains disposed of, any specific requests about a memorial or burial, and any other preferences they have about organ donation. Notice that the Wisconsin Authorization asks for information regarding religious preferences, memorial preferences, and a source for the funds to pay for disposition of the body. You might want to add those to your Authorization. Also, some states may dispense with the witness signatures if the document is notarized. Consult the laws of your state to ensure that your form is in compliance with whatever execution requirements exist.

When you are finished drafting these documents, and you have confirmed that Henry and Wanda are comfortable with them, put them aside. You will have your clients execute them all at the same time as they execute the will and any trust documents you prepare. Now you need to turn to management of the property during incapacity.

## MANAGEMENT OF PROPERTY DURING INCAPACITY

Many people, especially when they are young, view life and death as a fairly straightforward process: you are alive and then you are dead. Really, what else is there? But actually, when cases like that of Terri Schiavo are in the news, people do become aware that there can be a period of incapacity. Unfortunately, most people assume that those long, lingering periods of incapacity will happen to others and not to themselves. I know that I plan to die in my sleep at the ripe old age of 103 after running a marathon. But that really isn't very realistic, is it?

What most people do, if they do anything at all, is put some kind of language into their revocable trust to allow a successor trustee to take over management of their property at death *or incapacity*, and they feel like all their ducks are in a row and they can turn their attention to grocery shopping or playing golf. Then, disaster hits and they are completely unprepared because their checking account that they use to pay the utility bills is not in the trust, they forgot to change that beneficiary designation in a retirement plan to their trust, their annuities are paid to them individually and deposited into their checking account, along with their social security, the car insurance needs to be paid and, until death, there isn't much property in the trust for the trustee to manage during this period of incapacity because it is still owned individually. That trust beneficiary designation will have no effect on non-trust property. And frankly, what is usually in the trust are some securities accounts that don't need much attention during a relatively short period of incapacity; big ticket items like real estate, and all the probate property that will pour into the trust at death is sitting in grandma's apartment where the water and heat have been turned off for non-payment.

At that point, grandma's caretaker or the closest child who is handling her financial matters has to resort to a power of attorney. And often it has to be executed at the last minute because either grandma had been paying her own bills and managing her own affairs just fine until she had a stroke, or family members were writing the checks and collecting her mail and simply having her sign them whenever they visited her in the hospital. But you can't keep signing grandma's name to her checks indefinitely. Eventually, you will need some official paperwork to allow you access to grandma's accounts and, if she is permanently incapacitated when that time comes, your only recourse is a court ordered guardianship or conservatorship.

So what should Henry and Wanda do now while they are young and healthy to be prepared for any period of incapacity? First, joint bank accounts and adding both names on utilities, mortgages, and various accounts will ease the process when one spouse becomes incapacitated or dies. However, there will likely be some individual matters or accounts for which the surviving spouse cannot sign.

And when the surviving spouse becomes incapacitated or dies, that spouse most likely will have individual accounts.

The most common instrument to allow an agent to manage one's property, outside of a trust, is a power of attorney (POA). The POA is a simple instrument whereby the principal can appoint an agent to make a variety of property decisions on behalf of the principal, consistent with a pre-executed set of instructions. The only problem is that the typical POA terminates when the principal becomes incapacitated, which makes it completely unhelpful for the purpose of planning for incapacity. But most states permit execution of what is called a *Durable Power of Attorney*. It is *durable* because it survives a period of incapacity and terminates only upon death of the principal or agent if it is not revoked sooner. Durable POAs can be executed many years in advance, nominating an agent to make certain limited, or more extensive, property decisions only upon incapacity and the durable POA can supplement the powers of a successor trustee. Whenever you use a form POA check to see if it is durable or not.

But before you start executing form durable POAs, you need to study carefully the full scope of property powers that your client will be placing in the hands of his or her agent. These powers can be limited to only writing checks to pay utility or medical bills, or can be so extensive as to allow the agent to change beneficiary designations on various accounts, make amendments to trust documents, or perhaps even amend and execute a new will. The agent of a durable POA is a fiduciary, so if the agent misbehaves the principal or her executor can hold the agent accountable. But it's usually better to be well-prepared than to have to resort to litigation after the principal has died. Thus, your client needs to think carefully about who should be appointed an agent. It should be someone who is responsible and punctual paying bills, yet relatively near at hand. You don't want Uncle Bill having to fly in from Switzerland to manage grandpa's accounts. The person should be trustworthy and, perhaps more importantly, someone that the heirs and beneficiaries will trust. Even if Uncle Bill is a saint, there may be old hostilities between him and his siblings that will lead them to question every decision he makes. If that leads to litigation, he is not likely to be a good choice for the client's estate.

### Exercise 2—the Durable Power of Attorney

For this exercise, get together in pairs, one as attorney and the other as Henry or Wanda, to discuss the powers they would like to give to their agent(s) and discuss who they think would be the best agent to manage their property. Remember, you can designate numerous alternate agents if the primary agent predeceases the principal or is unwilling or unable to serve.

In deciding who to appoint, your client should consider a variety of factors, like:

- age of agent compared to age of principal
- relationship between agent and principal
- trustworthiness and reliability
- business acumen
- financial competence
- compassion and willingness to listen to the wishes of the principal
- flexibility and free time on the part of the agent

Below are two sample durable POAs. Go through them and decide how to cherry pick the provisions that Henry and Wanda are going to want. Discuss with your clients what powers over property each is willing to give an agent. Carefully parse the powers over property and ensure that you understand the contours of each power. If you aren't sure, you might want to either clarify the power or delete it. If you have taken Trusts and Estates, you have probably encountered cases in which a child is given a POA over a parent's financial affairs in the year or two leading up to death and the child gradually empties the parent's bank accounts, cashes in the securities, or sells the real estate and pockets the proceeds. The issue during litigation brought by the siblings is whether the agent took these actions at mom's behest, unduly influenced mom to accede to them, or just went out and did it without mom's approval at all. After the accounts are empty and the house is sold, it's hard to put that genie back in the bottle. Limiting the powers of the agent may make a lot of sense if you think there might be potential disagreements down the road. As long as the property is maintained and not wasted during mom's life, selling the house or cashing in the securities can probably wait until after she has died and her executor can make those decisions under guidance from her properly executed will or trust.

## STATUTORY FORM POWER OF ATTORNEY[8]

### DESIGNATION OF AGENT

I ____________________________________________ name the following

(Name of Principal)

person as my agent:

Name of Agent: ________________________________________

Agent's Address: ________________________________________

Agent's Telephone Number: ________________________________________

### DESIGNATION OF SUCCESSOR AGENT(S) (OPTIONAL)

If my agent is unable or unwilling to act for me, I name as my successor agent:

Name of Successor Agent: ________________________________

Successor Agent's Address: ________________________________

Successor Agent's Telephone Number: ________________________________

If my successor agent is unable or unwilling to act for me, I name as my second successor agent:

Name of Second Successor Agent: ________________________________

Second Successor Agent's Address: ________________________________

Second Successor Agent's Telephone Number: ____________________________

### GRANT OF GENERAL AUTHORITY

I grant my agent and any successor agent general authority to act for me with respect to the following subjects as defined in the Uniform Power of Attorney Act [insert citation]:

(INITIAL each subject you want to include in the agent's general authority. If you wish to grant general authority over all of the subjects you may initial "All Preceding Subjects" instead of initialing each subject.)

(___) Real Property

(___) Tangible Personal Property

(___) Stocks and Bonds

(___) Commodities and Options

(___) Banks and Other Financial Institutions

---

8 Uniform Law Commission, Uniform Power of Attorney Act § 301 (2022).

(___) Operation of Entity or Business

(___) Insurance and Annuities

(___) Estates, Trusts, and Other Beneficial Interests

(___) Claims and Litigation

(___) Personal and Family Maintenance

(___) Benefits from Governmental Programs or Civil or Military Service

(___) Retirement Plans

(___) Taxes

(___) All Preceding Subjects

**GRANT OF SPECIFIC AUTHORITY (OPTIONAL)**

My agent MAY NOT do any of the following specific acts for me UNLESS I have INITIALED the specific authority listed below:

(CAUTION: Granting any of the following will give your agent the authority to take actions that could significantly reduce your property or change how your property is distributed at your death. INITIAL ONLY the specific authority you WANT to give your agent.)

(___) Create, amend, revoke, or terminate an inter vivos trust

(___) Make a gift, subject to the limitations of the Uniform Power of Attorney Act [insert citation to Section 217 of the act] and any special instructions in this power of attorney

(___) Create or change rights of survivorship

(___) Create or change a beneficiary designation

(___) Authorize another person to exercise the authority granted under this power of attorney

(___) Waive the principal's right to be a beneficiary of a joint and survivor annuity, including a survivor benefit under a retirement plan

(___) Exercise fiduciary powers that the principal has authority to delegate

(___) Access the content of electronic communications

[(___) Disclaim or refuse an interest in property, including a power of appointment]

**LIMITATION ON AGENT'S AUTHORITY**

An agent that is not my ancestor, spouse, or descendant MAY NOT use my property to benefit the agent or a person to whom the agent owes an obligation of support unless I have included that authority in the Special Instructions.

**SPECIAL INSTRUCTIONS (OPTIONAL)**

You may give special instructions on the following lines:

______________________________________________
______________________________________________
______________________________________________
______________________________________________
______________________________________________
______________________________________________
__________

## EFFECTIVE DATE

This power of attorney is effective immediately unless I have stated otherwise in the Special Instructions.

## NOMINATION OF [CONSERVATOR OR GUARDIAN] (OPTIONAL)

If it becomes necessary for a court to appoint a [conservator or guardian] of my estate or [guardian] of my person, I nominate the following person(s) for appointment:

Name of Nominee for [conservator or guardian] of my estate:

______________________

Nominee's Address: ______________________

Nominee's Telephone Number: ______________________

Name of Nominee for [guardian] of my person: ______________________

Nominee's Address: ______________________

Nominee's Telephone Number: ______________________

## RELIANCE ON THIS POWER OF ATTORNEY

Any person, including my agent, may rely upon the validity of this power of attorney or a copy of it unless that person knows it has terminated or is invalid.

## SIGNATURE AND ACKNOWLEDGMENT

______________________ __________

Your Signature Date

______________________

Your Name Printed

______________________

Your Address

______________________

Your Telephone Number

State of ______________________________

[County] of______________________________

This document was acknowledged before me on ________________

(Date)

by __________________________________________.

(Name of Principal)

________________________________________________ (Seal, if any)

Signature of Notary ________________________________________________

My commission expires: ________________

## DURABLE POWER OF ATTORNEY[9]

I, *[NAME OF PRINCIPAL]*, of *[name of city]*, *[name of state]*, appoint my *[husband/wife]*, *[name of spouse]*, of *[name of city]*, *[name of state]*, my Attorney in Fact. In the event of the resignation, death or incapacity of *[name of spouse]*, as determined in writing by *[his/her]* primary care physician, then I appoint my *[relationship to alternate Attorney in Fact]*, *[name of alternate Attorney in Fact]*, of *[name of city]*, *[name of state]*, as my successor Attorney in Fact. I grant to my Attorney in Fact full power, unless I otherwise direct, to conduct all of my affairs the same as I could do if personally present and with full legal capacity, including the power:

**Section A.** To collect, hold, manage, maintain, improve, invest, insure, sell, mortgage, lease, exchange, abandon, convey and otherwise deal in any way with any of my real or personal property or any interest in, any proceeds of and the income from this property, in the manner and on the terms as my Attorney in Fact deems advisable, and to transfer any of my property to the trustee of any trust created by me or for my benefit;

**Section B.** To deposit in and withdraw from any bank, savings and loan association, credit union, financial institution, brokerage firm or other custodian of my assets, any moneys, time certificates, negotiable paper or securities, which I may now or later have on deposit or be entitled;

**Section C.** To institute, defend or compromise any legal or administrative claims in connection with my affairs;

**Section D.** To borrow money in amounts and on terms as my Attorney in Fact deems advisable and to give collateral or other security interest;

**Section E.** To make, endorse, negotiate and accept checks, drafts, money orders, promissory notes and other obligations;

**Section F.** To access any safe deposit box of which I am a tenant or co-tenant with full power to withdraw or change the contents; and to exchange or surrender any box and keys, renew any rental contract, and to do and perform all things which any depository agency, association or bank or its agents may require, releasing the lessor from all liability;

**Section G.** To exercise all powers and options, including distribution elections, and beneficiary designations, involving any of my life insurance policies, retirement programs, compensation plans, individual retirement accounts, pension, profit sharing and other employee benefit plans;

**Section H.** To prepare, execute and file all tax returns and obtain refunds, compromise liabilities and appear for and represent me in connection with any tax matter;

**Section I.** To vote at any corporate meeting and to otherwise act as my proxy with respect to any shares of stock, bonds, or other investments I may now or later hold and to exercise any options, warrants or rights;

**Section J.** To engage and terminate employees, agents, professional advisors and medical personnel;

**Section K.** To disburse funds as may be necessary in the sole discretion of my Attorney in Fact for my maintenance and support, to continue any support that I may be giving to any members of my family, and to meet any emergencies which befall me such as illness or other misfortune and to act as my health care personal representative under the Health Insurance Portability and Accountability Act (my Attorney in Fact will consult with my Patient Advocate if I have designated a Patient Advocate who is then authorized to make decisions concerning my care, custody and medical treatment);

**Section L.** To consent to my placement in a home or hospital for care and to consent to and authorize medical and surgical treatment as may be necessary and advisable in the discretion of my Attorney in Fact on consultation with my attending physicians (unless I have designated a Patient Advocate who is then authorized to make decisions concerning my care, custody, and medical treatment);

**Section M.** To make gifts of my property, including to my Attorney in Fact, in a manner consistent with a pattern of gifting established by me or in annual amounts which do not exceed the annual exclusion for federal gift tax purposes;

---

[9] West Family Estate Planning Guide, Appendix 11. Westlaw. © 2023 Thomson Reuters. No Claim to Orig. U.S. Govt. Works.

Section N. To perform all other acts necessary or incident to the execution of the above powers; and

Section O. To disclaim, in whole or in part, any property and any interest in property, including but not limited to the right to receive or control property, a fiduciary power, and a power of appointment.

Any lawful act performed by my Attorney in Fact will bind me, my heirs, beneficiaries, personal representatives and assigns. I reserve the right to amend or revoke this Durable Power of Attorney at any time. However, any financial institution or other party dealing with my Attorney in Fact may rely on this Durable Power of Attorney until receipt by it of an executed copy of my revocation. Subject to the above powers, I retain all legal title to my property. I do not intend by this Durable Power of Attorney to create a trust or to hold my Attorney in Fact responsible as a trustee.

My Attorney in Fact will have no legal liability, in the absence of bad faith or willful default, for failing to act under this power or for acting according to my specific written instruction.

My Attorney in Fact is entitled to receive reasonable compensation for any services rendered as Attorney in Fact.

In addition to the above powers, if I am incompetent or unable to provide instruction, I grant to my Attorney in Fact all of the same powers and discretion and all of the same legal and investment protection provided for a duly qualified conservator of an estate and guardian of a person with full powers under *[name of state whose law will apply]* law.

This Durable Power of Attorney is in addition to any other specific power of attorney which I may have previously executed or may later execute for any bank account or safe deposit box. Any other specific power of attorney, to the extent not inconsistent with this Durable Power of Attorney, will remain in full force and effect.

Any photocopy of this signed original will be deemed an original counterpart of this Durable Power of Attorney. This Durable Power of Attorney shall not be affected by my legal incapacity during my lifetime, except as provided by statute.

This instrument was acknowledged before me on *[date of execution]*, by *[name of principal]*.

____________________________ ____________________

Principal's Signature Date

**Statement and Signature of Witnesses.**

We sign below as witnesses. This declaration was signed in our presence. The declarant appears to be of sound mind, and to be making this designation voluntarily, without duress, fraud, or undue influence. (Two witnesses at least 18 years of age are required by Pennsylvania law and should witness your signature in each other's presence. A person may not be a witness if he/she signs this document on behalf of and at the direction of a Principal.

____________________________ ____________________________

Witness Signature Witness Signature

____________________________ ____________________________

Print Name Print Name

**Notarization (Optional)**

Notarization of document may not be required in your state, but if the document is both witnessed and notarized, it is more likely to be honored in some other states.

On this ______ day of ____________________, 20____, before me personally appeared the aforesaid declarant, to me known to be the person described in and who executed the foregoing instrument and acknowledged that he/she executed the same as his/her free act and deed.

IN WITNESS WHEREOF, I have hereunto set my hand and affixed my official seal in the County of ___________________________, State of __________________________, the day and year first above written.

________________________________

Notary Public

____________________

My Commission Expires

## Lessons Learned

Filling out these instruments is usually considered the easy part of a comprehensive estate plan. After all, most clients would want their surviving spouses to make health care decisions or manage property during a period of incapacity because they trust their spouse. But if there is no spouse, or the spouse might also be incapacitated, your client may need to rethink her plan. Also, one might not want to impose these burdens on an aging spouse and the spouse might not be able to undertake these duties. I can't tell you how many of my colleagues come by my office for advice, telling me that their mom or uncle is in hospice and is about to die and they are just now thinking about getting their estates in order. At that point it is usually too late to do any really sensible estate planning. At that point we are scrambling around trying to download documents off the internet, locate a notary, and get to grandma's hospital room before she gets her next series of pain killers that make her fall asleep. And it's only at that time that people realize that grandma inherited a bunch of property from grandpa that she didn't put into the trust, or that there was a glitch in her social security payments and they were being put into an account that isn't in the trust.

Once grandma is incapacitated, it is usually too late to do much until she passes on and a court-appointed executor has the legal authority to untangle her affairs. Just think, though, how much easier administration of the estate will be if all of grandma's finances are being properly managed by a knowledgeable and responsible agent before she dies. It would be even better if that agent kept impeccable records. And it would be better still if grandma can answer questions and direct how she wants her affairs taken care of, even if she cannot take care of them herself, she can tell her agents where her papers are and how she wants her affairs managed.

Be aware that the durable POA operates usually only during the principal's life, the will operates only at death, and the revocable trust can operate during both periods. But for the reasons mentioned earlier, there is likely to be property that isn't in the trust during the settlor's life, and the client's financial affairs can be thoroughly fouled up by the time the client has died and an executor is appointed. The durable POA is effective for giving someone power to manage all of the client's property, but it can only work well in conjunction with other powers granted under other instruments. Now that Henry and Wanda have these documents in order, we can turn to the big ones—the will and the revocable trust.

### *PRACTICE PROBLEMS*

In thinking about Henry's and Wanda's estate plans, and what would happen to each during a period of incapacity, consider whether any of the documents that were just executed are appropriate or would change under the following circumstances:

1. Henry and Wanda are in a car accident and Henry dies immediately, but Wanda lives in a coma for 5 more weeks.
2. Wanda's father dies and she inherits his entire estate, including the Montana property, that is about to go into a tax sale because her father forgot to pay three years' worth of property taxes. Should Wanda have different durable POAs or change the powers of her agent?
3. Henry is paying all of his mom's bills because she put his name on her accounts, but now Henry is incapacitated with a terminal illness.

Don't forget to fill in your time sheet!

# CHAPTER 5

# THE BASIC WILL

In this exercise you will draft a basic will for Henry or Wanda. And although you may feel a bit out of your depth jumping into a will at this point, you don't have to reinvent the wheel entirely. In the first exercise, you will draft the executorship and guardianship provisions of Henry's or Wanda's will, including the powers given to the executor, plus some introductory boilerplate provisions. In the second exercise you will draft the property provisions. These will include a few specific bequests, a pour over for the residue, and a provision for any property passing to minor children. And in the third you will draft provisions to deal with lapsed gifts, simultaneous death, and decide whether to include an exculpatory or no-contest clause.

To get you started, we have reproduced here 3 different wills drafted by three celebrities.[1] If you want, you can copy some of the boilerplate language from each of the wills as you think best fits your clients' intentions. Many law firms have will and trust software that allows you to simply check a bunch of boxes and then a nifty, completed will pops out of the printer. Since that is probably how you will begin your Trusts and Estates practice, we want you to start thinking about why you would check certain boxes over others. And since we can't give you all of the possible options here in this book, we instead are providing some actual wills so you can start thinking about which types of provisions make the most sense for different types of clients.

The three wills have some basic differences and many similarities. All three have pour over provisions that pour some or all of the decedent's property into a trust. Michael Jackson's will is very short, simply appointing an executor, a guardian, and pouring all of his probate property into his trust. Whitney Houston's will doesn't refer to a revocable trust. Instead, she gives everything to her children if they are above age 30, but if not it establishes a testamentary trust for certain property that would otherwise pass to the children. She also establishes testamentary trusts for her brothers. She has included spendthrift provisions and tax apportionment provisions that are usually located in the trust document and not the will. James Gandolfini's will is interesting as it makes a number of specific bequests, some rather generous pecuniary bequests, and pours some of his property into a trust he already established for his son by an earlier marriage. He has a blended family like Henry, including a second wife and children by two different wives. But his will has many provisions that might more appropriately have been put in his trust. This will has a spendthrift provision, spells out the executor and trustee duties for any testamentary trusts, has an exculpatory clause, and a simultaneous death provision. Gandolfini's will establishes testamentary trusts for underage beneficiaries and only pours some property into the trust for his son. One can only assume that because his current wife and daughter were provided for expressly in the will, Gandolfini may have had separate obligations to provide for his son in his divorce agreement, or he felt that his current wife would not be an appropriate trustee or guardian for his son.

As you begin to work through these wills with the idea of borrowing language for Henry's or Wanda's will, figure out how they differ, why, and what the benefits of the different styles might be. Note too that Gandolfini had a second wife, Houston had an ex-husband, and Jackson was unmarried, although all three had children at the time of their deaths. Gandolfini's will created a lot of publicity that might be worth perusing.

---

[1] There are numerous other wills of famous people at: http://www.doyourownwill.com/famous-wills.html. Admittedly they are not necessarily indicators of sound estate planning, but they are amusing and provide some other examples you might find helpful.

## THE EXECUTOR AND THE GUARDIAN

The most important part of most people's wills is identifying who they want to serve as guardians for their minor children and their children's property. Because children cannot manage their own property, they need a guardian of the property as well as someone who will have custody of the child's person and make decisions about education, medical care, and religious upbringing for the child. Historically, the custody of children was not given to the person who would be the legal heirs of the child, as the temptation to neglect the child was deemed too great if the guardian would benefit financially from the child's death. And for many children, control over the property was viewed as a benefit while custody of the child was a burden, leading the courts to subordinate the interests of the child's physical custody to the interests of the child's estate.

Today, however, custody of the child is the primary concern of courts, and guardianship over the property will follow the physical custody if the testator/parent does not make separate arrangements. In 1646, Parliament gave fathers the sole right to make testamentary appointments of guardians for their children, and if they did so and the mother was still alive, the guardian had priority over the mother and could dictate the removal of the child from the mother's custody. Mothers did not receive the right to make testamentary guardianship appointments until the late nineteenth century, by which time the law treated both parents as having co-equal rights to appoint guardians.

Under the law of today, both parents can name guardians for their children, but those guardians will not be appointed by a court unless both parents are deceased **and** the judge feels that the nominated guardian will be in the child's best interests. Regardless of whether family members challenge the guardianship nomination or fully support it, judges will make individual determinations of the child's best interest before formally appointing any guardian. This means that the guardianship nomination in a testator's will is not binding on the probate judge, but it will be given great weight. Remember how some family members challenged Michael Jackson's appointment of his mother as guardian for his minor children? If your client's children are going to inherit millions of dollars, as did Michael Jackson's children, you can be pretty sure there is going to be someone challenging both the property and the custodianship provisions of the will.

Let's first get some terminology down. The term *guardian* applies to an adult who has the legal right to manage a child's (or an incapacitated adult's) property. The term also is often used to identify the person who has control over the physical care and custody of a child. In some states the term *custodian* may be used to identify the person with legal rights to make decisions about the physical care and custody of a child. The term *conservator* is usually used for the person who has the physical care and custody of an incapacitated adult. In the context of divorce, we often speak of which parent has the physical *custody* of a child, and that usually implies the legal right to make decisions about the child's upbringing, education, medical treatment, religion, and the like, as well as control over the child's property. The law of guardianship determines who will have the guardianship of the child's property upon the parent's death, and the custody of the child's person upon the death of both parents.

Today, both parents are entitled to the physical custody of their children, unless they have been determined to be unfit by a court or have otherwise relinquished their parental rights (through surrogacy agreements or consent to adoptions for example). If one parent dies, the other parent has full, sole, and complete rights to custody of any children, and management over the property belonging to those children. Thus, if Henry dies first, and Gillian and Benjamin are still minors, Wanda will have sole custody of them and will serve as guardian for any property they might inherit from Henry unless Henry specifies otherwise. If Henry dies intestate, and half of his net probate estate passes to his surviving spouse and the other half to his children, then Wanda will serve as a guardian for the half that passes to the minor children. As a guardian of the property, she functions as a trustee, owing fiduciary duties to the beneficiaries during their minority. When they reach age 18, however, she must relinquish control over their property to them, and the guardianship terminates.

If Henry makes a will, however, and designates his daughter Doris to be the guardian of his children, then Wanda will continue to have the custody of the children, but Doris may serve as guardian of the property until the children reach 18, or later if Henry creates a trust and thereby postpones giving them outright ownership of any property until they reach a more mature age. If Wanda predeceases Henry, and then Henry dies leaving minor children and appointing Doris the guardian, she will be entitled to serve as both the guardian of the property and the custodian of the children, although a probate judge will have to approve her appointment for both. If Steve challenges Doris' appointment, the judge may decide that Steve would be a better guardian of the property or of the children and completely ignore Henry's will. But in most cases, judges try to respect the wishes of parents and, unless there is some serious reason why Doris should not serve as guardian, a judge would most likely approve her appointment. But at any later time, Steve may come back to court and request that Doris be deprived of her guardianship if he has evidence that she is neglecting the children or is squandering their property.

It is also important to note that a guardian is not a parent, and does not have the full range of parental rights that a parent has. For this reason, many children who have lost one parent may be adopted by a later spouse of the surviving parent. Children do not inherit from guardians, and vice versa, nor do wards of guardians receive homestead, family allowance, or exempt property from their guardians. Although guardians make a lot of the practical decisions for a child, the guardian is not a parent.

One of the most important reasons for executing a will is to nominate guardians for the physical care and custody of minor or incapacitated children. This cannot be done in a trust document. So when a client is thinking about who should have the physical care and control of minor children, the client should consider who should serve if the other parent predeceases the testator, or if both parents die simultaneously in an accident. In thinking about who to appoint, you might want to discuss with your client things like parenting styles, temperament, career demands, age, and resources of potential guardian nominees.

The next important question is whether the guardian of the person will need resources to take care of the children from the property the children will inherit from the parent. In all cases, children are entitled to being supported, if possible, in the style to which they have become accustomed. Thus, if Michael Jackson's children are used to a very wealthy life-style, they are entitled to continue that life-style. But if the guardian cannot fund that life-style adequately, the court will grant a certain amount of support from the children's estates to be paid to the guardian. If the guardian of the children also has control over the children's estates, then that person will need to keep track of how much money was spent on their support and be prepared to make an accounting when the children come of age and they receive whatever property is left.

Where there is a sizable estate, however, few parents want their children to receive full control over their inheritances at age 18. In most cases, they would rather put the property into a trust, with directions to the trustee to pay for the support of the children during their minority, and then to pay for their college education or to buy a house or to set them up in a trade. Few parents think their children are capable of managing an inheritance at age 18. But maybe at age 25, or 30, or 35 they can handle it. But *legal* guardianships of the person and the property must end at age 18 unless the property is put into trust or the child is incapacitated. This means that your client needs to consider the many different ways in which property can be held, and by different people, when they think about how to set up their estates to support their children into adulthood. In many respects, the property considerations are the more complicated aspects of estate planning, and the custodianship of the children is more easily settled upon. However, the relationship between the custodian of the children and the guardian of the children's property is one that must be carefully thought out.

Wills also should appoint an executor, or personal representative, to administer the estate. This person should be detail-oriented, efficient, and capable of managing the money, locating the assets, hiring an attorney, contacting potential beneficiaries, filling out all the forms for the probate court, and paying the decedent's bills ON TIME. The executor also serves as a fiduciary and, because he or she will have control over all the decedent's probate property during the period of administration, courts usually require that they post a bond (an insurance policy to ensure that they won't misbehave). Usually, testators will include in their wills a provision that the executor need not post a bond if the nominated individual is a close and trusted family member. But just like the guardian nomination, the judge does not have to appoint the nominated person as executor if there are serious questions about that person's qualifications. If the nominated executor predeceases the testator, declines to serve, or is unfit, the court will appoint someone else executor. Many states preclude felons, minors, and those suffering mental or physical disabilities that interfere with effective service from being appointed executors. Usually, testators will name at least two and sometimes three or four potential candidates for executor, and will indicate which, if any, are relieved from having to post a bond. If none of the nominated executors are appointed, the court will appoint someone else, and that person will likely have to post a bond.

### Exercise 1—Introduction, Guardian, Executor, Debts and Funeral Arrangements

Assuming that Henry and Wanda would each serve as sole custodians of Gillian and Benjamin were the other to die, and that each trusts the other to manage the children's share of property during their minority, draft the relevant language accordingly. But also consider whether Henry and/or Wanda would like to delay giving any property to the children until they are older than 18 by establishing a trust for the property. Also draft the relevant language to appoint a guardian in case Henry and Wanda die simultaneously and determine who should have control over the minor children's estates, and until when, if neither parent is alive. Although we will be drafting the property provisions in the next exercise, be thinking about whether Henry and Wanda are going to want to use a trust to manage any property that may pass to their children. A trust is usually a good idea at least until the children reach a suitable age.

Next, draft the executorship/personal representative provision. The executor is the person the testator believes will do a good job administering the estate. You also need to consider what powers your client wants to give to the executor to manage the property. In the case of Michael Jackson and Whitney Houston, their estates continue to receive millions of dollars yearly in royalties from their music. Should the executor be given the power to grant licenses or to invest the money in certain types of investments? Should Henry and Wanda's executors be empowered to sell any real estate, trade in certain stock, or otherwise manage the estate long-term? What if there isn't enough cash on hand to pay medical bills? Should the executor be given sole discretion as to what assets should be liquidated to pay debts and/or estate taxes. Look at the examples in the wills below and draft the appropriate powers language for the executor. As part of this exercise, discuss with your client some priorities in case both Henry and Wanda die simultaneously, either dies with extensive medical debts, the stock market tanks, or the house has to be sold.

The decedent's debts also need to be paid. Although many wills direct the executor to pay all *just debts*, that isn't really necessary as the executor must pay them regardless of the will. However, if there is any property that is indebted, and for which the estate is not going to pay off the debts, this is a good time to mention it. *Exoneration* is the doctrine that allows a will beneficiary to ask the estate to pay off debts on property specifically devised. But most people don't think the estate should pay the mortgage on the house, or perhaps even a car loan. Today, non-exoneration is the default rule, but it's always best to be specific. So think about that loan on Doris' car.

It's also a good time to mention what property should be used to pay final debts. Many wills that simply pour over probate assets into a trust direct that the trustee will pay the debts and that the trust is liable for them. Unless the trust instrument acknowledges that the trustee can use trust assets to pay off debts, it would be a breach of the trustee's fiduciary duty to pay the estate's debts. This would mean that the payment of the debts would have to come out of the probate property and might result in the forced sale of assets that the decedent would not wish to have sold. Discuss with Henry and Wanda their debts, and discuss the likelihood of future debts, especially medical costs, and what property they think should be available to pay for those debts. What happens if that property doesn't exist? Where should the property come from to pay debts? Look at the examples below and draft either a generic just debts clause, or be more specific if you think that is appropriate.

Funeral directions are non-binding as well, especially because in many cases the decedent's body has already been buried or cremated before the will is even discovered, and certainly well before the will is filed for probate. But funeral directions help ease the mind of the testator, who may want his or her body disposed of in a particular way. Although you had Henry and Wanda draft funeral instructions, and appoint a decision-maker to make decisions about disposition of their bodies, this is a nice time to repeat some aspects of those instructions (perhaps not every detail about what songs are to be played at the memorial) and to remind everyone that the testators have made separate arrangements for disposition of their bodies or have stated who they want to make disposition decisions.

In drafting funeral directions, think about the ability (or inability) of the executor to comply with the decedent's wishes in Gary Coleman's will. He wrote:

> I direct my personal representative to cause my personal remains to be cremated and to plan a wake for me conducted by those who have had no financial ties to me and can look each other in the eyes and say they really cared personally for Gary Coleman. I direct my personal representative to permit no members of the press to be present at my wake or funeral.[2]

It is tempting to want to express one's personal grievances with the world or with one's family in the funeral instructions, but is that sound? How would Coleman's executor know who could be invited and who could not be invited, or whether people had financial ties to Coleman or not? Is there anyone who could complain if the executor held a public funeral open to the whole world? What purpose does a statement like this serve? A private letter to family is a much more effective mechanism for providing funeral instructions.

Also, as you draft these important provisions of Henry's or Wanda's will, go ahead and draft the other boilerplate provisions, like whether they are married, have children, the identity of their children, and make provision for afterborn children. Did you note that Whitney Houston's will was written about a month before the birth of her only child back in 1993. She did not update it upon her divorce, when her father died, or when it became clear that she would not have any additional children. If you make provisions for afterborn children, then they cannot take intestate shares under the state's pretermitted child statute. What if Henry and Wanda have more children, or adopt a child? Think about how their situations could change in the future and draft language that you think might be relevant to their situations. You should notice in these three wills reproduced below that less than half is spent making actual property dispositions. Make mention of debts and anything else you spot that you think should be included. Discuss these with your client too before

---

[2] https://www.megadox.com/Gary-Coleman-Last-Will-and-Testament.

you assume that they will, or won't, want to exercise powers of appointment they may later acquire, for instance.

## Drafting Considerations

As you review the wills and begin to pick and choose certain language to copy, and draft other more customized language, you may be wondering where to start. What considerations should guide your drafting, other than avoiding confusion and keeping your work out of litigation? Here are some basic things you should keep in mind:

### *Avoid Ambiguity*

Practitioners often start drafting a will from an existing document. However, it is important that each time you draft a will for a client, you review and edit it as if you were drafting it from scratch. Nothing could be more embarrassing, or potentially disastrous, than having a client execute a document that does not say what you think it should say.

When drafting wills, trusts, or any other document, keep in mind that you are creating a set of rules; rules that govern the administration and disposition of a testator's estate, or a Settlor's trust. The biggest pitfall in any document you draft is the creation of an ambiguity—any statement that could reasonably be read to mean more than one thing, or one in which the testator's meaning is obscured. While perfect clarity may be difficult to achieve, every step in that direction can lessen the likelihood of litigation over a will or trust.

In order to avoid ambiguity, there are simple steps you can take. First, clearly identify any person, thing or concept, and then consistently use that same name or terminology throughout the will. For instance, once you choose to refer to the administrator of the estate as the personal representative, do not use any other term (administrator or executor) when referring to that person. By using inconsistent terminology, you are telling your reader that you are not talking about the same idea or the same person. Your best bet, in selecting terminology, is to look at your state's probate code and use the same terms it uses.

Consistency is also important for references to beneficiaries. In most instances, a testator's intent is to benefit a class of people—children, grandchildren, siblings, or parents. By identifying these people early in the document, you can refer to the class, rather than the individuals throughout the documents. Keep in mind, however, that these classes can change over time (children are born, people die), and that your document needs to be flexible enough to account for those changes. For instance, had Henry and Wanda executed wills after the birth of Benjamin, but before Gillian was born, it would make sense to mention the existence of Benjamin, while also allowing the will to provide for later born children. You might write something like this: *As of the date of this will, my only living child is Benjamin Higgins, but any references to my children refer to him, as well as any child of mine born or adopted after the date of this will.*

Another possible source of ambiguity is the verbs of authority in the document. For instance, in directing the Executor to act, be clear when you are making that action mandatory (my executor will [or shall]) or you are making the action discretionary (my executor may. . .). In establishing a distribution, use the language of gifting—give, devise or bequeath. As you will see, attorneys are never happier than when they can use three words when only one is necessary. Does saying *"I hereby give, devise and bequeath my pocket watch to my eldest grandson, Jack McManus"* provide greater clarity than "I give my pocket watch to Jack McManus." If you believe that each additional word is necessary, you should know what each word means, and what it adds to the clarity of your document. The IRS and court rulings on validity or tax treatment of a trust or estate often will become the source of language that practitioners use to draft these documents. While these rulings are very important, beware of the kitchen sink approach to drafting. Just because XYZ language worked for one trust and ABC language worked for a second trust, using both XYZ and ABC won't necessarily work for you.

When drafting specific devises, it is especially important to be clear. For instance, if the Testator leaves his 'art collection' to his sister, but his home and its furnishings to his wife, what does that mean for the artwork in his home? What happens if the Testator sells the home and most of the furnishings, and moves to a smaller home? Did the testator intend for his wife to receive less? Did he intend that she would also be entitled to the proceeds from those sales? Either result is likely, but you as the attorney need to be able to anticipate this contingency and to draft a document to reflect these changes.

### *Organizing a Will*

While there is not one standard way to organize a will, think about the types of topics your will covers. Normally, you will start with the who—identify the testator, the classes of heirs and other beneficiaries, the executor, the trustee of any testamentary trust, and the guardian, as well as any successors. Next, as discussed in the exercise below, the will is likely to discuss the payment of taxes and debts. These provisions are generally written as directions to the executor and for now you can skip the tax apportionment clause as we will come back to that in Chapter 9. Next, a will normally will address specific devises, including any devise of the estate to a testamentary or existing trust. Last, assuming the will includes the possibility of a testamentary trust, the will discusses the administration of the trust, and the trustee's responsibilities.

One other consideration in organizing a will is to decide if the document you have created is 'user friendly.' Look at the examples provided below and ask yourself how easy it is to find a specific piece of information. If you were the executor of one of those estates, would you easily be able to find the sections addressing your powers? One often overlooked tool for making a document easy to use is the creation of headings and subheadings. Consider using them if the document you are drafting is likely to be used as a regular source of information or rules.

**LAST WILL AND TESTAMENT**

**of**

**MICHAEL JOSEPH JACKSON[3]**

I, MICHAEL JOSEPH JACKSON, a resident of the State of California, declare this to be my last Will, and do hereby revoke all former wills and codicils made by me.

I

I declare that I am not married. My marriage to DEBORAH JEAN ROWE JACKSON has been dissolved. I have three children now living, PRINCE MICHAEL JACKSON, JR., PARIS MICHAEL KATHERINE JACKSON and PRINCE MICHAEL JOSEPH JACKSON,II. I have no other children, living or deceased.

II

It is my intention by this Will to dispose of all property which I am entitled to dispose of by will. I specifically refrain from exercising all powers of appointment that I may possess at the time of my death.

III

I give my entire estate to the Trustee or Trustees then acting under that certain Amended and Restated Declaration of Trust executed on March 22, 2002 by me as Trustee and Trustor which is called the MICHAEL JACKSON FAMILY TRUST, giving effect to any amendments thereto made prior to my death. All such assets shall be held, managed and distributed as a part of said Trust according to its terms and not as a separate testamentary trust.

If for any reason this gift is not operative or is invalid, or if the aforesaid Trust fails or has been revoked, I give my residuary estate to the Trustee or Trustees named to act in the MICHAEL JACKSON FAMILY TRUST, as Amended and Restated on March 22, 2002, and I direct said Trustee or Trustees to divide, administer, hold and distribute the trust estate pursuant to the provisions of said Trust, as hereinabove referred to as such provisions now exist to the same extent and in the same manner as though that certain Amended and Restated Declaration of Trust, were herein set forth in full, but without giving effect to any subsequent amendments after the date of this Will. The Trustee, Trustees, or any successor Trustee named in such Trust Agreement shall serve without bond.

IV

I direct that all federal estate taxes and state inheritance or succession taxes payable upon or resulting from or by reason of my death (herein "Death Taxes") attributable to property which is part of the trust estate of the MICHAEL JACKSON FAMILY TRUST, including property which passes to said trust from my probate estate shall be paid by the Trustee of said trust in accordance with its terms. Death Taxes attributable to property passing outside this Will, other than property constituting the trust estate of the trust mentioned in the preceding sentence, shall be charged against the taker of said property.

V

I appoint JOHN BRANCA, JOHN McCLAIN and BARRY SIEGEL as co-Executors of this Will. In the event of any of their deaths, resignations, inability, failure or refusal to serve or continue to serve as a co-Executor, the other shall serve and no replacement need be named. The co-Executors serving at any time after my death may name one or more replacements to serve in the event that none of the three named individuals is willing or able to serve at any time.

The term "my executors" as used in this Will shall include any duly acting personal representative or representatives of my estate. No individual acting as such need post a bond.

[3] See more at: https://www.documentcloud.org/documents/19395-michael-jacksons-will.

I hereby give to my Executors, full power and authority at any time or times to sell, lease, mortgage, pledge, exchange or otherwise dispose of the property, whether real or personal comprising my estate, upon such terms as my Executors shall deem best, to continue any business enterprises, to purchase assets from my estate, to continue in force and pay insurance premiums on any insurance policy, including life insurance, owned by my estate, and for any of the foregoing purposes to make, execute and deliver any and all deeds, contracts, mortgages, bills of sale or other instruments necessary or desirable therefor. In addition, I give to my Executors full power to invest and reinvest the estate funds and assets in any kind of property, real, personal or mixed, and every kind of investment, specifically including, but not by way of limitation, corporate obligations of every kind and stocks, preferred or common, and interests in investment trusts and shares in investment companies, and any common trust fund administered by any corporate executor hereunder, which men of prudent discretion and intelligence acquire for their own account.

VI

Except as otherwise provided in this Will or in the Trust referred to in Article III hereof, I have intentionally omitted to provide for my heirs. I have intentionally omitted to provide for my former wife, DEBORAH JEAN ROWE JACKSON.

VII

If at the time of my death I own or have an interest in property located outside of the State of California requiring ancillary administration, I appoint my domiciliary Executors as ancillary Executors for such property. I give to said domiciliary Executors the following additional powers, rights and privileges to be exercised in their sole and absolute discretion, with reference to such property: to cause such ancillary administration to be commenced, carried on and completed; to determine what assets, if any, are to be sold by the ancillary Executors; to pay directly or to advance funds from the California estate to the ancillary Executors for the payment of all claims, taxes, costs and administration expenses, including compensation of the ancillary Executors and attorneys' fees incurred by reason of the ownership of such property and by such ancillary administration; and upon completion of such ancillary administration, I authorize and direct the ancillary Executors to distribute, transfer and deliver the residue of such property to the domiciliary Executors herein, to be distributed by them under the terms of this Will, it being my intention that my entire estate shall be administered as a unit and that my domiciliary Executors shall supervise and control, so far as permissible by local law, any ancillary administration proceedings deemed necessary in the settlement of my estate.

VIII

If any of my children are minors at the time of my death, I nominate my mother, KATHERINE JACKSON as guardian of the persons and estates of such minor children. If KATHERINE JACKSON fails to survive me, or is unable or unwilling to act as guardian, I nominate DIANA ROSS as guardian of the persons and estates of such minor children.

I subscribe my name to this Will this __7__ day of __July__, 2002

______________________________

MICHAEL JOSEPH JACKSON

On the date written below, MICHAEL JOSEPH JACKSON, declared to us, the undersigned, that the foregoing instrument consisting of five (5) pages, including the page signed by us as witnesses, was his Will and requested us to act as witnesses to it. He thereupon signed this Will in our presence, all of us being present at the same time. We now, at his request, in his presence and in the presence of each other, subscribe our names as witnesses.

Each of us is now more than eighteen (18) years of age and a competent witness and resides at the address set forth after his name.

Each of us is acquainted with MICHAEL JOSEPH JACKSON. At this time, he is over the age of eighteen (18) years and, to the best of our knowledge, he is of sound mind and is not acting under duress, menace, fraud, misrepresentation or undue influence.

We declare under penalty of perjury that the foregoing is true and correct.

Executed on ___July 7th___, 2002 at ___5 p.m.___, ___Los Angeles, CA___

______________________ Residing At ______________________

______________________ Residing At ______________________

______________________ Residing At ______________________

**LAST WILL AND TESTAMENT**

**of**

**WHITNEY E. HOUSTON**[4]

I, WHITNEY E. HOUSTON, residing in the State of New Jersey, declare this to be my Last Will and Testament and revoke all my prior wills and codicils.

FIRST: I direct that my funeral and cemetery expenses, the expenses of my last illness, all expenses of administration of my estate and all my debts (except mortgage indebtedness and indebtedness secured by any life insurance policy or otherwise secured) that are just and not barred by time be paid by my Executors from my residuary estate.

SECOND: (A) I give my entire interest in all my household furniture and furnishings and other articles of household use or ornament located at any real estate used by me on a full or part-time basis for my residential purposes, together with all my clothing, personal effects, jewelry, and automobiles, and all insurance policies thereon, if any (hereinafter referred to as my "tangible personal property"), to any children of mine who survive me, in such portions as my Executors, in their sole discretion may deem advisable, or sell the same, or any balance thereof, and add the proceeds to my residuary estate.

(B) If no child of mine survives me:

(1) I give all jewelry I own at my death to my mother, EMILY CISSY HOUSTON, if she survives me; and

(2) I give the rest of my tangible personal property (or all of my tangible personal property if my mother does not survive me) to those of my mother, EMILY CISSY HOUSTON, my father, JOHN R. HOUSTON, my husband, ROBERT B. BROWN, my brother, MICHAEL HOUSTON, and my brother, GARY HOUSTON, as survive me, to be amicably divided among them as they might agree, in shares as nearly equal as possible.

If my mother, my father, my husband and my said brothers cannot agree on the distribution of any property which would otherwise be distributed to them under this Article SECOND, I direct that such property be sold and the proceeds be added to my residuary estate.

THIRD: The balance of my estate, whether real or personal and wherever situate (referred to as my "residuary estate") shall be disposed of as follows:

(A) If any issue of mine survive me, my residuary estate shall be paid to my issue living at my death, per stirpes; provided that any part of my residuary estate passing to a child or more remote descendant of mine who is younger than thirty (30) years of age at my death shall not be paid to him or her outright, but rather I give the same to my Trustees to hold in a separate trust for his or her benefit pursuant to Article FOURTH.

(B) If I leave no issue at my death, my residuary estate shall be paid, in equal shares, to those of my mother, EMILY CISSY HOUSTON, my father, JOHN R. HOUSTON, my husband, ROBERT B. BROWN, my brother, MICHAEL HOUSTON, and my brother, GARY HOUSTON, who survive me; provided, however, that as to each of my said brothers (regardless of his age), his share of my residuary estate shall not be paid to him outright, but rather the same shall be paid to my Trustees to hold in a separate trust for the benefit of such brother pursuant to Article FIFTH.

FOURTH: The following are the terms of the separate trusts for the respective benefit of any child or more remote descendant of mine who is younger than thirty (30) years of age, each of whom is hereinafter referred to as the "Beneficiary" of his or her separate trust:

(A) My Trustees may, at any time or from time to time, pay to the Beneficiary, or apply for his or her benefit, upon such occasions as my Trustees in their sole discretion shall deem advisable, so much or all (or

[4] See more at: https://abcnews.go.com/images/Entertainment/Whitney%20Houston%20Will.pdf.

none) of the entire net income and so much or all (or none) of the principal of the separate trust held for the Beneficiary as my Trustees may deem desirable. At the end of each trust year, my Trustees shall add to the principal of such separate trust any net income not so paid or applied and thereafter the same shall be dealt with as principal for all purposes. Without limiting my Trustees as to occasions upon which payments may be made and without requiring them to make any payment if they deem it inadvisable, I suggest that purposes for which distributions of income and principal might be made include maintenance, educational requirements, engagement, marriage, acquisition of a home, birth of a child, commencement of a new business enterprise or continuance of an existing one, and medical requirements. In granting discretion to my Trustees to make such payments, it is my desire that such discretion be liberally exercised when the occasion, whether one previously specified or not, is such that the interests of the Beneficiary would, in my Trustees' judgment, be best served thereby.

(B) My Trustees shall make the following distributions of principal to the Beneficiary from his or her separate trust:

(1) One-tenth (1/10) of the then principal when the Beneficiary reaches the age of twenty one (21) years;

(2) One-sixth (1/6) of the then principal when the Beneficiary reaches the age of twenty-five (25) years; and

(3) The entire remaining principal, together with all accrued and undistributed income, when the Beneficiary reaches the age of thirty (30) years, whereupon the separate trust held for the Beneficiary shall terminate; provided that if the Beneficiary is at least twenty-one (21) years of age at the time the separate trust is set aside for his or her benefit, one-tenth (1/10) of such separate trust shall then be paid to him or her in lieu of the payment specified in subparagraph "(1)" above; and provided further that if the Beneficiary is at least twenty-five (25) years old at the time the separate trust is set aside for his or her benefit, one-fourth (1/4) of such separate trust shall then be paid to him or her in lieu of the payments specified in subparagraphs "(1)" and "(2)" above.

(C) If the Beneficiary dies before reaching the age of thirty (30) years, the separate trust held for him or her shall terminate and my Trustees shall pay the remaining principal, together with all accrued and undistributed income, to my issue then living, per stirpes; provided, however, that any property payable to a child or more remote descendant of mine who is younger than thirty (30) years of age at the Beneficiary's death shall not be paid to him or her outright, but rather the same shall be paid to my Trustees to hold in a separate trust for his or her benefit pursuant to this Article FOURTH; and provided further that all property payable pursuant to this paragraph to a person who is the Beneficiary of a trust under this Will which is then in existence shall, irrespective of the age of such person, be added in its entirety to the principal thereof to be administered therewith and shall not be paid to him or her outright.

(D) If there be no issue of mine living at the Beneficiary's death, such property shall be paid, in equal shares, to those of my mother, EMILY CISSY HOUSTON, my father, JOHN R. HOUSTON, my husband, ROBERT B. BROWN, my brother, MICHAEL HOUSTON, and my brother, GARY HOUSTON, who survive the Beneficiary; provided, however, that as to each of my said brothers (regardless of his age), his share of such property shall not be paid to him outright, but rather the same shall be paid to my Trustees to hold in a separate trust for the benefit of such brother pursuant to Article FIFTH.

(E) Notwithstanding any contrary provision in this Will, the separate trust held for the Beneficiary shall terminate, to the extent that it shall not have previously terminated, twenty-one (21) years after the death of the last survivor of my father, JOHN R. HOUSTON, as were living at the date of my death. Upon the termination of such separate trust pursuant to this provision, my Trustees shall pay the entire then principal, together with all accrued and undistributed income, to the Beneficiary thereof.

FIFTH: The following are the terms of the separate trusts for the benefit of each of my brothers, MICHAEL HOUSTON and GARY HOUSTON (each of whom shall be referred to in this Article as the "Beneficiary" of his separate trust):

(A) My Trustees may, at any time or from time to time, pay to the Beneficiary, or apply for his benefit, upon such occasions as my Trustees, in their sole discretion shall deem advisable, so much or all (or none) of the net income and so much or all (or none) of the principal of the separate trust held for the Beneficiary as my Trustees may deem desirable. At the end of each trust year, my Trustees shall add to the principal of such separate trust any net income not so paid or applied and thereafter the same shall be dealt with as principal for all purposes. Without limiting my Trustees as to occasions upon which payments may be made and without requiring them to make any payment if they deem it inadvisable, I suggest that purposes for which distributions of income and principal might be made include maintenance, support, care, engagement, marriage, acquisition of a home, birth of a child, commencement of a new business enterprises or continuance of an existing one, medical requirements and vacations. In granting discretion to my Trustees to make such payments of income and principal, it is my desire that such discretion be liberally exercised when the occasion, whether one previously specified or not, is such that the interests of the Beneficiary would, in the judgment of my Trustees, be best served thereby, and that the interests of remaindermen in the principal of the trust shall be disregarded in connection therewith.

(B) Upon the Beneficiary's death, the separate trust held for the Beneficiary shall terminate and my Trustees shall pay the remaining principal, together with all accrued and undistributed income, to the same persons, and in the same proportions, as would have inherited such property from me had I then died intestate, the absolute owner thereof, and a resident of the State of New Jersey; provided, however, that notwithstanding the foregoing, under no circumstances shall any part of my estate or the property held in trust under this Will be paid to JOHN R. HOUSTON III.

SIXTH: (A) No assignment, disposition, charge or encumbrance of the income or principal of any trust created herein for the benefit of any beneficiary, or any part thereof, by way of anticipation, alienation or otherwise, shall be valid or in any way binding upon my Trustees and I direct that no beneficiary may assign, transfer, encumber or otherwise dispose of such income or principal, or any part thereof, until the same shall be paid to him or her by my Trustees. No income or principal or any part thereof shall be liable to any claim of any creditor of any beneficiary.

(B) If any beneficiary of this Will dies within thirty (30) days after the date of my death or after the date of death of any other person upon whose death such beneficiary would, but for this paragraph, become entitled to receive either income or principal under this Will, then I direct that for the purposes of his Will, such beneficiary shall be deemed to have predeceased me or such other person, as the case may be.

(C) Whenever used in this Will, the word "issue" shall include, for all purposes, persons attaining that status by formal adoption, it being my intention to expressly include any extension of the line of descent by means of adoption.

SEVENTH: Distribution of any property under this Will to a person who is a minor or who is under some other legal disability may be made by my Executors and Trustees directly to such person or to any one with whom such person resides or, in the sole discretion of my Executors and Trustees, may be made to such person's parent or spouse or Guardian, Conservator or Committee in whatever jurisdiction appointed, or, in the case of any such person who is younger than twenty-one (21) years of age, whether or not a minor, to a Custodian for such person's benefit under the Uniform Gifts to Minors Act or Uniform Transfers to Minors Act of any of the following States: the State in which I am a resident at my death; the State in which such person resides; the State in which any Executor or Trustee serving hereunder resides; or the State in which any ancestor, sibling, uncle or aunt of such person resides. The receipt by the one to whom distribution is made pursuant to this Article shall be a full discharge in respect of any property so distributed even though such payee may be a fiduciary here under. Reference in this Will to a "minor" shall mean a person younger than twenty-one (21) years of age.

EIGHTH: I direct that there shall be no apportionment of any estate, inheritance, transfer, succession, legacy or other death taxes levied or assessed by reason of my death by any governmental authority, domestic or foreign, with respect to any property passing under this Will, or any Codicil hereto, or in respect of any other property passing apart from this Will which may be subject to such taxes. All such taxes, together with interest and penalties thereon, if any, shall be paid as an administration expense from my residuary estate disposed of in Article THIRD, without apportionment among the beneficiaries of my residuary estate. For purposes of this paragraph, such taxes shall not include any generation skipping transfer taxes which may be payable under Chapter 13 of the Code. I expressly recognize that any reduction in tax attributable to property qualifying for the Federal estate tax marital deduction shall inure to the benefit of all recipients of my residuary estate, and not just to the benefit of the recipient of the property qualifying therefor.

NINTH: I confer upon my Executors and Trustees all powers and discretion conferred generally upon fiduciaries by Section 3B:14–23 of the Statutes of the State of New Jersey, and other provisions of this Will, and in addition, without limiting the foregoing, my Executors and my Trustees shall have the following powers and discretion with respect to all property of whatever kind at any time held by them, including income held by them until its distribution, which they may exercise as they deem advisable:

(A) To retain, sell (at private or public sale), purchase, exchange, invest and reinvest in bonds, preferred or common stocks, money market funds, certificates of deposit, mortgages, interests in any kind of investment trust, or other evidences or rights, interests or obligations, secured or unsecured, foreign or domestic, or any other property, real or personal and whether or not in the nature of a wasting asset; and to retain and insure the same for any period of time without liability therefor;

(B) To retain investments, cash or property of which I may die possessed, or which may be received by them, for such length of time as to them may seem proper, without liability by reason of such retention and without limitation as to the length of such time;

(C) To employ and to pay the compensation of such agents, accountants (including any firm with which a fiduciary hereunder may be associated), and to delegate discretionary powers to, and rely upon information or advice furnished by, such agents, accountants, custodians, experts or counsel;

(D) To improve, lease (for any term, whether or not beyond the term of the administration of my estate or of any trust created hereunder or the term fixed by any law), partition or otherwise deal with or dispose of any real or personal property or any interest therein; to make alterations in, renovations, and extra ordinary improvements to any building now or hereafter located on any such property or to demolish the same; to construct new buildings; and to enter into contracts or grant options (for any period) with respect to any of the foregoing;

(E) To consent to the modification, renewal or extension of any note, whether or not secured, or any bond or mortgage, or any term or provision thereof, or any guarantee thereof, or to the release of such guarantee; to release obligors on bonds secured by mortgages or to refrain from instituting suits or actions against such obligors for deficiencies; to use property held under this Will for the protection of any investment in real property or in any mortgage on real property;

(F) To abandon any property, real or personal, which they shall deem to be worthless or not of sufficient value to warrant keeping or protecting; to abstain from the payment of taxes, water rents, assessments, repairs, maintenance and upkeep of such property; to permit such property to be lost by tax sale or other proceeding, or to convey any such property for nominal or no consideration;

(G) To exercise or dispose of any or all options, privileges or rights appurtenant or incident to the ownership of any property; to vote, assent, subscribe, convert property of any other nature; to become a party to, or deposit securities or other property under, or accept securities issued under, any voting trust agreement;

(H) To oppose, assent to or participate in any reorganization, readjustment, recapitalization, liquidation, partial liquidation, consolidation, merger, dissolution, assets, lease, mortgage, contract sale or purchase of or other action or proceeding by any corporation and, in connection therewith, to subscribe to new securities issued pursuant thereto or exchange any property for any other property or pay any assessments or other expenses; to delegate discretionary powers to any reorganization, protective or similar committee;

(I) To borrow money from any party, including any fiduciary hereunder, whether for the purpose of raising funds to pay taxes, to purchase property, to exercise stock options, or otherwise, and to give or not to give security therefor;

(J) To consent to the election by any corporation to be taxed as an "S" corporation under the Internal Revenue Code as it may from time to time exist (or to continue any such election if such election is in effect at the time of my death);

(K) To make any loans, either secured or unsecured, in such amounts, and upon such terms, and at such rates of interest, and to such persons, firms or corporations as in the exercise of their discretion they may determine;

(L) To invest, reinvest, exchange and carry on any business conducted by me or in which I may be interested as a shareholder, partner or otherwise, for any period of time; to sell or liquidate the same; or to incorporate any such business;

(M) To hold property in the name of a nominee or unregistered or in such form as will pass by delivery;

(N) To foreclose any mortgage or mortgages, and to take title to the property or any part thereof affected by such mortgage or, in their discretion, to accept a conveyance of any property in lieu of foreclosure, and to collect the rents and income therefrom, either through a receiver or directly, and to protect such property against foreclosure under any mortgage that shall be a prior lien on said property, or to redeem from foreclosure under any such mortgage, as well as to protect any such property against nonpayment of taxes, assessments or other liens;

(O) To claim administration and other expenses and losses as deductions either in income tax returns of my estate and/or in any estate tax return, whichever would in their opinion result in the payment of the lowest aggregate of such taxes, without requiring reimbursement of the principal of my residuary estate because of any increase in the estate tax caused by deducting the same in income tax returns, or without making any other adjustments of income or principal, and regardless of the effect that such action on their part may have on the interest of the various beneficiaries under this Will, although my Executors may make such adjustments if they so determine in their absolute discretion;

(P) To satisfy any legacy hereunder, whether such legacy be general, pecuniary, residuary or otherwise, with any property, including an undivided interest in property, and to allot any property, including an undivided interest in property, to any separate trust created here under whether or not the same kind of property is used in the satisfaction of any other such legacy or as allocated to other trusts created hereunder;

(Q) To allocate any federal exemption from the federal generation-skipping transfer tax to any property with respect to which I am the transferor for purposes of said tax, whether or not such property passes under this Will or outside this Will, including, but not limited to, any property which I have transferred during my life to which I did not make an allocation and any property over which I have a general power of appointment, regardless of whether I exercise such power of appointment, and to exclude any such property;

(R) My Executors and my Trustees shall be deemed to have acted within the scope of their authority, to have exercised reasonable care, diligence and prudence, and to have acted impartially as to all persons interested including, but not limited to tax elections, unless the contrary be proved by affirmative evidence, and in the absence of such proof shall not be liable for loss arising from depreciation or shrinkage in value of any property herein authorized to be held or acquired.

TENTH: In addition to the powers and discretion conferred upon my fiduciaries by Article NINTH, as to each and any corporation, partnership or other business entity, public or private (including any successor thereto), in which my fiduciaries, as such, hold or acquire any interest (each such corporation, partnership or other business entity being hereafter referred to as the "Entity"), I authorize my fiduciaries to retain the shares thereof or interest therein for as long as they deem it to be in the best interests of my estate or the trusts held under this Will, regardless of the fact that such shares or interest might produce no income, regardless of any duty to diversify investments, and notwithstanding any other fiduciary obligation which might require them to dispose of such shares or interest, other than the obligation to act with reasonable care.

In addition, I authorize my fiduciaries, to the extent permitted by law, to exercise their rights and powers as holders of such shares or interest to effect the continued operation of the Entity or the sale or other disposition of the Entity or of its assets or business, or, in their sole discretion, to sell, exchange, offer for redemption or otherwise dispose of the shares or interest in the Entity owned by my estate or the trusts held under this Will, or to effect the liquidation or dissolution of the Entity, at such time or times and upon such terms and conditions as shall, in the opinion of my fiduciaries, be in the best interests of my estate or of the trusts held under this Will.

So long as my fiduciaries continue to hold any interest in the Entity, I authorize and empower them to participate in the management of the Entity to the extent that their interest therein enables them to do so without liability or responsibility for any loss resulting from the exercise of the powers hereby granted, or they may delegate their managerial authority to others, whether by means of employment agreements or other arrangements, and they may enter into voting trusts and grant irrevocable proxies, as they deem advisable.

Consequently and to these ends, I expressly authorize my fiduciaries to select, vote for and remove directors of the Entity (if the Entity is a corporation); to take part in the management of the Entity and, to the extent permitted by law, in their managerial capacity to fix, determine or change the policy thereof; to name or change officers, the managing personnel and/or the operating personnel; to employ new management; to reduce, expand, limit or otherwise change the business or type of merchandise dealt in or property invested in and investments held by or product manufactured by or service rendered by the Entity; to require the employees and/or the officers of the Entity to file bonds for the faithful performance of their duties; to determine the amount of bond or bonds to be secured; to select the bonding company; to employ expert outside and disinterested accountants or engineers to make a full and complete survey or appraisal of the Entity's business and its prospect in the trade; to employ investment or legal counsel (including any firm with which a fiduciary hereunder maybe associated) whenever my fiduciaries shall deem it advisable; to charge the cost of all such services against the interest in the Entity held by my fiduciaries or to vote or take other action to require the Entity owning said business to pay such expenses; to contribute additional working capital or to subscribe to additional stock as they may see fit; and to take all steps and perform all acts which they shall deem necessary or advisable in connection therewith.

Any one or more of my fiduciaries may act as an officer, director, manager or employee of the Entity, and my fiduciaries are specifically authorized to exercise their rights inhering in their ownership, as such fiduciaries, for the election or appointment of any person or persons, including themselves, as directors, officers, managers and the like. Any such fiduciary who may serve as an officer, director, manager or employee of the Entity shall be entitled to receive compensation for such services not withstanding that my fiduciaries may themselves (whether individually or as fiduciaries hereunder) be in a position to determine or control the determination of the amount of such compensation, and direct that no such person shall be required to furnish any bond in connection with any such employment.

In providing as I have, I am aware that conflicts of interest may arise by reason of service hereunder on the part of my fiduciaries and as an officer, director, manager or employee of the Entity. Nevertheless, I have so provided because I have absolute confidence in their business judgment and integrity. It is my intentions that any such fiduciary shall, in all respects, be free to exercise the powers and discretion herein conferred as fully and unrestrictedly as if there were no such conflicting interests. With this thought in mind, I expressly exempt my fiduciaries from the adverse operation of any rule of law which might otherwise apply to them in the performance of their fiduciary duties by reason of a conflict of interest. Without limiting the generality of the foregoing, I specifically direct that they shall not have any greater burden of justification in respect of their duties as fiduciaries by reason of a conflict of interest than they would have in the absence of any such conflict.

For purposes of this Will the term "fiduciaries" shall include my Executors, my Trustees, and any one or more of them and any Successor Executor or Successor Trustee.

ELEVENTH: I appoint my attorney, SHELDON PLATT, as Executor of my Will.

I appoint my sister-in-law, DONNA HOUSTON, and my attorney, SHELDON PLATT, as Trustees under this Will.

I appoint my husband, ROBERT B. BROWN, as Guardian of the person and property of my minor children. If my husband shall fail or cease to act for any reason, I appoint my sister-in-law, DONNA HOUSTON, as Guardian in his place.

If ancillary probate of this Will in any jurisdiction is required, I appoint as my Ancillary fiduciaries the same persons who are then serving as my Domiciliary fiduciaries. My Ancillary fiduciaries shall have the same powers and discretion as are conferred upon my Domiciliary fiduciaries.

Except as herein above provided in this Article, the last acting individual sole Trustee for whom no designated successor shall be available to act for any reason whatsoever may designate pursuant to a written instrument executed by him or her during his or her lifetime, one or more individuals and/or corporate banking institutions as co-Trustee, to serve with such individual or to succeed such individual as Trustee, in the event he or she shall cease to act for any reason whatsoever.

I direct that no fiduciary (including an Ancillary fiduciary) serving hereunder, whether as Executor, Trustee or Guardian, or as successor thereto, shall be required to file or furnish any bond or other security, any provision of law to the contrary notwithstanding.

All references in this Will to my "Executors", "Trustees" and "Guardians" and the pronouns and verbs corresponding thereto, shall be deemed to include all Successors, and shall be deemed to refer to each Executor, Trustee and Guardian serving hereunder at any time and shall be construed in the masculine or feminine and in the singular or plural, whichever construction is consistent with facts prevailing at any given time.

IN WITNESS WHEREOF, I have hereunto set my hand and seal this 3rd day of February, One Thousand Nine Hundred and Ninety-Three.

______________________________(L.S.)

SUBSCRIBED, PUBLISHED and DECLARED by the above-named Testatrix, WHITNEY E. HOUSTON, as and for her Last Will and Testament in the presence of us, who at her request, in her presence and in the presence of each other, have hereunto subscribed our names as witnesses, this 3rd day of February in the year One Thousand Nine Hundred and Ninety-Three.

______________________ residing at ______________________

______________________ residing at ______________________

______________________ residing at ______________________

I, WHITNEY E. HOUSTON, as testatrix, sign my name to this instrument this 3rd day of February, 1993, and being first duly sworn, do hereby declare to the undersigned authority that I sign and execute this instrument as my Last Will and Testament and that I sign it willingly, that I execute it as my free and voluntary act for the purposes therein expressed, and that I am 18 years of age or older, of sound mind, and under no constraint or undue influence.

______________________________

Whitney E. Houston, Testatrix

SILVIA M AYALY VEJA, THOMAS L. WEISENBER and JEROME H. LIST, the witnesses, being first duly sworn, do each hereby declare to the undersigned authority that the testatrix signs and executes this instrument as her Last Will and Testament and that she signs it willingly, and that each of us states that in the presence and hearing of the testatrix he hereby signs this Will as witness to the testatrix's signing, and that to the best of our knowledge the testatrix is18 years of age or older, of sound mind, and under no constraint or undue influence.

______________________________
Witness

______________________________
Witness

______________________________
Witness

STATE OF NEW JERSEY

COUNTY OF MORRIS

Subscribed, sworn to and acknowledged before me by WHITNEY E. HOUSTON, the Testatrix, and subscribed and sworn to before me by SILVIA M AYALA VEJA, THOMAS L. WEISENBECK and JEROME H. LIST, Witnesses, this 3rd day of February, 1993.

______________________________
Joseph S. Weitberg
An Attorney-at-Law of New Jersey

**LAST WILL AND TESTAMENT**

**OF**

**JAMES GANDOLFINI[5]**

I, JAMES GANDOLFINI, a resident of the City, County and State of New York, and a citizen of the United States of America, being of full age, sound mind, memory and understanding, do hereby make, publish and declare this to be my Last Will and Testament, hereby revoking all Last Wills and Testaments and Codicils thereto attached, heretofore made by me.

FIRST: I direct that all of my just debts, funeral expenses, last illness expenses, if any, and the cost of administration of my estate be paid out of the assets of my estate as soon after my demise as may be practicable. Such debts shall not include obligations secured by mortgages on real property and loans secured by a cooperative apartment.

SECOND: I direct that all inheritance, estate, transfer, succession and other death taxes and duties (including any interest or penalties thereon) imposed by any jurisdiction whatsoever by reason of my death (exclusive of any tax imposed as a result of any generation-skipping transfer under the Internal Revenue Code of 1986 as amended or a corresponding provision of state law) upon or with respect to any property includible in my estate for the purpose of any such taxes or duties, whether such property passes under or outside, or has passed outside the provisions of this Will or any Codicil hereto, be paid from the principal of my residuary estate without apportionment.

THIRD: A) I give all my clothing and jewelry to my son, MICHAEL GANDOLFINI, to be his absolutely, if he survives me, and which property he may distribute, in his sole determination, and if he does not survive me, then to my wife, DEBORAH LIN, to be hers absolutely, if she survives me, and which property she may distribute, in her sole determination, and if she does not survive me, to my Executors to be divided as my Executors shall determine, which determination shall be conclusive and binding upon all persons interested in my estate.

B) I give all my other tangible personal property (other than currency) to my wife, DEBORAH LIN, to be hers absolutely, if she survives me, and which property she may distribute, in her sole determination, and, if she does not survive me, then to my Executors to be divided as my Executors shall determine, which determination shall be conclusive and binding upon all persons interested in my estate.

C) Any expenses which may be incurred in selling, storing, packing, shipping and insuring any of such tangible property, including any expense which may be incurred in delivering such property to the designated beneficiary or beneficiaries thereof shall be charged against the principal of my estate and treated as an expense of administering my estate.

FOURTH: I devise and bequeath the following:

A) To my assistant, PAULETTE FLYNN BOURNE a/k/a TRIXIE FLYNN, the sum of Two Hundred Thousand ($200,000.00) Dollars, provided she shall survive me;

B) To my friend, FATIMA BAE, the sum of Fifty Thousand ($50,000.00) Dollars, provided she shall survive me;

C) To my niece, LAURA ANTONACCI, the sum of Five Hundred Thousand ($500,000.00) Dollars, provided she shall survive me;

D) To my niece, JENNA ANTONACCI, the sum of Five Hundred Thousand ($500,000.00) Dollars, provided she shall survive me;

E) To my godson, ROBERT JOSEPH PARISH, the sum of One Hundred Thousand ($100,000.0.0) Dollars, provided he shall survive me.

---

[5] See more at: https://www.bellenews.com/wp-content/uploads/2013/07/James-Gandolfini-Will.pdf.

F) To my friend, Thomas A. Richardson, the sum of Two Hundred thousand ($200,000.00) Dollars, provided he shall survive me;

G) To my friend, Doug Katz, the sum of Fifty Thousand ($50,000.00) Dollars, provided he shall survive me with the hope that he will use it for the benefit of his son.

FIFTH: I direct my Executors to and I give and grant to the Trust which I have created for the benefit of my beloved son, Michael GANDOLFINI, a first option to purchase all my right, title and interest in Condominium Unit No. 5C, together with Parking Space Number 9, located at 429 Greenwich Street, New York, New York at its fair market value. In .the event that said trust does not purchase from my estate Condominium Unit No. 5C, together with Parking Space Number 9, located at 429 Greenwich Street, New York, New York then the same shall be a part of my residuary estate and be disposed of in accordance with the provisions hereinafter contained in this my, Last Will and Testament, regarding the disposition of my residuary estate.

SIXTH: I have provided for my wife, DEBORAH LIN, as set forth in Articles Third and Eighth (B) herein. I have also made other provisions for DEBORAH LIN and therefore, I am not making any further provisions for her under this, my Last Will and Testament.

SEVENTH: I give, devise and bequeath to my Trustees, hereinafter named, IN TRUST NEVERTHELESS, all of my right, title and interest in and to the house and land which I own in Italy. My Trustees shall hold the same for the benefit of my son, Michael Gandolfini and my daughter Liliana Ruth Gandolfini. The interest of my son, Michael Gandolfini in this Trust shall be fifty (50%) percent and the interest of my daughter, Liliana Ruth Gandolfini shall be fifty (50%) percent. Upon both beneficiaries of this trust reaching the age of twenty-five (25) said property shall be transferred to them in such percentages. It is my hope and desire that they will continue to own said property and keep it in our family for as long as possible.

EIGHTH: A) I give, devise and bequeath all the rest, residue and remainder of my estate, of whatsoever nature and wheresoever situate, including any lapsed legacies, bequests and devises, (sometimes referred to herein as my "residuary estate") as follows:

I) Thirty Percent (30%) to my sister, LETA GANDOLFINI;

II) Thirty Percent (30%) to my sister, JOHANNA ANTONACCI;

III) Twenty Percent (20%) to my wife, DEBORAH LIN;

IV) Twenty Percent (20%) to my daughter, LILIANA RUTH GANDOLFINI.

B) In the event that any of the above-named beneficiaries shall predecease me or die with me in or as the result of a common accident or disaster or under such circumstances that It is doubtful who died first, then the interest of such a deceased residuary estate beneficiary I give devise and bequeath to the remaining residuary estate beneficiaries in equal shares, share and share alike. In the event that any two of the above-named beneficiaries shall predecease me or die with me in or as the result of a common accident or disaster or under such circumstances that it is doubtful who died first, then the interest of such a deceased residuary estate beneficiaries I give devise and bequeath to the remaining residuary estate beneficiary.

NINTH: I have in mind my beloved son, MICHAEL GANDOLFINI, but I am not providing for him other than as set forth in this my Last Will and Testament because I have made other provisions for him.

TENTH: Whenever, pursuant to the provisions of this, my Will, any share of my estate or any income therefrom shall be payable or distributable to any beneficiary who is under twenty-one (21) years of age, the same shall absolutely vest in and belong to such beneficiary, but payment thereof may be deferred, and I authorize my Trustees, in their sole and uncontrolled discretion, to hold the same and to retain the custody and control thereof, and to administer the same on the beneficiary's behalf, and to accumulate the income therefrom, If any, with all the investment and other powers hereinafter granted to them as Trustees, and I direct that they shall apply so much of the income and principal thereof as in their discretion they may deem advisable and proper from time to time for the support, education and maintenance of such beneficiary, and upon such beneficiary's attaining the age of twenty-one (21) years, to pay over to such beneficiary whatever principal and income may then remain in their hands, or in the event such beneficiary shall die prior to attaining the age of twenty-one (21) years, then to the estate of such beneficiary.

ELEVENTH: Any income or corpus to be applied for the use and benefit of a beneficiary under the age of twenty-one (21) years, under the provisions of this Will, may be so applied by the Executors and Trustees either directly or by making payment, without bond, to such beneficiary, or to a guardian of the person or of the property of such beneficiary, or to any head of any household with whom such beneficiary resides, for the use of such beneficiary, in which event the receipt of such beneficiary, parent, guardian or person, as the case may be, shall be a complete discharge to the Executors or Trustees making such payment; such person need not be legally appointed the guardian of such beneficiary, nor shall such beneficiary, guardian or person be obligated to give any accounting for the disposition of said income or corpus except on the written request of the Executors or Trustees hereunder.

TWELFTH: No principal or income payable or to become payable under any trust created by this Will shall be subject to anticipation or assignment by any beneficiary thereof, or to attachment by or to the interference or control of any creditor of any such beneficiary, or to be taken or reached by any legal or equitable process in satisfaction of any debt or liability of such beneficiary prior to its actual receipt by the beneficiary.

THIRTEENTH: In addition to, and not in limitation of, the powers and discretions elsewhere herein granted and conferred by law, I give and grant to my Executors and Trustees, in the administration of my estate and the Powers-in-Trust hereunder and, insofar as pertinent, in the administration of accumulated income held hereunder, the following powers and discretions:

A) To retain, in their absolute discretion and for such period or periods as shall seem advisable to them, all or any part of the property owned by me at the time of my death, the property received at the commencement of any Trust and the property received in substitution therefore.

B) To Invest and reinvest the funds of my estate or of any Trust, in property of any kind, real, personal, mixed or chooses in action, irrespective of any statute, case, rule or custom limiting the investment of estate or Trust funds.

C) To continue and to operate any business or interest therein I may own at the time of my death for such time as they shall deem advisable; to engage in any other business; to become or remain a partner, general or special, in any business; to incorporate any such business and hold the stock thereof as an investment; and to provide capital for and employ agents to manage and operate any such business without liability or indebtedness resulting from the operation thereof if the management is selected with reasonable care.

D) To sell at public or private sale, exchange, mortgage, lease (although the term of the lease may extend beyond the term of any Trust) and otherwise manage and deal with real estate and rights below and above its surface.

E) To exercise all rights as the owner of securities including, among others, the right to vote by proxy, participate in reorganizations and voting Trusts and hold stock in their own names, jointly or severally, or in the name of a nominee, with or without disclosing the fiduciary relationship.

F) To carry out the terms of any agreement I may have entered into to sell all or any part of any property or any interest I may own in any business at the time of my death.

G) To borrow money and mortgage or pledge the property of my estate or any Trust as security therefor; to advance money for the protection of my estate or any Trust and secure such advances by a lien on the property of my estate or any Trust; and to advance income to beneficiaries and secure such advance by a lien on the future benefits of such beneficiaries.

H) To make allotments and distribution in kind without regard to the income tax basis of any assets.

I) To compromise and arbitrate claims in favor of or against my estate or any Trust.

J) To determine, in their sole discretion, what is income or corpus of my estate or any Trust and to apportion and allocate all receipts, credits, disbursements, expenses and charges to income or corpus as they shall deem proper and, except insofar as they shall exercise such discretion, matters relating to the rights of beneficiaries among themselves as to corpus and income shall be governed by the rules of law applicable from time to time.

K) To deduct from the income of my estate or any Trust a reserve for depreciation of any depreciable asset and to authorize the income beneficiary thereof to take such deduction or to apportion such deduction between themselves, as fiduciaries, and the income beneficiary in such manner as they shall deem proper.

L) To sell property to or purchase property at public or private sale from any Trust created hereunder with the proceeds or funds from any such other Trust for a consideration equal to the then fair market value of the property notwithstanding that they may be the fiduciaries of both the selling and purchasing Trust.

M) To execute and deliver any written instruments which they may deem advisable to carry out any power, duty or discretion granted to them, and all persons shall be fully protected in relying upon their power to execute every such instrument and no one shall be obligated to see to the application by them of any money or property received by them pursuant to the execution and delivery of any such instrument.

N) Whenever they shall have the right to elect whether any item of expense connected with the administration of my estate or of any Trust shall be claimed as a deduction for income tax purposes or claimed, instead, as a deduction for estate tax purposes to exercise such right of election in such manner as they may, in their absolute discretion, determine to be advisable even though the manner in which such election is exercised may result in an advantage or disadvantage to any beneficiary as compared with any other beneficiary.

O) Whenever required to make a distribution or transfer of all or a part of the assets of my estate or of any Trust, to retain therefrom assets sufficient, in their judgment, to cover any liability which may then or later be imposed upon them including, but not limited to, their liability for estate, inheritance, income or other taxes, until such liability shall have been finally determined.

P) The Executors and Trustees shall have sole custody of all securities, papers, personal property and cash comprising my probate or Trust estate and solely perform all ministerial duties. No individual Executor or Trustee shall be obligated, but may if he wishes to sign or countersign checks for the disbursement of estate or Trust funds.

Q) All powers, duties and discretionary authority granted to the Executors and Trustees may be exercised by them without posting any bond, without obtaining any order from or the approval of any Court and without any notice to or consent of anyone. The Executors and Trustees are not to be answerable for any loss that does not occur through their own default or negligence. A successor Executor or a successor Trustee shall succeed to all the powers, duties and discretionary authority of the original Executors and Trustees.

R) To hold, manage, invest and account for the Trusts created hereunder, in whole or in part, in solido, in one or more consolidated funds as they, in their sole discretion, may from time to time determine. In such event, the division of such funds into the Trusts need be made only on the Trustees' books of account in which each Trust shall be proportionately charged and credited. No such consolidation holding, however, shall be deemed to defer or postpone the vesting or distribution, in accordance with the terms of this, my Will, of any property held in Trust.

S) Any Executor or Trustee may, with the consent of the other, delegate any or all of his or her or its powers, duties and discretions to any other Executor or Trustee by an instrument in writing and may revoke such delegation at will in the same manner.

T) To employ brokers, banks, custodians, investment counsel, attorneys, accountants and such other agents, professional or otherwise, and to delegate to them such of their duties, rights and powers as they may determine and for such periods as may be deemed proper without liability for any mistake or default of any such person selected or retained with reasonable care and prudence and to pay them, or any of them, reasonable compensation which shall be deemed part of the expenses of my estate or of the Trusts or Powers-in-Trust hereunder, as the case may be.

U) In case it shall become necessary or proper to divide all or any part of my estate or any Trust hereunder into parts or shares or to distribute the same, to make such division or distribution, in their discretion, in money, in kind, or partly in money and partly in kind; and, if such division is for the purpose of enabling any asset to be held pursuant to a Trust or a Power-in-Trust, to effect such division, in whole or in part, in their sole discretion, by allocating to each part or share an undivided interest in such asset.

V) In the event it shall be necessary or proper for my Executors or Trustees to distribute any part of my estate or any Trust hereunder, then and in their sole and absolute discretion, they shall have the power to make non-pro-rata distributions.

W) To join with my wife in filing any income tax return for any year in which such joinder is permitted by law and to pay all or such ratable share of any taxes thereon as they shall deem proper and to consent to any gifts made by my wife during my lifetime as having been made one-half by me for the purpose of any gift tax law, and the exercise of such authority shall be final and conclusive and not subject to question by any persons.

FOURTEENTH: A) I hereby nominate, constitute and appoint my wife, DEBORAH LIN, my sister, LETA GANDOLFINI, and my attorney and friend, ROGER S. HABER, as Co-Executors of this, my Last Will and Testament. In the event that DEBORAH LIN or LETA GANDOLFINI or ROGER S. HABER shall predecease me, fail to qualify, resign or to act as Executor for any reason whatsoever, then I direct that the Co-Executors or sole remaining Co-Executor may continue to act as such without the necessity of appointing substitute or successor Co-Executors in the others place and stead. I direct that my Co-Executors, whether acting together or singly or in any combination, shall not be required to furnish any bond or other security for the faithful performance of their duties in any jurisdiction whatsoever, any law to the contrary notwithstanding.

B) I hereby nominate, constitute and appoint my wife, DEBORAH LIN, my sister, LETA GANDOLFINI, and my attorney, ROGER S. HABER, Co-Trustees of the Powers-in-Trust created under this, my Last Will and Testament. In the event DEBORAH LIN or LETA GANDOLFINI OR ROGER S. HABER shall predecease me, resign, fall to qualify or cease to act as Co-Trustee for any reason whatsoever then I nominate, constitute and appoint my sister, JOHANNA ANTONACCI, as substitute or successor Co-Trustee hereunder. I direct that my Co-Trustees, whether serving together or singly or in any combination, shall not be required to furnish any bond or other security for the faithful performance of their duties in any capacity in any jurisdiction whatsoever, any law to the contrary notwithstanding.

C) No individual Executor or Trustee acting hereunder shall be liable or responsible for the neglect or default of any other Executor or Trustee nor for the neglect or default of any agent selected or appointed with reasonable care, and my individual Executors and Trustees shall not be liable or accountable for any act performed, permitted or omitted by them, or by reason of any loss or diminution in value suffered by my estate or any Trust herein established except for acts of fraud or gross negligence. No fiduciary at any time acting hereunder shall be required to file periodic accountings in the court in which this Will shall be admitted to probate, but such fiduciary may do so at any time or times if he or she shall deem the filing of any such accounting advisable.

FIFTEENTH: In the event that the mother of a minor child of mine, predeceases me or cannot serve as guardian of such child for any reason whatsoever, then I appoint my sister, LETA GANDOLFINI, as Guardian of my minor children. In the event the mother of a minor child of mine and LETA GANDOLFINI, both predecease me or cannot serve as guardian of such child for any reason whatsoever, I hereby appoint my sister, JOHANNA ANTONACCI, as substitute or successor Guardian hereunder. I direct that my Guardian and my substitute or successor Guardian shall not be required to furnish any bond or other security for the faithful performance of her duties in any jurisdiction whatsoever, any law to the contrary notwithstanding.

SIXTEENTH: No person dealing with my Executors, Trustees or Guardians shall be required to see to the application of any property paid or delivered to them, or to inquire into the expediency or propriety of any transaction, or the authority of my Executors or Trustees or Guardians to enter into and consummate the same upon such terms as they may deem advisable.

SEVENTEENTH: If any beneficiary or beneficiaries under this Will, and I, or any person upon whose death such beneficiary or beneficiaries would have otherwise become entitled to receive any income or principal hereunder should die in a common accident or disaster, or as a result of a common accident or disaster, or under such circumstances that it is doubtful who died first, then all of the provisions of this Will shall take effect in like manner as if such beneficiary or beneficiaries had predeceased me or such other person, as the case may be.

IN WITNESS WHEREOF, I have subscribed and sealed and do publish and declare these presents as and for my Last Will and Testament in the presence of the witnesses attesting the same the 19th day of December in the year Two Thousand and Twelve.

______________________________ (L.S.)

______________________________ residing at ______________________________

______________________________

______________________________ residing at ______________________________

______________________________

The above instrument, consisting of fifteen (15) pages, of which this is the fifteenth (15th) page, was, at the date thereof, subscribed, sealed, published and declared by the Testator, JAMES GANDOLFINI, as and for his Last Will and Testament in the presence of us and each of us, who, at his request, in his presence and in the presence of each other, have hereunto subscribed our names as witnesses thereto the 19th day of December in the year Two Thousand and Twelve.

State of )<br>
) ss.<br>
County of )

Each of the undersigned, individually and severally, being duly sworn, deposes and says:

The within Will was subscribed in our presence and sight at the end thereof by JAMES GANDOLFINI, the within named Testator on the 19th day of December, 2012, at _______

Said Testator at the time of making such subscription, declared the instrument so subscribed to be his Last Will.

Each of the undersigned thereupon signed his or her name as a witness at the end of said Will at the request of said Testator, in his presence and sight and in the presence and sight of each other.

Said Testator was, at the time of so executing said Will, over the age of eighteen years and, in the respective opinions of the undersigned, of sound mind, memory and understanding and not under any restraint or in any respect incompetent to make a Will.

Said Testator, in the respective opinions of the undersigned, could read, write and converse in the English language and was suffering from no defect of sight, hearing or speech, or from any other physical or mental impairment which would affect his capacity to make a valid Will. The Will was executed as a single, original instrument and was not executed in counterparts.

Each of the undersigned was acquainted with said Testator at such time and makes this affidavit at his request.

The within Will was shown to the undersigned at the time this affidavit was made and was examined by each of them as to the signatures of said Testator and of the undersigned.

The foregoing instrument was executed by said Testator and witnessed by each of the undersigned affiants under the supervision of ________________, an attorney-at-law.

Sworn to before me this 19th day of December, 2012.

______________________________

Notary Public

State of )

) ss.

County of )

I, JAMES GANDOLFINI, have designated my attorney ROGER S. HABER an Executor in my Last Will and Testament dated December 19, 2012.

Prior to signing my Last Will and Testament, I was Informed that:

1. Subject to limited statutory exceptions, any person, including an attorney, is eligible to serve as my executor;

2. Absent an agreement to the contrary, any person, including an attorney, who serves as an executor for me is entitled to receive statutory commissions for executorial services rendered to my estate;

3. Absent execution of this disclosure acknowledgement, the attorney who prepared the Will, a then affiliated attorney, or any employee of such attorney or a then affiliated attorney, who serves as an executor shall be entitled to one-half the commissions he or she would otherwise be entitled to receive and;

4. If such attorney serves as my executor, and he or she or another attorney affiliated with such attorney renders legal services in connection with the executor's official duties, he or she is entitled to receive just and reasonable compensation for those legal services, in addition to the commission to which an Executor is entitled.

Dated December 19, 2012.

______________________________ (L.S.)
JAMES GANDOLFINI

WITNESSES:

______________________________

______________________________

______________________________

Sworn to before me this 19th
day of December, 2012.

______________________________

Notary Public

## DISPOSING OF THE PROPERTY

A testator can make numerous dispositions of property within a will, or may simply pour all of his or her property into a pre-existing trust that will govern the disposition of the property once the trust is funded. Doing so does not avoid probate, however, for all property owned at death by the testator will need to be administered, and will be considered probate property for elective share purposes. While it may seem sensible to put everything into a revocable trust before the testator dies, so there is no probate property to be administered, that's not only difficult to maintain, but may be counter-productive. Remember, as we mentioned earlier, there needs to be property available to pay the family set-asides and final debts. And it's unlikely that a testator will remember to acquire all property in the name of the revocable trust. So the sofa, television, and perhaps even the car, will be held in individual names and need to be probated. The will is an important document precisely because it catches all left-over property and funnels it back into the trust, it makes guardianship and executorship appointments, and it ensures that the total estate plan comes together and works in sync.

As you should remember from your Trusts and Estates class, there are four types of bequests:

- Specific—specific items of property intended to pass to designated beneficiaries regardless of their change in value between the time of execution and death (includes real estate, items of tangible personal property, or specific items of intangible property named with precision, like my Citibank retirement account)
- Demonstrative—a particular value or cash bequest to be paid from specific items of property (like $5000 worth of XYZ stock, or a selection of paintings equal in worth to the value of my real estate)
- General—monetary devises of specified amounts (like $10,000)
- Residuary—all property left in the estate not otherwise disposed of by one of the prior three bequests, including lapsed or failed bequests.

In many cases, testators make a series of specific small bequests to friends, grandchildren, caretakers, or charities, and then leave the residue of their estates to their immediate primary beneficiaries. Look at James Gandolfini's will for an example of this. But if the estate is facing extensive debts and can't cover all the bequests, abatement statutes generally will cause the residue to abate before specific or general bequests. This means that that small gift to the testator's alma mater will get paid before the surviving spouse and minor children, if they are the residuary legatees. Sometimes this order of abatement does not result in furthering the testator's intentions, especially if the testator wants to benefit the spouse primarily and only the alma mater if the spouse is adequately provided for. So you should be thinking about alternative plans (and alternative language) regarding all the devises in a will in case the property has been adeemed (isn't in the estate anymore), in case there is far more property than originally planned for (the testator acquires lots of additional property, say through an inheritance), or the estate is not large enough to pay for the debts, set-asides, or the specific and general bequests.

In the case of testators like Henry and Wanda who have minor children, you will certainly want to think about a trust for any gifts that would otherwise go to the children outright and would therefore necessitate a guardianship. And although you don't need to establish the trust during life, it generally makes sense to go ahead and put large items of property (like a home, perhaps some investment accounts, and maybe even the cars) into a revocable trust during life, and then pour the relatively smaller items of property, especially tangible personal property, into the trust at death. The trust can make provisions for retaining the property in trust and using it for the benefit of minor children until they reach a certain age, and management of the property can be given to a spouse, adult child, or family friend rather than a corporate trustee if you want that person to make judgments about paying out assets on behalf of the minor children. Corporate trustees are generally very good at safeguarding property and investing it well, but are less adept at making decisions about whether ballet lessons are better than karate lessons, or whether a child should get a car at age 16 or have to wait until they can purchase it themselves. Before you settle down to actually draft the property provisions of a will or a trust, you need to think about the myriad benefits and costs of the different mechanisms for holding property and which are most important to your client. They include:

- Probate avoidance—minimizing the hassle of administration by having property pass automatically at death through a right of survivorship, trust provision, joint tenancy, or beneficiary designation (i.e., a will substitute).
- Maximum control until death—there is likely to be some property that the client wants complete unfettered control over up until death, either for ease of use or as insurance against not having enough property to support oneself.
- Flexibility—utilizing various mechanisms to maximize the flexibility of the estate plan in case the client has very large end-of-life debts, inherits a sizable amount of property, a beneficiary has special needs, or unexpected debts arise.
- Tax minimization—certain types of transfers have beneficial tax implications if your client's estate is large enough to face estate taxes (greater than $12.92 million).
- Spendthrift protections—some trusts can be established to protect the assets from creditors of the beneficiaries.
- Postponed decision-making—powers of appointment are particularly useful in postponing decisions about gifts until more facts are known (the entire class is ascertained, a beneficiary's wealth status is known, etc.).
- Management ease during incapacity or after death—some property may need to be in a form, or subject to an appropriate power, that allows someone else to manage the property for the client's behalf.

There are many other benefits and considerations you should take into account when recommending an estate plan for any client. For clients like Henry and Wanda, however, the main concerns are likely to be flexibility for potentially significant changes in wealth or marital status (odds are they will get a divorce before one dies), provision for minor children in the unlikely event both die, and maximum continued control during life since they are both young and actively managing their property.

### Exercise 2—Drafting the Property Provisions

Now that you have the guardian, executor, debts, and other boilerplate provisions drafted, let's move to the actual property dispositions. The only property that Henry and Wanda can dispose of by this will is property owned outright by them at their death (i.e., their net probate estates). For this exercise, you will need to meet with your clients, once again, to determine exactly how they would like their estates to pass to their beneficiaries. This time split up into teams of two, one lawyer and one client for each team. And we leave the details to the students playing Henry and Wanda. As you role-play and together draft the property provisions, be sure that you discuss with your clients the legal implications of some of their bequests and take copious notes so you can compare how well the plan fits the clients' wishes.

To help with this exercise, we have given those of you playing Henry and Wanda some public facts and some private facts. Again, these are not to be kept secret, but are to help you provide a plan for your lawyer. In the end, however, you may choose to prioritize some of these outcomes over others.

## The Public Facts

### *Henry*

Henry knows that Wanda is likely to be well-provided for by her parents and so he would like to ensure that Wanda is comfortable, but that the remainder of his property passes to his four children equally. Anything passing to Wanda that she does not consume during her life, however, he would like to have pass to all four children rather than to her devisees, especially if Wanda gets remarried. Because Gillian and Benjamin are minors, he would like that any bequests to them be placed into a trust, with Wanda as trustee, until each either graduates from college or reaches age 25. Steve and Doris can have their shares outright, although he would be amenable to some kind of spendthrift provision for Steve. He would also like to make small bequests to his siblings in case he inherits any of his mother's property, to the Sierra Club so long as there is at least plenty to pay the bequests to his family, to his alma mater the State University where he got his MBA, and anything he might get from his brother Bob he wants to have pass to Bob's children, if any.

### *Wanda*

Wanda secretly figures she will outlive Henry and will survive until Gillian and Benjamin are adults, but she wants them to have the lion's share of her property. She also wants to provide a trust for her cousin Susan. She doesn't want any of her property to benefit Steve and Doris in any way, as she thinks Steve is a loser and Doris is too bossy. She hasn't thought very carefully about what she might do if she does inherit her father's fortune, since her father seems so healthy and the prospect so remote. She was a bit scared last year, however, when her father had a heart attack at 65. Wanda is very happy with Henry, but he does annoy her, and the age difference is something that has started to bother her a bit more, especially when strangers ask if he is her father and the kids' grandfather! Wanda would like to make a large bequest to the Atlas Foundation and she wants to minimize any property passing to Henry as she believes he 1) has enough money of his own, and 2) shouldn't get any of her family's property.

---

In drafting the property provisions think especially about two things. First, the will affects only the probate property. Do you think either Henry or Wanda should consider putting any property into outright ownership so that it will be subject to the will, or can all of their goals be achieved with the property titled as it is? Chances are they will both need trusts, which we will draft in the next Chapter. Should some or all of these property instructions be in the trust and not in the will? Think about what property can or should be put in trust now and what property can or should remain outside the trust in order to maximize ease of use.

Second, think carefully about how to treat after-acquired property, especially any outright gifts from Henry's mother's estate or Wanda's father's estate. What happens if either acquires a power of appointment over property in one or the other estate? Should they capture that property and dispose of it according to their wills, or not?

Finally, it makes sense to pour the residuary probate property into the revocable trust you are going to draft in the next Chapter. So you don't need to spend a lot of time worrying about the primary bequests to the surviving spouse and children because those most likely will be taken care of in the trust. But remember that any property put into trust before death avoids probate but may be more difficult to manage. Property that passes into trust upon the settlor's death becomes subject to fiduciary duties.

You will need to draft the residue clause that will ultimately pour over the residue into the revocable trust. Consider whether you want to capture any property over which either might have a power of appointment, or not, and be explicit! A sample clause might be: "I devise the rest and residue of my property, including any property over which I might have a power of appointment to . . ." Or, your client might not want to exercise that power if it means adding the property to the client's estate, in which case an appropriate clause might be: "I devise the rest and residue of my property to . . ., and I declare that I am intentionally choosing not to exercise any powers of appointment that I may have unless I refer to the power explicitly."

Finally, go back to the drafting considerations mentioned earlier in this Chapter. One of the most important considerations here is making sure that you have covered all the possible contingencies of things that can go wrong with a gift, from lapse to disclaimer to simultaneous death. Does the client want issue of predeceased beneficiaries to take their ancestor's share, or does he want the gift to lapse and pass to the residuary legatees? Discuss these contingencies with your client and draft them as clearly and carefully as possible. Draft alternate gift language for any special or general bequest.

### Exercise 3—Lapsed Gifts, Will Contests, and the Will Formalities

Many wills include provisions for lapsed gifts, usually that specific and general bequests that lapse fall into the residue if there are no alternate provisions in the bequest itself, and residuary gifts that lapse either pass to the other residuary beneficiaries or perhaps to the trust or a charity. In the case of Henry's and Wanda's wills, each should have the residuary pour over into their trust. So, lapsed gifts should probably go into the residue and thereby into the trust. You will also need to discuss with your clients whether they want to include a no-contest clause in their wills, exculpatory clauses to waive liability for their executors or trustees, a simultaneous death provision in case Henry and Wanda die simultaneously, boilerplate language to capture all property so that none passes by intestacy, and of course include the execution and attestation language.

Many of these provisions are available from the sample wills up above, and you might find others in your Trusts and Estates casebook or other will examples from the internet. Go through the sample wills to make sure that you aren't forgetting anything that looks like it could be important. The goal is not to make sure you've got every boilerplate provision ever written, but to make sure you've got all the ones that matter.

Finally, you will need to include the execution and attestation language. The UPC provides a sample that is valid in all states. So add that as well, personalizing it for Henry and Wanda. And in case you missed this detail, you need to make sure that each page of the will (and the trust) is paginated to prevent extra pages being added. This is usually done by a sentence at the beginning that this will consists of X pages, or by using page numbers at the bottom of the page that notes that it is page 1 of X pages, 2 of X pages, etc. You also need to provide a place at the bottom of each page for your testator to initial each page. You can easily imagine why this is done. With computers today it would be easy to print out a completely new page to substitute for an original page, but it's a lot harder to get the testator's initials after the testator has died (although that did occur in the curious case of *Est. of Beale*).[6] So be sure your will is properly formatted, titled, paginated, and has no spelling errors or typos.

[6] 15 Wis.2d 546, 113 N.W.2d 380 (1962).

**UPC § 2–504. Self-Proved Will.**

(a) A will that is executed with attesting witnesses may be simultaneously executed, attested, and made self-proved, by acknowledgment thereof by the testator and affidavits of the witnesses, each made before an officer authorized to administer oaths under the laws of the state in which execution occurs and evidenced by the officer's certificate, under official seal, in substantially the following form:

I, ________, the testator, sign my name to this instrument this _____ day of __________, and being first duly sworn, do hereby declare to the undersigned authority that I sign and execute this instrument as my will and that I sign it willingly (or willingly direct another to sign for me), that I execute it as my free and voluntary act for the purposes therein expressed, and that I am [18] years of age or older, of sound mind, and under no constraint or undue influence.

________________________

Testator

We, __________, __________, the witnesses, sign our names to this instrument, being first duly sworn, and do hereby declare to the undersigned authority that the testator signs and executes this instrument as (his)(her) will and that (he)(she) signs it willingly (or willingly directs another to sign for (his)(her)), and that each of us, in the presence and hearing of the testator, hereby signs this will as witness to the testator's signing, and that to the best of our knowledge the testator is [18] years of age or older, of sound mind, and under no constraint or undue influence.

________________________

Witness

________________________

Witness

State of __________

County of __________

Subscribed, sworn to and acknowledged before me by ______, the testator, and subscribed and sworn to before me by ______, and ______, witness, this ______ day of ______.

(Seal)

____________________________________

(Signed)

____________________________________

(Official capacity of officer)

(b) A will that is executed with attesting witnesses may be made self-proved at any time after its execution by the acknowledgment thereof by the testator and the affidavits of the witnesses, each made before an officer authorized to administer oaths under the laws of the state in which the acknowledgment occurs and evidenced by the officer's certificate, under official seal, attached or annexed to the will in substantially the following form:

The State of __________

County of __________

We, ________, ________, and _______, the testator and the witnesses, respectively, whose names are signed to the attached or foregoing instrument, being first duly sworn, do hereby declare to the undersigned authority that the testator signed and executed the instrument as the testator's will and that (he)(she) had signed willingly (or willingly directed another to sign for (him)(her)), that (he)(she) executed it as (his)(her) free and voluntary act for the purposes therein expressed, and that each of the witnesses, in the presence and hearing of the testator, signed the will as witness and that to the best of (his)(her) knowledge the testator was at that time [18] years of age or older, of sound mind, and under no constraint or undue influence.

________________________ Testator

________________________ Witness

________________________ Witness

Subscribed, sworn to and acknowledged before me by ______, the testator, and subscribed and sworn to before me by ______, and ______, witnesses, this ______ day of ______.

(Seal)

________________________

(Signed)

________________________

(Official capacity of officer)

(c) A signature affixed to a self-proving affidavit attached to a will is considered a signature affixed to the will, if necessary to prove the will's due execution.

Once you have completed the final draft of the will, go over it with your client to ensure that it adequately reflects his or her intentions. If not, fix those provisions and meet again with your client until all is right.

## Lessons Learned

Besides the obvious benefit of actually getting to draft real will language, we want you to use the exercises in this Chapter to think carefully about what you should do with boilerplate provisions. You are likely to see some wills that appear to consist of page after page of boilerplate that is unlikely to have any actual purpose in your client's life. Others are likely to be very short, like Michael Jackson's will, despite the fact that it might be disposing of millions of dollars' worth of property. Which is better? There is really no easy answer to that question. Alternative bequests and a lot of boilerplate can come in handy if the unexpected happens. But you don't want to be accused of throwing everything in but the kitchen sink because you get paid by the word. Learn to tailor the language to your clients' situations and anticipate which events are likely to occur, and which can be safely ignored. Your job here was to draft a relatively simple will because most of the complicated provisions will be put into the trust. But that doesn't mean the will isn't important. Besides the ritual and mythology surrounding one's last will, the will functions much like a safety-net. It won't do its job if it has too many holes in it.

### *PRACTICE PROBLEMS*

Now that you have gotten your feet wet drafting some basic will provisions, write provisions to deal with the following situations that may require modifications to Henry's or Wanda's wills:

1. Steve's band makes it really big and suddenly Steve is a multi-millionaire, but he's getting too much into drugs.
2. Doris ends up marrying her partner, Patricia, but Henry and Wanda both know it's just not going to last. They seem to fight all the time and Patricia appears to be involved with Doris just because she's convinced Doris will make a lot of money.

3. There are rumors that the directors of the Atlas Foundation are likely to be indicted for embezzlement from the Foundation's endowment and might have to close, but the members are vowing to keep it open, or set up a different organization to further its policy goals.
4. Wanda's mother has a stroke and is in a nursing home, requiring round-the-clock care, and her father has divorced her in order to protect the family's wealth. Wanda is horrified and wants to help provide for her mother as much as she can.

Don't forget to fill in your time sheets!

# CHAPTER 6

# THE BASIC REVOCABLE TRUST

The basic revocable trust has become the bread and butter of most estate plans, in large part because it is especially flexible during the trust settlor's life, it can provide for an agent to manage the property during a period of incapacity, and it disposes of the property at the settlor's death according to the trust provisions without requiring that the property go through probate. If the trust settlor still has minor children at death, the trust can continue until a point in the future when the beneficiaries are capable of taking the property outright. And, in most instances, the trust can be set up, amended, and maintained without having to comply with all of the will formalities.[1] It is private and gives the settlor almost complete control until death over any property in the trust.

So, if a person could easily manage her property during life, with full dominion and control, have it pass smoothly to a successor trustee when she becomes incapacitated and dies, and then have it pass smoothly to the next takers without any court interference, why doesn't everyone have a revocable trust? The answer is that the revocable trust is actually a bit more complicated to establish, it takes some significant maintenance during life if it is going to be truly beneficial, and the legal drafting of the trust needs to be very carefully done if it is going to continue in existence past the settlor's death. The great thing about revocable trusts is their flexibility; the bad thing about revocable trusts is that if their flexible terms are not drafted just right, they can become very inflexible. And the trust has to be maintained. It's not something you just put in a drawer and pull out when the time comes, which you can do with a will. Property has to be retitled, property in the trust may have to be managed according to fiduciary obligations, and revoking the trust isn't as easy as snapping your fingers.

In this Chapter you are going to draft a revocable trust for Henry and/or Wanda (or both if you feel particularly ambitious!) But before you start drafting anything, you need to understand the legal parameters and conditions, as well as the advantages and disadvantages, of revocable trusts. In the first exercise, you are going to draft the provisions of the trust that deal with your client's lifetime powers and appoint a successor trustee to manage the property if your client becomes incapacitated or dies. In the second exercise, you are going to draft the property provisions naming who will take your client's property at death. In the third exercise, you will draft the property provisions for Gillian and Benjamin, in the unlikely event that they are still minors at your client's death. To avoid a court ordered guardianship of Gillian and Benjamin's property, you will want the trustee to manage anything the children inherit until they reach a suitable age (most likely higher than 18). And, if your client is Henry, you might also want to provide that some of the property that Steve and Doris might inherit stay in trust until they are a bit older as well.

## The Law of Revocable Trusts

Every state allows a property owner to place his property in trust, name himself as trustee during his own life, and retain the power to revoke the trust and thereby remove the property back to his own individual ownership where he can dispose of it freely. As you recall, the person who sets up the trust is called the *settlor*, the person who acquires the legal title to the property but under a duty to manage it for the benefit of another is called the *trustee*, and the person or persons who are to receive the benefit of the property are the equitable title holders, called the *beneficiaries*. The testator, in our case Henry or Wanda, can be settlors, trustees, and beneficiaries, so long as there is

[1] This is not true in Florida and New York, however, which require that dispositive provisions of a revocable trust be executed with the will formalities. See NY EPTL § 7–1.1; Fl. Stat. § 737.111.

at least one other person—a successor trustee and/or successor beneficiaries—who can enforce the terms of the trust in case they decide to squander the property in violation of the trust terms. This is important, because without someone else who has an interest in the trust property there is no trust. The courts will deem the trust illusory and rule that the settlor owns it outright, which means the trust property becomes part of the settlor's net-probate estate. This result would undermine one of the most important points of the trust—to facilitate the passing of the property to others at death, without having to go through probate.

When a trust is established, the settlor must "put the property into the trust" by transferring legal title to the trustee. If the settlor and the trustee are the same person, it's kind of like saying aloud to the whole world that "I, Henry, hereby give myself my sofa and television as trustee of my revocable trust, and if I don't revoke it before I die, then the sofa and television are to pass to my wife Wanda." Oral trusts can be established for personal property without any documentation, but you can imagine the evidentiary headaches that would arise if Henry did this and there were no witnesses or a writing to spell out exactly what personal property was in the trust and would therefore pass to Wanda. Would the trust include a television he bought to replace the old one, after he declared the trust? What would happen if he revoked the trust without telling anyone? As with most legal transactions, it's always better to have it in writing.

With real property, securities, cars, boats, RVs, bank accounts, and other property that has some kind of title document (like deeds, car titles, bank statements, and the like), the property must be *retitled* in the name of the trustee. Any future property that is acquired by the trust must be taken in the name of the trustee. This is one of the reasons that revocable trusts are somewhat expensive to set up and can be a pain in the neck to maintain. Property should be titled in the name of the trust all the time. Thus, if Henry and Wanda want to establish revocable trusts, they need to retitle their assets. The house will have to be transferred, the cars will have to be retitled, the bank accounts will have to be changed, and the retirement accounts will have to be changed over. And although most banks, stock companies, and county recorders' offices are used to seeing property taken in the name of "Henry Higgins as trustee of the Henry Higgins Revocable Trust established January 15, 2020, and subsequent amendments" it is absolutely imperative that the property be correctly retitled in the name of the trustee and that the trust be correctly identified so that there is no confusion when Henry dies and the successor trustee takes over. If Henry trades in his car and buys a new one, he needs to make sure that it is correctly titled in the name of the trust or else it will be deemed part of his net probate estate at death and will not pass according to the terms of his trust, defeating the purpose of all of that expensive estate planning you are providing for him now.

We will work on retitling some property in the next Chapter. For now, however, we need to focus on: who Henry and Wanda want to serve as their successor trustees, what powers they want to give their trustees, what property they want to put into the trust, what property they want to leave out of the trust, and how they want to have the trust property pass at their deaths.

Once the trust is established, and the property has been titled in the name of the trustee, Henry and/or Wanda can revoke the trust as to certain property simply by transferring it to others, retitling it back in their own names, or consuming the property. Some settlors make it more difficult to revoke the trust so that they don't inadvertently remove some property that they didn't want to remove.[2] In that case, they might include a provision that states that the revocation of the trust with regard to any property must be done in writing by a letter to the trustee. In that case, if the settlor tries to

[2] In *Heaps v. Heaps*, 124 Cal.App.4th 286 (Ct.App.Ca. 2004), the trust permitted the trustees to take title in their own names individually, in their names as trustees, or in any other form. Because of the flexibility in how the property could be titled, the court held that to revoke the trust the settlor had to do something more than just change the title documents. When the settlor and his wife sold the house, which was the trust's principal asset, and took title in their own name, the court ruled that no effective revocation had occurred because they needed to do something more significant than merely changing the name on the title to effectively revoke the trust.

revoke the trust with regard to certain property and fails to follow the requisite procedure, the trust is not revoked and the settlor may be liable to the beneficiaries for mismanaging trust property. At the same time, if it's really easy to revoke the trust, you can imagine that intestate or will beneficiaries will claim that the trust was revoked with regard to certain property as a result of a simple action of the settlor that may not have been intended to revoke the trust.

For instance, imagine that Henry acquires a valuable painting that he takes ownership of as trustee of his revocable trust. He includes the painting as part of his assets with his homeowner's insurance. But the insurance policy doesn't indicate that the painting is owned in trust. Then, a few years later, he loans the painting to the local museum of art, and the loan documents indicate that Henry is the owner. Of course, he is the owner, but he is the legal owner of the painting that he owns in trust for the benefit of others who have the equitable title. The little metal plaque on the painting indicates that Henry is the owner now, but all four of his children are his successor beneficiaries of the trust. If Henry gives possession of the painting to Doris, telling her that he wants her to have it early, has Henry revoked the trust with regard to the painting? Doris will say yes, and the other kids will say no unless there is clear written evidence indicating whether Henry is revoking the trust and making a lifetime gift to Doris, or is simply allowing Doris to have possession until his own death.

Trusts are great mechanisms, but they can become problematic and controversial if the settlor treats the property exactly as he would property he owns fully outright. If Henry writes himself a letter stating that he is revoking the trust for the painting when he gives it to Doris, then all is well and good (unless of course he was unduly influenced to make the gift to Doris). At the end of the day, trusts are not very good for people who are bad at paperwork, are disorganized, or who like to cut corners. They are great for people who don't change their property a lot, are methodical and consistent record-keepers, and who understand the importance of maintaining the trust form to get the eventual probate avoidance benefits down the road.

One of the best things about revocable trusts, however, is that when the settlor/trustee becomes incapacitated, the successor trustee can simply take over management of the property without needing a court order, a court-imposed conservatorship, or any delay. This means that if Henry is in a car accident and is in a coma for two weeks, his successor trustee can pay bills, invest the trust property, and otherwise manage it seamlessly. If Henry recovers, he can go back to managing the property himself, or he can allow his successor trustee to continue to manage it. If he recovers, and he doesn't like what his successor trustee did while he was injured, he can replace the trustee, revoke the trust, or amend the trust to write that person out. He can also give the successor trustee only limited powers during his period of incapacity, but greater powers after his death. So providing for management of the trust property during a period of incapacity is very important.

Trusts are also wonderful mechanisms for avoiding probate altogether. Thus, any property that is titled in the trust prior to the settlor's death will automatically be exempted from probate and can pass according to the terms of the trust. Any property that a testator wishes to have poured over from his will into his trust (i.e., any property still owned individually by the decedent at his death) will have to be probated before it can be titled in the name of the trust and pass according to the trust's terms. But as you noticed from the wills in Chapter 5, many testators have any residual property left over at their death, which is not already in the trust, poured into the trust via their will to pass according to the trust's terms. However, only property in the trust prior to the settlor's death will pass completely outside probate. The rest will be catalogued and inventoried with probate court supervision before it can be disposed of to beneficiaries named in the trust.[3]

[3] This was the subject of much controversy surrounding James Gandolfini's will. Pundits speculated that if all of his possible $70 million estate was going to be disposed of by the terms of the will, then he would have some significant estate taxes to pay.

The probate avoidance benefit means that most of the big-ticket items (houses, cars, bank accounts, stock accounts, and the like) should be titled in the name of the trust before the settlor's death. Once the settlor dies, in most instances, the trust becomes irrevocable. This means that after the settlor's death, the terms of the trust are no longer flexible unless appropriate flexibility is given to the successor trustee. This is usually done in the form of a discretionary trust. In the case of Henry, he might want Wanda to serve as successor trustee to manage the property for the benefit of his four children, but he wants her to use her discretion in whether she gives the property to any of them outright, or holds it in further trust until they reach a sufficiently mature age. He may want her to expend the property for their education, buying a house, or setting up a business, but not to go on a grand cruise or gamble it away in the local casino. How he drafts the successor trustee's powers and discretion, and the rights of the successor beneficiaries are therefore very important. And what is he going to do if Wanda predeceases him and he needs an alternate trustee, or if one of his children predeceases him leaving minor issue? You have to work through the contingencies with your client carefully in order to keep this trust out of litigation and out of future casebooks.

Giving a certain amount of discretion to the successor trustee is imperative if the trust is going to successfully provide for minor beneficiaries. The settlor will want to ensure that the children do not take outright ownership until they are mature enough to handle the property. Giving that discretion to the trustee usually entails creating a power of appointment. As you should remember from Trusts and Estates, powers of appointment are precisely what the term implies: a power to appoint property to oneself or to others. In the case of powers, the property owner who creates the power is called the *donor*, the person who possesses the power to decide who will take ownership or possession next is called the *donee*, and the group of people for whom the power may be exercised are called the *permissible appointees*. Normally the donee of a power of appointment is not a fiduciary and does not have a legal obligation to exercise the power. But if this power is given to a trustee, the power must be exercised with the requisite care.

If Henry wants to create a trust with Wanda as the successor trustee, and he wants to give her the discretion to disperse principal to any of his four children or to their issue only, he has given her a *special* power of appointment. If he gives her the power to invade the principal for her own benefit, for the benefit of her creditors, her estate or the creditors of her estate, then it is called a *general* power of appointment. There are some important reasons why donors would use a general rather than a special power of appointment for their trustees that we don't have time to discuss here. Suffice it to say that if the trustee has a general power to invade the principal of the trust, most state laws consider that power to be "ownership equivalent." This means that the trust property will be deemed part of the donee's estate at the donee's death if it has not been appointed before that, it will be available for the creditors of the donee's estate if the estate is not large enough to pay all the donee's debts, and it may be available to a surviving spouse of the donee as part of the elective estate. Depending on your comfort level with powers of appointment. You may want to draft appropriate language for the successor trustees to have adequate discretion to invade principal for the benefit of the minor children, and perhaps for the benefit of the surviving spouse, depending on your client's wishes.

## Drafting Considerations

Again, we want you to think about the purpose of the trust and the skills that go into drafting effective trust terms. Review the discussion of will drafting considerations in Chapter 5, and keep the following in mind:

---

But if, as later turned out to be the case, he had a relatively small percentage of his property pass according to his will, and the rest passed according to other mechanisms and instruments, then the will wasn't so bad.

- Even if you are using a sample document, review it as if you wrote it entirely on your own.
- Avoid ambiguity by using consistent terminology and references; review your state's probate and trust law to identify the best terminology to use.
- Look at your verbs of authority and determine if your instructions reflect the clients' wishes (is the direction mandatory or discretionary?). What happens if some of the trust property is sold or spent entirely?
- Ask yourself if you are saying what you truly intend, and remove unnecessary language that may confuse the reader or contradict other provisions.
- Look to see if your document can be used easily by a trustee or trust beneficiary, neither of whom may be an attorney.

### Exercise 1—the Trustee and the Trustee's Powers

As with the wills, you don't have to reinvent the wheel. Below we have reproduced two standard revocable trusts, the kind that are easily available on the internet. For this exercise, we want you to meet with your client to determine who should serve as successor and alternate trustees, and what powers you want those trustees to have in the case of your client's incapacity and at your client's death. You also want to discuss with your client what kind of documentation should be necessary to prove incapacity. You don't want to impose such onerous conditions that the successor trustee will need three doctor statements, a signed affidavit by the U.S. Surgeon General, and a court order in order to find that the settlor is incapacitated. On the other hand, your client probably doesn't want the successor taking over every time he pops a sleeping pill or leaves the country. Should the successor beneficiaries have to agree with the trustee that the settlor is incapacitated? Should there be a required psychiatric exam? The answer may depend on your client's beneficiaries as well as on your client's own mental and physical health.

Also, consider whether you want the trustee(s) to have discretion to appoint any trust property into further trust for the benefit of minor or disabled beneficiaries. Do you want the trustee to have a general power of appointment to invade the trust property for the trustee's own benefit, or should the invasion power be limited to benefitting the other beneficiaries? What standard of care should the trustee exercise when deciding to exercise discretion? Do you want to build into the trust limits on the trustee's actions, so that the power can only be exercised for certain ascertainable reasons, like the health, support, maintenance, or education of the beneficiaries? Should the trustee have the power to modify or amend the trust after the settlor's death?

In this exercise, we will draft individual trusts for Henry and Wanda. Although some couples use a joint trust, especially when the trust contains jointly-owned property, Henry and Wanda have very little jointly-held property. Henry may prefer to put the home in his trust but with instructions about who gets it at his death rather than adding Wanda's name to the title now. Do you understand why he might prefer one or the other approach?

Draft the trustee language, the powers of the trustee(s), and the conditions for a finding of incapacity for Henry or Wanda using the models below as a guide. You will notice that one of the samples below spends nearly 3 pages on what you might think of as boilerplate, and only two paragraphs (10 & 11) on actual property disposition. This should tell you something about the importance of those trustee powers. For this exercise, be sure you draft appropriate provisions for:

1. Henry or Wanda as principal trustee of their own trusts
2. At least 1 successor trustee and at least 1 alternate successor trustee

3. Powers of the trustee (you can spell them out or group them together under more general powers)
4. Ability to revoke or remove a trustee or appoint a new trustee (who can/should be able to remove, revoke, or appoint a trustee?)
5. Does Henry or Wanda want an exculpatory clause for the trustee?
6. Identify if the trustee will have to post a bond or shall be compensated for performing the duties of trustee, knowing that trustees are legally-entitled to trustee fees
7. Identify what happens upon the incapacity and death of the settlor, including what documentation is necessary to prove incapacity.

When you are thinking about the powers of the trustee, think about not only Henry's and Wanda's current property, but also any property they might later acquire, either through their own hard work or through an inheritance. Should that property be included in the trust, and how do you get it there?

## THE [NAME OF TRUST] UNDER AGREEMENT DATED [DATE OF TRUST AGREEMENT][4]

*[Name of settlor]*, of *[name of city]*, *[name of state]*, as Settlor, and *[name of settlor as initial trustee]*, as initial Trustee, establish by this Agreement the *[NAME OF TRUST]* TRUST for the benefit of the beneficiaries identified in Article ONE. "Trustee," unless otherwise stated, refers to the initial trustee and to all successor trustees, whether individuals or corporate trustees and regardless of number and gender.

Settlor, or any other person, may at any time assign, transfer, convey, deliver, give or devise property to the trust. The property, on receipt by the Trustee, will be held, managed and distributed under this Agreement.

### ARTICLE ONE DISTRIBUTION OF TRUST INCOME AND PRINCIPAL

#### Section A. During Settlor's Lifetime

During Settlor's lifetime, the Trustee will pay the trust income to Settlor or for Settlor's benefit. Settlor may withdraw any amount of trust principal at any time.

If Settlor becomes physically or mentally incapacitated, the successor Trustee named in Article TWO is nominated to replace the initial Trustee. Article TWO will then become effective as if Settlor were deceased. Settlor is "physically or mentally incapacitated" if in the written opinion of Settlor's primary care physician, Settlor is physically or mentally unable to hold and manage the trust principal and income or unable to withdraw trust principal. If Settlor's primary care physician cannot be readily found or identified, then the written opinion may be obtained from two physicians selected by Settlor's patient advocate. If Settlor has not designated a patient advocate, then the written opinion may be obtained from two physicians selected by a majority of the adult members of Settlor's immediate family.

During Settlor's incapacity, the Trustee will distribute so much trust income and principal as is necessary to maintain Settlor in the standard of living to which Settlor had been accustomed prior to becoming incapacitated. To the extent funds are available, and taking into consideration funds available from other sources, the Trustee may also distribute trust income and principal for the benefit of those persons who were receiving the majority of their support from Settlor at the time of Settlor's incapacity to maintain them as nearly as possible in the standard of living to which they were accustomed prior to Settlor becoming incapacitated.

#### Section B. At Settlor's Death

At Settlor's death, the Trustee, after making payments under Article FOUR, Section D, will hold, administer and distribute the remaining property as follows:

1. *Household Furnishings and Other Tangible Personal Property*

The Trustee will distribute tangible personal property held in the trust according to a written list or statement signed and dated by Settlor which describes the items and the distributees with reasonable certainty, according to the list or statement. In the event of a conflict among or between lists or statements, the most recent list or statement will control.

The Trustee will distribute to Settlor's *[husband/wife]*, *[name of spouse]*, if *[he/she]* is then living, all remaining tangible personal property, including all remaining jewelry, apparel, household furniture and furnishings, books, art works, collections, sporting equipment, water craft and vehicles, and all rights under any insurance policies relating to this property. The Trustee will not claim an interest in any property which may already belong to Settlor's *[husband/wife]* and the Trustee will honor any reasonable claim of ownership *[he/she]* asserts.

If Settlor's *[husband/wife]* is not then living, the Trustee will distribute all remaining tangible personal property to Settlor's then living children, and not to the descendants of any deceased child, to be divided as they agree. The Trustee will sell any property Settlor's children do not desire, or which is not distributed for any reason, and will distribute the proceeds from the sale with the remaining trust property. At any sale, Settlor's children will have the first right to purchase any of the property to be sold.

[4] West Family Estate Planning Guide, Appendix 5. Westlaw. © 2023 Thomson Reuters. No Claim to Orig. U.S. Govt. Works.

The Trustee will pay the reasonable expenses of packing, shipping and delivering the tangible personal property to any distributee at his or her residence or place of business as an administration expense.

2. *Remaining Trust Property*

If Settlor's *[husband/wife]*, *[name of spouse]*, survives Settlor, the remaining trust property will consist of two portions, the "Qualified Share" and the "Nonqualified Share." The Qualified Share will be that fractional portion of the trust property that Settlor's executor elects to treat as qualified terminable interest property. The Nonqualified Share will be the balance of the trust property. The terms "executor" and "qualified terminable interest property" are used as defined for federal estate tax purposes. Trust property will be valued as finally determined for federal estate tax purposes. The Trustee will hold in this trust only property that qualifies for the marital deduction and will distribute to Settlor's *[husband/wife]* any property that does not qualify. The Trustee will charge all payments made under Article FOUR, Section D, including all payments deducted for trust income tax purposes, first to the Nonqualified Share and any balance to the Qualified Share. The Trustee will administer this trust as a single trust, without distinguishing between the Qualified Share and the Nonqualified Share.

Settlor anticipates that the executor will elect to treat as qualified terminable interest property that fractional portion of the trust property which will eliminate Settlor's federal estate tax, taking into consideration the applicable exclusion amount and all deductions and credits allowed on the return. The executor may elect a fractional portion which does not entirely eliminate Settlor's federal estate tax if the executor determines in its discretion that election of a different fractional portion is in the best interests of the trust beneficiaries. In making the election, the Trustee will consider the value of all other property qualifying for the marital deduction that passes for federal estate tax purposes to Settlor's *[husband/wife]*.

a. If Settlor's *[husband/wife]*, *[name of spouse]*, survives Settlor, the Trustee will, beginning as of Settlor's death, pay to *[him/her]* or apply for his or her benefit all trust income at quarterly or more frequent intervals until *[his/her]* death.

b. The Trustee, in its discretion, may distribute trust principal as necessary for the health, education, maintenance, and support of Settlor's *[husband/wife]* in *[his/her]* accustomed standard of living, and for his or her medical, dental, hospital and nursing expenses and expenses of invalidism. The Trustee will, if permissible, charge these distributions for tax purposes against the Qualified Share until it is exhausted.

c. At the death of Settlor's *[husband/wife]* or, if *[he/she]* predeceases Settlor, at Settlor's death, the Trustee will divide the remaining trust property, including any accrued and undistributed income, into as many equal shares as Settlor has (i) children then living and (ii) deceased children with descendants then living. The Trustee will hold these shares as follows:

(1) One share will be held in a separate trust for the benefit of each of Settlor's then living children. If the child is age 24 or younger, the Trustee, in its discretion, may distribute trust income from the child's trust as necessary for the child's health, education, maintenance and support, in the child's accustomed standard of living. The Trustee will add undistributed income to trust principal at the end of each trust accounting year. After the child reaches age 25, the Trustee will pay to the child or apply for his or her benefit all income from that child's trust at quarterly or more frequent intervals until the child's death or termination of the trust.

(2) At any time after the child reaches age 25, or at any time after the child's trust is established if he or she is then age 25 or older, he or she may withdraw by written notice to the Trustee any amount of principal from the trust which is not, when taken together with all prior withdrawals made under this paragraph, greater than 50% of the sum of: (i) the market value of trust principal determined at the time the Trustee receives written notice of the withdrawal and (ii) all prior withdrawals made under this paragraph. The child may make no more than one withdrawal during each trust accounting year.

(3) At any time after the child reaches age 30, he or she may withdraw by written notice to the Trustee any part or the entire balance of trust principal.

(4) The Trustee, in its discretion, may distribute trust principal from the child's trust as necessary for the health, education, maintenance and support of the child in his or her accustomed standard of living, and for the child's medical, dental, hospital, and nursing expenses and expenses of invalidism.

(5) The child's trust will continue until he or she has withdrawn all the principal of the trust or the principal has been exhausted by discretionary distributions or until the child's death, whichever occurs first.

(6) At the child's death, the Trustee will distribute the remaining trust property, in trust or otherwise, as the child appoints in his or her Last Will and Testament admitted to probate, provided that specific reference is made in the Will to this power of appointment. Any trust created under this power of appointment may be subject to any powers the child may confer, except a further power to appoint, and may contain any lawful trust provisions which the child incorporates, including a spendthrift clause. This power may not be exercised in any manner which would result in a violation of the *[name of state whose law will apply]* statutory Rule Against Perpetuities.

(7) To the extent a child of Settlor dies without validly and completely exercising his or her power of appointment, the Trustee will distribute the trust property remaining in the child's trust to the child's then living descendants per stirpes. If a distribution is to be made to any descendant then under age 21, the Trustee will hold that descendant's share in a separate trust under Section C.

(8) To the extent a child of Settlor dies without validly and completely exercising his or her power of appointment and dies without leaving descendants surviving, the Trustee will distribute the trust property remaining in the child's trust in equal shares to Settlor's other children who are then living, and to the then living descendants of any deceased children of Settlor, per stirpes. If a distribution is to be made to any beneficiary of an existing trust under this Agreement, the Trustee will add the distribution to the principal of that trust.

(9) If, prior to the time of division of trust property into equal shares for Settlor's children, any child of Settlor has died, the Trustee will distribute any share created for the then living descendants of a deceased child of Settlor to those descendants per stirpes. If a distribution is to be made to any descendant then under age 21, the Trustee will hold that descendant's portion in a separate trust under Section C.

**Section C. Trusts for Descendants of Settlor's Deceased Children**

Whenever any property is to continue in trust for the benefit of descendants of a deceased child of Settlor, the Trustee will hold, administer and distribute the property in a separate trust as follows:

1. The Trustee will apply income as necessary, in the Trustee's discretion, for the health, maintenance, education and support of the beneficiary. The Trustee will accumulate income not applied for these purposes. If income is insufficient, the Trustee may apply accumulated income or trust principal as necessary in the Trustee's discretion, for these purposes. In exercising its discretion the Trustee may consider the beneficiary's standard of living and other sources of financial support, and the amount of trust income and principal. The Trustee will distribute the remaining principal and accumulated income to the beneficiary at age 21, and the trust will then terminate.

2. If any descendant of a deceased child of Settlor dies before age 21, the Trustee will distribute the principal and accumulated income to that beneficiary's then living descendants per stirpes. If that beneficiary has no then living descendants, the Trustee will distribute the trust property in equal shares to that beneficiary's then living brothers and sisters who are Settlor's descendants and the then living descendants of a deceased brother or sister per stirpes. If none of the beneficiary's brothers or sisters nor their descendants are then living, the Trustee will distribute the principal and any accumulated income in equal shares to Settlor's other than living children and the then living descendants of any of Settlor's deceased children per stirpes. If a trust created by this Agreement is in existence for one of these beneficiaries, the Trustee will add that beneficiary's share to the principal of the beneficiary's trust.

**Section D. Distribution on Death of All Beneficiaries**

If, at the time of termination of any trust, there is no living beneficiary to whom the trust property will be distributed, then the Trustee will distribute the trust property to *[NAME OF FOUNDATION]* FOUNDATION, a *[name of state whose law will apply]* nonprofit corporation.

**ARTICLE TWO TRUSTEE APPOINTMENT, RESIGNATION AND REMOVAL**

**Section A. Appointment During Settlor's Life**

If any Trustee discontinues to serve during Settlor's life, Settlor may in writing appoint a successor Trustee. If Settlor is also serving as Trustee, Settlor may at any time resign and appoint a successor Trustee.

**Section B. Appointment On Settlor's Death**

On Settlor's death, Settlor's *[husband/wife]*, *[name of spouse]*, is nominated to become the Trustee. If *[name of spouse]* predeceases Settlor, fails to qualify, or for any reason discontinues to serve as Trustee, *[name of successor trustee]* is nominated to serve as the successor Trustee.

A nominated Trustee will act as successor Trustee only after signing a written acceptance of appointment which describes any property the Trustee refuses to accept. Acceptance of appointment as successor Trustee is not an acceptance, ratification or approval of any acts, omissions or defaults of any prior Trustee nor an undertaking by the successor Trustee to audit or verify any prior Trustee's records. Any successor Trustee is entitled to rely on statements and records concerning trust property found after a reasonable search. No successor Trustee will have responsibility or liability for trust property until it has signed an acceptance of appointment and the trust property is in the legal possession of the successor Trustee.

**Section C. Resignation of Trustee**

Any Trustee may resign by giving Settlor written notice. After Settlor's death any Trustee may resign by giving each current trust beneficiary written notice. The resignation will become effective 30 days after delivery of notice. A Trustee who has resigned must submit a final account within 60 days following the effective date of resignation.

**Section D. Appointment of Successor Corporate Trustee**

In the event there is no acting Trustee, or following the removal or resignation of a corporate Trustee, a majority of current trust beneficiaries may designate as successor Trustee a bank or trust company which is qualified to act in a fiduciary capacity and which has a minimum capitalization, either itself or together with its parent holding company, of $100,000,000. If a current trust beneficiary is a minor or is otherwise legally incapacitated, a parent, guardian, conservator, attorney-in-fact or other person having custody of the beneficiary may act for the beneficiary in appointing a successor Trustee. If the current trust beneficiaries do not designate a successor corporate Trustee within 30 days after the effective date of the prior Trustee's vacancy, removal or resignation, a Trustee will be appointed in accordance with *[name of state whose law will apply]* law. A successor corporate Trustee must submit to each current trust beneficiary a written acceptance of appointment.

**Section E. Removal of Corporate Trustee**

After Settlor's death, a majority of the current trust beneficiaries of any trust having a corporate Trustee may remove that Trustee by giving written notice. The Trustee's removal will become effective 30 days following delivery of notice. A corporate Trustee who has been removed must submit a final account to each current trust beneficiary within 60 days following the effective date of removal. If a current trust beneficiary is a minor or is otherwise legally incapacitated, a parent, guardian, conservator, attorney-in-fact or other person having custody of the beneficiary may act for the beneficiary in removing a corporate Trustee.

**Section F. Appointment of Successor Trustee After Environmental Investigation**

Prior to signing an acceptance of appointment, any nominated successor Trustee may conduct such environmental investigations as it considers appropriate. Based on such investigations, a nominated successor Trustee will have the right to decline to act as successor Trustee. If no nominated successor Trustee will act due to the results of an environmental investigation, or if a Trustee refuses to accept property because of possible liability due to an environmental hazard and only under these circumstances or as otherwise provided in this Agreement, then a majority of current trust beneficiaries may nominate a successor Trustee for that trust, including any Trust for Real Estate under Article THREE. If no successor Trustee is nominated, a Trustee will be appointed in accordance with *[name of state whose law will apply]* law.

**ARTICLE THREE TRUST ADMINISTRATION**

The following provisions apply to the administration of any trust created by this Agreement.

**Section A. Amendment and Revocation**

Except during Settlor's incapacity, Settlor may amend or revoke this Agreement or any part of it at any time by written amendment. If Settlor is not acting as Trustee at the time of amendment, the duties, powers and liabilities of the Trustee may be increased only with the Trustee's written consent. After Settlor's death, this Agreement will be irrevocable. The interest of every beneficiary is subject to Settlor's power to withdraw trust principal and to amend or revoke this Agreement.

**Section B. Insurance and Death Benefits**

Settlor or any other person may designate the trust as beneficiary of any insurance policy or any plan paying death benefits. Any insurance policy proceeds or death benefits payable to the trust are subject to the terms of this Agreement when received by the Trustee. The owner of any policy or the participant under any plan paying death benefits retains all incidents and obligations of ownership. Designation of the trust as beneficiary of any insurance policy imposes no obligation on the Trustee to maintain the policy in force or to pay premiums.

**Section C. Trustee's Account**

In lieu of any applicable provisions of *[name of state whose law will apply]* law regarding accounts by Trustees, the Trustee will submit an account at least annually to each beneficiary who is currently entitled or, in the Trustee's discretion, eligible to receive distributions of trust property or have trust property applied to his or her use and to each beneficiary who possesses a testamentary or presently exercisable general or special power of appointment. The account will include a statement of all receipts, disbursements, gains and losses, significant transactions, and distributions of trust property and an inventory of trust property at both current and carrying values. The Trustee may submit an account, in its discretion, to other Interested Trust Beneficiaries, as defined under *[name of state whose law will apply]* law. If any beneficiary is a minor or is otherwise legally incapacitated, a parent, guardian, conservator, attorney in fact or other person having custody of the beneficiary may act for the beneficiary in receiving the Trustee's account and objecting to the account with the same legal effect as if the account had been submitted to the beneficiary as an adult with full legal capacity. The Trustee's account will be deemed accepted and approved by a beneficiary unless the beneficiary delivers a written objection to the Trustee within 90 days after receipt of the account. Settlement of any account to which a beneficiary has objected will be in accordance with *[name of state whose law will apply]* law. Any beneficiary or the Trustee may initiate these proceedings. When the account has been settled or when the 90 day period for filing objections has passed without any objection having been delivered to the Trustee, the Trustee will be released and discharged as to all matters included in the account as if the account had been approved by court order.

**Section D. Spendthrift Provision**

No beneficiary may sell, assign, transfer, encumber or in any manner dispose of his or her interest in trust property, including income from trust property, until it is distributed outright to the beneficiary. Trust property is not subject to garnishment or attachment by any creditor of any beneficiary and is not subject to any legal proceedings designed to prevent the distribution of principal or income to any beneficiary. This provision does not restrict a beneficiary's right to disclaim an interest in any portion of the trust property.

**Section E. Early Termination**

The Trustee, other than a sole Trustee who is also a beneficiary of trust income, may in its discretion terminate any trust prior to the time provided in this Agreement if the principal of the trust is so small that continuation is impractical because of expense of administration or otherwise. The Trustee will then distribute the principal and any undistributed income to each beneficiary who is then entitled or, in the Trustee's discretion, eligible to receive trust income or have trust income applied to his or her use. All future interests in the trusts will then be terminated.

**Section F. Maximum Duration**

Every trust will terminate 21 years after the death of the last surviving beneficiary living at Settlor's death or within 90 years after Settlor's death, whichever is longer, regardless of any other provision in this Agreement. The Trustee will then distribute the principal and any undistributed income to each beneficiary who is then entitled to receive trust income or, in the Trustee's discretion, eligible to receive trust income or have trust income applied to his or her use. All interests in the trusts will then be terminated.

**Section G. Beneficiary Serving As Trustee**

After Settlor's death, whenever a discretionary payment or application of income or principal is contemplated with respect to a beneficiary who is serving as Trustee, the decision will be made only by the Trustee other than that beneficiary, unless the beneficiary is the sole Trustee.

**Section H. Per Stirpes**

Any share of trust property to be distributed to the descendants of any person per stirpes will be divided into as many equal shares as there are surviving children of that person and deceased children who left surviving descendants. Each surviving child, if any, is allocated one share. The share of each deceased child with surviving descendants is divided in the same manner, with subdivision repeating at each succeeding generation until the property is fully allocated among surviving descendants. A deceased individual who left no surviving descendant is disregarded, and an individual who leaves a surviving ancestor who is a descendant of the designated ancestor is not entitled to a share.

**Section I. Real Estate Outside *[Name of State Whose Law will Apply]***

If any trust includes real estate outside *[name of state whose law will apply]* and the Trustee is unable or unwilling to act as Trustee of that property, the Trustee will appoint a Special Trustee with full power and authority as to that property. The Special Trustee will have no power or authority over, or liability for, any other trust property at any time. The Special Trustee will act only as long as the real estate outside *[name of state whose law will apply]* remains trust property or until the Special Trustee is removed by written notice from the Trustee. The Special Trustee will pay all net income from the real estate to the Trustee at least annually. When the real estate is sold or distributed, the Special Trustee will distribute all remaining trust property in its possession to the Trustee, and the Special Trustee will then be discharged with no further liability.

**Section J. Custody of Documents**

Any Corporate Trustee will have custody of all securities, notes, mortgages, insurance policies, contracts and other instruments reflecting ownership of trust property.

**Section K. Applicable Law**

*[Name of state whose law will apply]* law governs the validity, interpretation and administration of this Agreement regardless of the residence of Settlor or any beneficiary. Any trust created by this Agreement is exempt from registration.

**Section L. Indemnification of Trustee**

Settlor and Settlor's successors-in-interest jointly and severally indemnify and hold harmless Trustee (individually and in a fiduciary capacity, including any officer, director, employee, agent, successor and assign of a corporate Trustee) from and against all "liabilities" incurred due to an environmental hazard associated with the holding of trust property. "Liabilities" includes all claims, demands, interests, charges, damages, losses, causes of action, fines, penalties, judgments, injunctive relief, costs, expenses of every kind whatsoever, whether known or unknown, contingent, liquidated or otherwise, including reasonable attorney and environmental consultant fees. A Trustee may require that a beneficiary indemnify and hold harmless the Trustee in a similar manner before trust property is distributed to the beneficiary, regardless of any other provision in this Agreement. "Environmental hazard" is defined as any actual, perceived or threatened violation of federal, state or local environmental or human health law, statute, regulation, rule, ordinance or court order.

**Section M. Trust for Real Estate**

If the Trustee refuses to accept any property because of the possibility of liability due to an environmental hazard, such property will be held, as of Settlor's death or physical or mental incapacity, in a separate trust known as the "Trust for Real Estate." The Trustee of the Trust for Real Estate will administer any Trust for Real Estate according to the same terms that would apply under Article ONE, Section A, if Settlor is then living, or which would otherwise apply to the trust property under Article ONE if Settlor is then deceased. However, if trust property held under Article ONE, Section B, is divided into separate trusts, the Trustee of the Trust for Real Estate will likewise divide and hold the Trust for Real Estate in separate trusts in the same proportions that the trust property held under

Article ONE, Section B, is divided. By creating the Trust for Real Estate, Settlor does not intend to change the disposition of trust property or the treatment of trust property for tax purposes.

**Section N. Lapse of Pecuniary Distributions**

No antilapse provision or provision for substitute gift under any state law, whether enacted before or after the execution of this Agreement, will apply to any specific pecuniary distribution under this Agreement. It is Settlor's intent that only the beneficiary identified to receive a specific pecuniary distribution shall receive that distribution, unless otherwise indicated in this Agreement.

**Section O. S Corporation Stock**

If any trust established under the terms of this Agreement holds stock that is S corporation stock ("S corporation stock"), the following special provisions apply with respect to that stock:

1. If the trust S corporation stock has only one current income beneficiary and such beneficiary is a citizen or resident of the United States, Settlor desires such beneficiary make in a timely manner an election necessary for the trust to be treated as a qualified subchapter S trust (QSST). The terms of the QSST will be the same as the terms of the trust, except that so long as the QSST holds S corporation stock: (i) during the life of the QSST beneficiary, there shall be only one income beneficiary of the QSST; (ii) any principal distributed during the life of the current QSST beneficiary may be distributed only to such beneficiary; (iii) the income interest of the current QSST beneficiary will terminate on the earlier of the death of such beneficiary or the termination of the QSST; and (iv) upon the termination of the QSST during the current QSST beneficiary's life, the QSST will distribute all of its assets to such beneficiary.

2. If the trust holding S corporation stock has more than one current income beneficiary or only one current income beneficiary but the election to treat such trust as a QSST is unavailable or it appears that the QSST election will not be timely made, and the current and contingent beneficiary or beneficiaries of such trust consist only of individuals who are U.S. citizens or residents, estates, organizations described in Section 170(c)(2) to (5) of the Internal Revenue Code, or a combination of them, none of which acquired their interest in the trust by purchase, the Trustee will make the election necessary for the trust to be treated as an electing small business trust (ESBT). The terms of the ESBT will be the same as the terms of the trust.

3. In addition to the powers provided elsewhere in this Agreement, the Trustee will have the following powers with respect to any S corporation stock, QSST, or ESBT: (i) to distribute S corporation stock to Settlor's probate estate if this trust is the residuary beneficiary of the estate and the retention of the stock could, through lapse of time or otherwise, result in the loss of S corporation status; (ii) to refuse to make directed payments of obligations of the estate of Settlor's spouse if such directions are received more than two years from the date of the spouse's death, but only to the extent that payment would require the disposition of S corporation stock and such directed payments could result in the loss of S corporation status; (iii) to allocate S corporation stock away from a disqualified trust, whether to a qualified trust or to an individual beneficiary outright; and (iv) to divide the trust assets and allocate the S corporation stock to a separate trust or trusts that will qualify as a QSST or an ESBT.

4. The provisions of any trust established under this Agreement that hold S corporation stock will be construed and may be amended by a court as necessary to permit a trust holding S corporation stock to qualify as a QSST or an ESBT, except to the extent such construction or amendment would result in the loss to Settlor's estate of a deduction or credit against federal estate tax. For purposes of example and not by way of limitation, such construction and amendment shall include the removal or modification of powers contained in the trust instrument.

**ARTICLE FOUR TRUSTEE'S POWERS**

In addition to any inherent or implied powers of a trustee, Settlor grants to the Trustee the power to manage and control all the trust property to the fullest extent permitted a trustee or a fiduciary under *[name of state whose law will apply]* law. This power includes:

**Section A. Selling Property**

The power to sell, convey, mortgage and lease any real or personal property which is held as trust property, with the discretion to determine all terms such as price, rate of interest, and contract period.

**Section B. Prudent Investor Rule**

The power to invest the trust property in accordance with the prudent investor rule, including the power to invest in commercial and savings accounts, money market certificates and funds, cash management accounts, common and preferred stocks, bonds, U.S. governmental obligations, mutual funds, notes, debentures, and common trust funds and to delegate investment and management functions. However, the Trustee may retain all property in the form in which it is received without liability for any resulting loss and without regard to the proportion that any one asset or class of assets bears to the whole. While Settlor is acting as Trustee, the Trustee is authorized to buy, sell and trade assets of any kind, including securities, options and futures contracts, and to sell short, trade on margin, maintain and operate margin accounts and pledge any securities as collateral.

**Section C. Borrowing**

The power to borrow money in an unsecured transaction or in a transaction using trust property as security. While Settlor is living, the Trustee may guaranty the obligations of third parties and may execute and deliver such other documents as the Trustee deems necessary and appropriate in connection with such guaranty.

**Section D. Payment of Claims, Taxes and Expenses**

The power to pay the following: (1) Settlor's funeral expenses; (2) claims against Settlor's estate; (3) specific devises included in Settlor's Last Will and Testament, regardless of whether it is admitted to probate, if Settlor's probate estate is insufficient to satisfy the specific devises; (4) reasonable administration expenses of Settlor's estate; (5) any statutory allowances for Settlor's dependents; and (6) all estate taxes assessed by reason of Settlor's death which are either the legal obligation of the trust or Settlor's estate or whose payment is requested by the personal representative of Settlor's estate and approved by the Trustee. The estate taxes referred to in item (6) and Section E will include all federal, state, or foreign estate, inheritance, and succession taxes, but will exclude any generation-skipping transfer taxes, which will be paid from the property giving rise to such taxes.

**Section E. Apportionment of Taxes**

Unless otherwise provided in this Agreement or Settlor's Last Will and Testament, these taxes will be apportioned as follows: (1) any estate taxes attributable to Settlor's tangible personal property and/or tangible personal property owned by this trust, will be excluded from apportionment; (2) any estate taxes attributable to property not transferred under this Agreement will be apportioned to and paid by the recipient of that property; (3) any estate taxes attributable to property transferred under this Agreement will be paid proportionately from the shares or distributions under this Agreement; (4) any estate taxes attributable to property disclaimed under a qualified disclaimer will be paid from the disclaimed property; (5) any estate taxes chargeable under items (2) and (3) above will be equitably apportioned by applying any available deduction, credit, or rate differential attributable to such transfer; and (6) any estate taxes excluded from apportionment by this Agreement will be paid from the residue of the trust property after payment of all debts, last illness, funeral and administration expenses, and non-residuary devises.

**Section F. Settlement of Disputes**

The power to settle, litigate, submit to arbitration, or release any claim in favor of or against the trust; and to prosecute and defend any legal proceedings on behalf of the trust or the Trustee in the performance of its duties.

**Section G. Distribution of Property**

The power to distribute trust property in divided or undivided interests, in disproportionate shares or in different kinds of property, and to adjust resulting differences in valuation.

**Section H. Voting Securities**

The power to vote securities in person or by proxy, to grant discretionary proxies, to elect an individual Trustee or any officer or director of a Corporate Trustee as officer or director; to exercise options, warrants, or other rights with respect to any stock or any employee benefit plan, and to participate in a voting trust or similar agreement.

**Section I. Corporate Transactions**

The power to participate in any reorganization, consolidation, merger, dissolution, sale, purchase, or lease of assets, or similar transaction, by any corporation whose securities or obligations are trust property.

**Section J. Principal and Income**

The power to apportion between income and principal all receipts and expenditures without regard to any specific requirement of *[name of state whose law will apply]* statutory law on allocations between income and principal, but subject to any legal requirement for the qualification of trust property for the marital deduction. The surviving spouse has the power, exercisable annually, to compel the Trustee to withdraw from an individual retirement account an amount equal to all the income earned on the assets held in the individual retirement account during the year and to distribute that amount to the surviving spouse as a beneficiary of the trust.

**Section K. Consolidation of Trusts**

The power to consolidate separate trusts for administrative convenience, each trust having an undivided interest in the consolidated fund.

**Section L. Securities Registration**

The power to register any security in the name of a depository trust or a nominee without indicating a fiduciary capacity.

**Section M. Safe Deposit Boxes**

The power to lease safe deposit boxes and to appoint an agent or grant power of attorney for access to the safe deposit boxes.

**Section N. Transactions with Related Parties**

The power to engage in any transaction with the Personal Representative of Settlor's estate or a fiduciary of a member of Settlor's family, as the fiduciaries agree, even if the fiduciaries are identical.

**Section O. Payment of Administration Expenses**

The power to pay reasonable expenses of administration, including reasonable Trustee fees.

**Section P. Employment of Agents**

The power to employ agents, attorneys, investment counsel, financial planners and other professional advisors to advise or assist the Trustee in the exercise of its investment powers or in the performance of its administrative duties. The Trustee may pay reasonable compensation and costs for their services, and may act on their recommendations without independent investigation. The Trustee may rely on information or advice from these advisors, and the Trustee will not be liable for any action taken or omitted in reliance on their opinions or advice or for the default or misconduct of any advisor.

**Section Q. Refusal to Accept Property**

The power to refuse to accept property as trust property when, following such environmental investigations as it considers appropriate, the Trustee, in its discretion, considers such acceptance as causing the possibility of liability to the Trustee due to an environmental hazard associated with the holding of the property; the power to take all actions the Trustee considers appropriate concerning an environmental hazard associated with the holding of trust property, including the power to employ environmental consultants.

**Section R. Division of Trusts**

The power to divide any trust into two or more trusts for any reason the Trustee considers desirable in carrying out the provisions of this Agreement.

**Section S. Gifts by Trustee**

The power to make any distribution intended as a gift if authorized by Settlor or the authorized agent of Settlor.

**Section T. Disclaimers**

The power to disclaim, in whole or in part, any property and any interest in property, including but not limited to the right to receive or control property, a fiduciary power, and a power of appointment.

In the exercise of any power which requires or involves discretion by the Trustee who is not also a beneficiary of trust principal, the Trustee's decision will be final and conclusive on all persons (whether alive or not) who, at that time or in the future, may have an interest in the income and/or principal of the trust. The Trustee will not be required to obtain the approval of any court in the exercise of these powers.

This Trust Agreement is signed by *[name of settlor]*, Settlor and Initial Trustee, on the date written on the first page of this Agreement.

*IN WITNESS WHEREOF*, the parties hereto have signed this Trust Agreement on the ____________ day of ____________________, 20__.

________________________________ ________________________________

Settlor Trustee

________________________________ ________________________________

Witness Witness

STATE OF ________________________ )

) ss.

COUNTY OF ________________________ )

City of ____________, this __________ day of ______________, 20__.

Personally appeared ______________, known to me (or satisfactorily proven) to be the person whose name is subscribed to the within instrument and acknowledged that he executed the same, as Settlor, for the purposes therein contained.

____________________________________

Notary Public

[Whew—that is a very long trust. Do you think all of those provisions are necessary?]

## JOINT REVOCABLE TRUST AGREEMENT[5]

Trust agreement made [*date of agreement*], between [*name of trustor 1*], of [*address of trustor 1*], and [*name of trustor 2*], of [*address of trustor 2*] ("trustors"), and [*name of trustee*], of [*address of trustee*] ("trustee").

In consideration of the mutual promises set forth in this agreement, trustors and trustee agree as follows:

**SECTION ONE. TRUST ESTATE**

Trustors have transferred and delivered to trustee *[OPTIONAL: without consideration]* all of the property described in Exhibit *[designation of exhibit]*, which is attached and incorporated by this reference. Trustee acknowledges receipt of the described property. All of that property and all property later subject to this trust shall constitute the trust estate, and shall be held, managed, and distributed as provided in this agreement.

**SECTION TWO. DISTRIBUTION OF TRUST PRINCIPAL AND INCOME**

Trustee shall apply and distribute the net income and principal of the trust in the following manner: [*statement of provisions regarding distribution of principal and income*].

**SECTION THREE. REVOCATION AND AMENDMENT OF TRUST**

During the joint lives of both trustors, this trust may be amended, altered, or revoked, in whole or in part, by an instrument in writing signed by both trustors and delivered to trustee. After the death of either trustor, the surviving trustor may amend, alter or revoke the trust by an instrument in writing signed by the surviving trustor and delivered to the trustee. On revocation by both trustors, the trust estate shall be paid to them in the proportions in which they have made contributions to it, based on values at the time or times of contribution. If the trust is revoked after the death of either trustor by the surviving trustor, the trustee shall transfer to the surviving trustor all of the trust estate. On any revocation under this agreement, the trustee shall execute and deliver to trustors or the surviving trustor all instruments that are necessary or appropriate to release all interests of trustee in the trust. The trust may not be amended to change the obligations, duties, or rights of trustee without the written consent of trustee to such amendment.

**SECTION FOUR. ADDITIONS TO TRUST**

Either trustor shall have the right at any time, either during his or her life or by will at his or her death, to add other property acceptable to trustee to the trust created by this agreement. This property, when received and accepted by trustee, shall become a part of the trust estate of this trust.

**SECTION FIVE. INVASION OF TRUST CORPUS**

Trustee shall at any time pay to or apply to the use of the person then entitled to the income of the trust, out of the principal of the trust, such sum or sums as either trustor may direct in writing.

**SECTION SIX. POWERS OF TRUSTEE**

[*Statement of provisions regarding powers of trustee*].

**SECTION SEVEN. COMPENSATION OF TRUSTEE**

[*[Statement of provisions regarding trustee's compensation]/[Statement of provisions regarding waiver of compensation]*].

**SECTION EIGHT. SUCCESSOR TRUSTEE**

If trustee resigns or is unable to continue to act as trustee, *[name of successor trustee]*, of *[address of successor trustee]*, is appointed as successor trustee. Any successor trustee, including *[name of successor trustee]*, shall succeed as trustee with like effect as if the successor were originally named as trustee. All other rights and powers conferred on trustee under this agreement shall pass to any successor trustee.

---

5 17B Am Jur Legal Forms 2d § 251.59 (2023).

**SECTION NINE. PERPETUITIES SAVINGS CLAUSE**

Notwithstanding anything to the contrary contained in this agreement, the trust created by this agreement shall cease and terminate *[number of years]* years after the death of the last survivor of trustors and all issue of trustors living at the date of this agreement. At the date of termination trustee shall distribute the trust estate as it shall then be constituted, together with any unpaid net income, to those beneficiaries who are then entitled to the income from the trust estate in the same proportions in which they are entitled to that income.

**SECTION TEN. GOVERNING LAW**

The trust created by this agreement has been accepted by trustee in *[name of state]*, and will be administered by trustee in that state. The validity, construction, and all rights under this agreement shall be governed by the laws of *[name of state]*.

**SECTION ELEVEN. SEVERABILITY**

If any provision of this agreement is, or becomes, invalid or unenforceable, the remaining provisions of the agreement shall be, and continue to be, fully effective.

Trustors and trustee have executed this agreement at *[place of execution]* the day and year first above-written.

[*Name of trustor 1*]

[*Name of trustor 2*]

[*Name of trustee*]

[*Acknowledgments*]

[*Attachment of exhibit*]

---

## Exercise 2—the Property Provisions

Now that you have provided for the settlor, the trustee, alternate trustees, how to determine incapacity, and the powers of the trustee, it is time to think about the property dispositions. In this exercise, draft the disposition language to provide benefits to the surviving spouse and any other living, adult persons that the client would like to benefit. For this exercise, you may want to use trust property to pay part or all of the surviving spouse's elective share or your client may want all of the trust property to pass to others. One of the nice things about a trust is that it can be kept entirely confidential, even from the beneficiaries. If Henry or Wanda wants to make some gifts that they don't want the other to know about, the best form to do so is in this trust.

We have given you some of the basic gifts Henry and Wanda want to make through their trust. But those of you role-playing the clients will receive additional information about some gifts you want to make that you might not want your spouse to know about. If you are being represented by a single lawyer, you have already waived your right to confidentiality. But if you went with sole representation, you may freely explain these gifts to your lawyer knowing that your lawyer has a duty of confidentiality to you that will prevent him or her from disclosing that information to your spouse. And as you have become more attuned to the interests of Henry and Wanda you may decide that some of these gifts are not that important to you and you want to change your plan entirely.

This exercise concerns just the property that Henry and Wanda want to have pass to living adult beneficiaries (i.e., people who will take immediately upon their deaths). It is possible, however, that some of these beneficiaries will in fact predecease Henry or Wanda. Think about, and draft appropriate language for, this possibility after determining from your clients whether they would want those gifts to lapse and remain in the trust to pass to other beneficiaries, or whether they want those gifts to pass to alternate beneficiaries like the issue of the primary named beneficiary. To the greatest extent possible, one does not want to rely on the state's anti-lapse statute to deal with lapsed gifts, especially if your state's statute does not apply to trust interests. If it does not apply to gifts in trust, any gifts to predeceased beneficiaries will lapse and pass to residuary beneficiaries, or possibly fall outside the trust to pass by intestacy (which will entail probate and all of the hassle that involves).

## The Public Facts

### *Henry*

Henry wants his property to pass as follows:

- The house should go to Wanda for her life or until she remarries or decides to move, at which point she can sell the house, but the proceeds need to go back into the trust. The trust is to provide her with appropriate housing until her death, with some flexibility and discretion in the trustee to decide how best to accomplish this. But at her death, the proceeds from the sale of the house (if it is still owned by the trust at Wanda's death, it should be sold) should be distributed evenly for the four children.
- All personal property except a list of family heirlooms and mementos is to pass outright to Wanda, but anything left at her death is to pass to the four children.
- Any life insurance payable to the trust and any securities accounts owned by the trust or payable to the trust on Henry's death are to be retained, invested, and the income paid to Wanda for life, at her death for the benefit of Gillian and Benjamin until they reach the age of 25, at which time the corpus is to be divided into 4 equal shares for the four children. Henry probably wants to change the beneficiary designation of his retirement account to pay to the trust and not to Wanda and/or the children.

### *Wanda*

Wanda wants her property to pass as follows:

- If she and Henry retitle the home in both names, she wants him to have her share of the house outright immediately upon her death, free from trust.
- All of her personal property, including her jewelry, she wants to be held in trust for the benefit of Gillian and Benjamin until they reach age 25, at which point they can dispose of the property entirely.
- Her share of the furniture is to pass directly to Henry outright immediately upon her death.
- Any life insurance proceeds payable on Wanda's life, securities accounts owned by the trust or payable on death to the trust, and any cash in any bank accounts owned by Wanda and payable on death to the trust she wants to be used to pay the income to Gillian and Benjamin until they reach 25 for their education and support only. At age 25, Henry may have the power to appoint this property into further trust for the benefit of Gillian and Benjamin only if he thinks it is in their best interests to do so.
- Wanda wants the Basquiat painting to go to her cousin Susan at her death.

## Exercise 3—Lapsed Gifts, Spendthrift Provisions, and Gifts to Minors

Now you need to think about what to do with property that might pass to underage or incapacitated beneficiaries. You generally don't want the property to pass outright to underage beneficiaries, because they will then need a court-appointed guardian to manage the property for them, and they will receive it outright when they reach age 18. The better practice is usually to have the property remain in trust, managed by the trustee, until the children are of a sufficiently mature age to be trusted with outright control of the property. In the meantime, however, your clients might want the income to be paid to the children at age 18, or that the trustee can pay the income to an educational institution for the children's behalf. Your clients might want to limit the uses of the property until it is paid outright to the beneficiaries. However, once the property passes out of the trust it will pass outright in fee simple absolute to the beneficiaries and the settlor no longer can dictate how it is to be used. Dead hand control can only continue so long as the property remains in the trust.

Go back through the trust and make sure that you have provided for all possible contingencies. Provide what will happen to any property passing to a beneficiary who predeceases the settlor. Thus, all the provisions to the surviving spouse will lapse if the settlor is the survivor. Usually, that property simply passes straight on through to the children, but what if Wanda and Henry both die simultaneously and Gillian and Benjamin are still minors? What if one of the children also dies in the car accident but not the other? What if Steve or Doris predecease the surviving spouse, or fail to survive until Gillian and Benjamin are 25, but they leave issue? Think about all the possible permutations and outcomes if Susan or Janet predecease the settlor but not the life tenants, or predecease both. Provide alternate bequests and/or expressly state whether your state's anti-lapse statute should or should not apply to save bequests to predeceased beneficiaries.

You also need to think about whether any or all of the trust beneficiaries should be precluded from alienating their trust interests prior to final termination of the trust through a spendthrift provision. It may be that only Steve is reckless and irresponsible, or perhaps so are Henry and Gillian. Typical spendthrift provisions are as follows:

> No interest of any beneficiary in the income or principal of this trust shall be voluntarily or involuntarily assignable or transferable in anticipation of payment or be liable in any way for the beneficiary's debts or obligations and shall not be subject to attachment.

Spendthrift provisions preclude a beneficiary from transferring his interest, encumbering it by borrowing against it, or making it available to creditors. For someone like Steve, a spendthrift provision may make sense if Henry believes Steve might have a lot of debts. But it also might make sense for the other beneficiaries to have spendthrift provisions imposed on their interests, especially if Henry and/or Wanda don't want trust assets available to a surviving spouse's potential new spouse. Discuss with your clients whether they believe a spendthrift provision makes sense.

Finally, draft any relevant language to provide interests for any minor children. These may be the most important provisions you draft because, if all contingencies are not provided for, the trust may end up paying out directly to minor children in a way that will require a guardianship. And to avoid that is precisely one of the main reasons for using a revocable trust. Thus, draft the relevant language (or check it if you have already drafted it in exercise 2 for Gillian and Benjamin), as well as for any minor children of other beneficiaries who might take as alternate beneficiaries (issue of Susan or Doris or Steve for instance) either by direct grant, or by application of your state' anti-lapse statute. Make provisions in case any of the people whose interests are held in trust predecease the settlor or the life tenant. What happens if, for example, Doris survives Henry but predeceases Wanda, leaving minor issue? Do those issue take their share of property outright, or is it held in further trust?

### Lessons Learned

We have not given you express direction regarding how to draft these provisions, or whether you even need to include them. If Henry and Wanda decided to simply give everything to the survivor, and then a trust would be established only at the death of the survivor, you don't need to draft a revocable trust at this time. However, a revocable trust is advantageous for dealing with the transition from incapacity to death because property management won't have to pass between an agent under a durable power of attorney and the executor of the estate. The revocable trust allows for probate avoidance for all property titled in the trust before the settlor's death, as well as for fairly straightforward revocation by the settlor to allow for maximum pre-death control. And the trust provides for minor children by allowing trust property to be spent on minor children for education and support until they reach a certain age, and only after they have reached a sufficient level of maturity does the trust pay out to them directly. We want you to be sure you have tried your hand at drafting the trustee's powers, the actual property dispositions, and the future interests necessary to create alternate gifts and contingent remainders. This latter exercise is quite elementary, as you are not drafting a dynasty trust to last for generations and you don't have to worry about estate taxes in case you do get the future interests wrong, as the lawyers did in *Est. of Houston*, 201 A.2d 592 (Pa. 1964). But we also assume that you will be working through this book in a class where you will benefit from a discussion about what types of remainders or present estates are preferred under the circumstances of Henry's and Wanda's special facts.

At this point, your main task is to ensure that all of Henry's and Wanda's property is appropriately provided for, either through their wills or their trusts, that you have provided adequately for contingencies, and that you have created an estate plan that satisfies their wishes, while also benefitting from having an advance plan. You know what property needs to be retitled in the name of the trust, and what other things Henry and Wanda need to do to make sure that their loved ones are taken care of. If beneficiary designations need to be made, you have that noted, and if the house needs to be retitled, you know what to do. You should also understand why you might recommend that they acquire additional life insurance, or change some of their beneficiary designations based not only on the elective share, but also on their preferred plans. You should now know enough about your clients that you can recommend changes to how they hold their assets in order to facilitate their estate plans.

The next step will be preparing any final documents, like deeds or changes to beneficiary designations and then scheduling a time for Henry and Wanda to execute their various estate planning instruments. You will do that in the next Chapter. But in case you want a little extra practice, here are some additional problems:

### *PRACTICE PROBLEMS*

Just for practice, draft the relevant trust provisions to take into account the following facts and your client's wishes (you might need to meet with your clients again to ascertain their intentions with regard to these additional facts):

1. Janet returns from Tibet to live in a small apartment near Henry and Wanda. Henry feels obligated to provide adequate income to her now, and upon his death.
2. Susan is killed skiing in Colorado, leaving minor children.
3. Henry's brother Bob dies, leaving him a controlling share of his business, which Henry feels he should continue to keep open for the benefit of Bob's spouse and minor children.
4. Wanda's half-sister Rosemary contacts her from her institution and tells Wanda that the institution has squandered the entire $3 million that Wanda's father gave them for her lifetime care and that their father is refusing to give them any more money. As a result, they are neglecting her without officially releasing her and she needs help.

Hey, did you remember to fill in your time sheet? Be sure it is complete! You are almost done with your representation.

# CHAPTER 7

# TRANSMITTAL LETTERS, EXECUTION OF THE PLAN DOCUMENTS, AND CONCLUDING THE REPRESENTATION

Now that you have completed Henry's and/or Wanda's estate planning documents, it is time to execute them. But before you call everyone together, locate a notary, and find the witnesses, you need to once again make sure that the plan works with the way the property is arranged. Often large items, like the house or certain securities accounts, will need to be retitled in the name of the trustee. Or, beneficiary designations will need to be changed. Although those can be done after the instruments are all executed, it is important that they get done right away, in case your clients meet with an unfortunate mishap on the way home from your office.

Finishing up the representation requires that you do three things. First, you will need to send drafts of all of the plan documents to your clients for their approval. And since most clients are not lawyers, you will need to write them a letter explaining what you have done. This letter, the *transmittal letter*, explains in plain English that you have prepared the incapacity documents, a will, and a trust, AND it explains what these documents do. In other words, you will need to summarize their contents so that your clients understand the key elements of these documents and what they will achieve. Few clients actually read all of the will and trust documents carefully; rather, they will depend on the transmittal letter and your ability to draft documents that actually do what the transmittal letter says they do.

Second, you will need to execute all the documents, including any real estate deeds, beneficiary designations, or other documents concerning the property that will fund the trust or otherwise effectuate your clients' estate plans. This might mean writing a deed to transfer the house into Henry's and Wanda's names as joint tenants or having the beneficiary designation forms available at the execution ceremony. Part of your job is ensuring that these final tasks are taken care of before you can lean back and reflect on a job well done.

Third, you need to send your clients a letter concluding your representation. This is another very important letter. It should:

1. Explain what you did for them (as well as what you did not do and expect them to do, or what they chose not to pay you to do).
2. Explain what they need to do now (give the health care proxy to various relatives, put the will and trust somewhere safe, make copies for the trustee and executors, etc.) including any title changes and what they need to do in the future to keep the plan functioning (take title to large items in the name of the trustee of the trust, add additional life insurance when Henry retires for instance).
3. Explain what life changes that might occur to them will necessitate their coming back to you to revise their plan. Of course, if they get divorced, have another child, lose a parent inherit a lot of property, get sued for a big tort claim, a child develops a need for on-going care, or they win the lottery, they are likely to need to revisit and change their estate planning documents.

Your clients need to know what events in their lives should send them back to your office, assuming they were satisfied with your work, or even to someone else's office if they weren't. But they also need to know what they can or should do on their own—revised medical powers of attorney, guardianship, or lists of specific bequests of personal property—now and in the future. You don't want to tell them they have to come back to you because future changes are complex and require the skills of an attorney if the changes are within their skills set. Their needs should be put before your own.

And for your own records you need to have all of these documents in your file, complete with accurate notes and a completed time sheet so the firm's records are complete. If Henry or Wanda dies suddenly and you get that call from the survivor, you need to have everything at hand to assist them immediately. And the firm will want to know whether you deserve a bonus this year.

### Exercise 1—the Transmittal Letter

The transmittal letter should accompany the final draft of all of the estates documents to the client, explaining what each accomplishes. For instance, you will want to explain that they are going to execute a heath care proxy, a living will, a durable power of attorney, a will, and a living trust. As you explain each, you will want to point out the important elements of each document. Many lawyers find this to be one of the most difficult parts of the representation. They know what they have done for their clients, what the provisions mean, and how the plan works together. But they often are not as adept at explaining what they have done in plain English so their clients understand the documents and are put at ease that their intentions are being carried out.

Obviously, the transmittal letter will accompany drafts of all of the documents in case Henry and Wanda want to spend a lot of time slogging through the tax apportionment or non-exoneration language. But most likely, your clients will only read and rely on the transmittal letter. This is also a good opportunity for you to do a final check that everything is in order and works as you intended it to do.

For this exercise, we have provided the first few paragraphs, including the discussion of the health care proxy, and you are to modify it as appropriate and continue the letter. Remember, in drafting client letters you want to be clear, accurate, thorough, and concise at the same time.

> Dear Henry and Wanda,
>
> Enclosed you will find copies of the estate planning documents I have prepared for you. We are scheduled to execute them in my office, next Friday, the __ day of ___________, 20__ at __ o'clock _.m. I look forward to seeing you then and to getting your estate plan in order and up to date.
>
> Before we meet, however, I want to take this opportunity to provide a final summary of the terms and provisions of your estate plan. Of course, if there are any provisions that do not accurately reflect your intentions in this regard, please let me know at your earliest convenience so I can take steps to correct them before Friday.
>
> First: I have drafted a Health Care Proxy for you that designates __________________ as an agent to make health care decisions for you in case you are unable to make them for yourself. You have appointed ___________ and _____________ to be successor agents. You have chosen to grant your health care agent (broad powers) (limited powers) and have provided instructions about artificial nutrition and hydration as follows: ___________________________. You have also indicated that you are willing to be an organ donor of (all) (some) organs and tissues. You have also given express instructions as follows: ___________________________. Please reflect on this once more and confirm that it adequately reflects your intentions on this important matter and that you do not wish to add or subtract any provisions herein.
>
> Second: I have drafted a Living Will for you that * * * * *

When you have completed your transmittal letter, give it to your client and ask him/her to read through it and compare it to the estate planning documents you have provided. You might also give it to a parent or friend to read to see if that person feels that you have explained the documents in plain terms. Ideally, the letter will accurately and comprehensively explain the documents you have provided for Henry and Wanda and the documents accurately reflect their intentions. But if not, it is far better to catch any problems now, before execution, than afterwards. And even if an error or problem isn't caught until after execution, that is preferable to catching the problem after your client has died, when litigation is the only remedy. For it is always better to double- or triple-check your documents, and redo or re-execute them, than to litigate them after your client has died.

## Exercise 2—the Execution Ceremony

You have drafted quite a number of documents for Henry and Wanda throughout this book and the best part is now at hand. You are ready to execute the incapacity documents (the health care proxy, living will, durable power of attorney) as well as the will and revocable trust documents. You will note that some require two witnesses, some require only a notary, some require witnesses and a notary, and the will must be executed in conformity with your state's will formalities statute. To be sure everything is ready, go through each document and indicate with sticky notes where people need to sign, which ones need witnesses, which ones need a notary, and which ones have to be executed in the presence of everyone. If you have drafted a new deed for the house, or have changes to beneficiary designations, be sure those documents are prepared as well.

Next, arrange a time and place for you, your co-counsel, Henry, Wanda, and two other classmates of yours to come together for the execution ceremony. For this exercise, assume that you will serve as the notary, but not as a witness. Once you have everyone in the room, you should take charge as the lawyer, to ensure that everything is done properly. You will need to instruct the group in the following ways:

1. Be sure to tell them what documents they are executing (a will, a trust, etc.) so that the witnesses know what the testators are signing and what they are signing.
2. Ask your clients to confirm that they understand that they are executing these documents, and that they are of sound mind and free will. Ask each client to confirm in front of the witnesses that they have read these documents, understand them, and that they intend to execute them so they will have legal force.
3. Ask the witnesses to confirm that they understand they are witnessing these documents and may have to appear in court to testify to the execution process, that the clients executed of their own free will, and were of sound mind.
4. Explain the process that will be followed to ensure that the witnesses see the testator sign, the testator sees the witnesses sign, and that no one is to leave the room until they are done.

Now, pass around a blue ink pen to each person, and begin signing, trying really hard to keep all the documents intact, and don't let loose pages get mixed up. Make sure that the witnesses are actually seeing the testator sign, and that the testator is watching the witnesses sign. Finally, when you are done, thank your witnesses, and give the original to your client with instructions about how to keep it safe. Be sure to keep a copy of the executed original for your files.

Now that the documents are executed, you should sit down with Henry and Wanda and go over them, giving them oral instructions as to how to keep them safe, who should get copies, and what needs to be done with retitling certain property. If you are recommending that they change their bank accounts, you are probably going to have to trust them that they will take care of it and that they understand the importance of doing it quickly. If you had them execute a new deed for the house, you will most likely take charge of having it recorded (and will add the recording fees to their final bill). But who should Henry and Wanda give copies to, and of which documents?

1. Health Care Proxy—the original should be filed safely away, but copies should be given to the primary and alternates designated in the proxy, and others who might be called upon to assist if Henry or Wanda is in the hospital. If they don't want to give everyone copies, they can simply tell Wanda's parents, their siblings, and Steve and Doris where to find these documents in case they are needed. They might also want to provide copies to their primary care doctors for their files.
2. Living Will and Designation of Agent for Disposition of Remains—the originals of these should also be filed safely away. But you probably do not need to promulgate copies to everyone who might be around if disaster strikes. As long as people know where to find these documents in the unlikely event that Henry or Wanda is in a persistent vegetative state, or dies suddenly, it's probably not necessary that the agents have the documents immediately at hand.
3. Will—the original should be filed safely away, but it is probably a good idea to give the executor a copy. Or, if they don't want to provide copies, they should tell their children and their parents where to find their will and who is appointed primary and alternate executor.
4. Trust—the original of the trust should also be filed safely away, but the trustee and successor trustee should have a copy. Because it is likely that Henry and Wanda will be taking title to subsequent property in the name of themselves as trustees for their trusts, they need to be sure they use the correct title and make the trust document available to title agencies, banks, or other account holders. Trusts are essentially private documents, but the trustee is under a fiduciary duty to manage the property in conformity with the trust terms. Thus, it is important that the trustee have ready access to the trust document to confirm the terms of the trust.
5. Deeds or Beneficiary Designations—the originals will need to be filed with the County Recorder's Office or sent to the companies that manage the insurance or the securities accounts. Keep copies safely filed with other estates documents so that beneficiaries know what accounts the testator has, and which ones to contact in case of death.

### Exercise 3—Concluding the Representation

By now, you should know an awful lot about Henry and Wanda, their property, their aspirations, their family situations, and their secrets. And you are probably relieved that you have done what they asked, quite competently, and that now you should get a nice fat check for all of your time. But you aren't done yet. Even if you have sent them home after the execution ceremony with their neat little packet of documents and kept copies for your files, you need to do a few more things.

First, be sure you clean up your file. Delete old drafts of the will and trust so they don't suddenly appear and cause embarrassment. Make sure your notes are complete and thorough. Be sure you've got the names and addresses of the witnesses and notary in your file (it's ok if they are on the documents themselves) in case you need to call them to testify. And lock any documents on your computer so they cannot be changed. Most law firms have software that locks official documents once they have been executed so they cannot be modified. They can be copied and new documents created from them, but they are dated and disabled so that you can attest that they have not been tampered with.

Second, be sure to follow up with recording any deeds, mailing beneficiary changes to the relevant entities, and sending copies of the trust to any companies that require it. If the car is being retitled, you need to be sure the Department of Motor Vehicles receives the right paperwork. Of course, in our exercises you don't actually have to do any of this, but still it is a good idea to make a list of what you need to do to wrap things up. Best practices in law firms would probably entail entering the tasks into a calendar and confirming each task when it has been accomplished.

Third, you need to draft a final letter and bill to send to your client(s), stating that you have concluded your representation, that you hope they are satisfied with what you have done for them, that if they have any questions they should not hesitate to contact you, and that if their life circumstances change they should get in touch. You might also want to inform them that they should revisit their plan yearly and meet with you every 2 or 3 years just to check up on things. You need to tell them what to do if they acquire new property, and what to do if their financial or family situation changes dramatically. You can thank them for their business and assure them that you will let them know if changes in the law occur that might have implications for their estate plan.

In drafting this final letter, you will want to look back at your retainer letter from Chapter 1 to make sure that this letter reflects all the work you said you would do in that first letter. You want to note anything that you did that wasn't in the retainer letter. And you want to confirm that you did everything you said you were going to do, and probably some additional tasks. Best of all, you can enclose that final bill.

And finally, be sure to complete your time sheet to record your time concluding the representation!

## Lessons Learned

This Chapter involved executing the various documents which, as you well know from Trusts and Estates, can create some very interesting will formalities challenges if they are not executed properly. More importantly, however, you have drafted two very important client letters. The first, the transmittal letter, was an exercise in explaining your legal work in plain English and offered one last opportunity to catch any errors or omissions. As you drafted the letter explaining what each document did, you should have checked with your notes to ensure that they matched up. This letter is important for multiple reasons. It offers a last chance to check your work. It is likely to be the only document the client actually reads and thus is the only opportunity for the client to catch any errors. It restates what services you provided your client and what you did not do. And it gives you practice in one of the most important aspects of lawyering—client communication.

Then, after you executed the documents, you drafted another letter: the letter concluding the representation. This letter has a different function from the transmittal letter. It informs your client about any actions he or she needs to take immediately to effectuate the estate plan. And perhaps most importantly, it identifies what life-changes affecting your client will require revision to the plan. If you have read ahead into Chapter 8, you will see that some of the possible life-changes have now occurred and Henry and Wanda are coming back to have their estate planning documents changed. But you know enough about their lives to predict what life-changes are likely to occur to them, and you can practice your diplomacy. You need to explain that if they get a divorce they need to revisit their plans. You need to explain that if either dies, a child dies, a child becomes a parent, or they lose their jobs, they need to revisit their plans. Many of the reasons for amending are happy events, but some may be sad or difficult events for a client to face. Be sensitive in your letter to the life-changes that we all face as we age, gracefully or not.

Best of all, however, you got to send out your very first bill for legal services rendered. In drafting your bill you don't need to include everything you did during every minute. But you also don't want to simply end your letter with "you owe me $8,900.00 for services rendered—please pay up!" Discuss with your professor and your classmates the appropriate level of detail to include in your bill. For instance, if your client insisted upon several in-person meetings, you might want to explicitly refer to that. You may also want to specify the time spent on each document, so that the client understands what you have billed. And be sure you decide how much of your time cruising the internet or calculating the elective share you will not charge the client, and instead chalk it up to continuing education.

# CHAPTER 8

# UPDATING THE PLAN

You have completed all of Henry's and Wanda's estate planning documents and have executed them. You have sent them on their way, feeling confident that they are well provided for in case either one dies in the near future. But you also have learned enough about your clients, and you drafted that final letter in light of this knowledge, to know that there are some changes to their lives and situations that might very likely affect their estate plan in the future. In fact, you told them to contact you if major life changes occurred. In this Chapter we will draft some amendments to their estate planning documents to deal with some pretty significant, and specialized, changes.

It is now three years after you sent Henry and Wanda home with all of their executed documents, and Henry has just contacted you about three major events in their lives that need to be accounted for. First, the mother of Steve's illegitimate child brought paternity proceedings against him and proved, through DNA evidence, that Steve is the father. As a result, Steve is spending more time with his daughter Rachel and is paying some small amount of child support. Doris has since given birth to twins with her unmarried partner, Patricia. Henry needs to think a bit harder about providing for his grandchildren and what, if anything, he should do about Doris' significant other.

Second, Wanda's father has since died and Wanda has inherited about $4 million worth of assets, both in the form of the Montana property and in cash and securities. She is also the trustee of her father's trust and has a power to appoint over $10 million in assets among herself, her siblings, and their children.

Third, Wanda has recently discovered that she is pregnant with their third child but, because of her age, this child has been diagnosed with Downs Syndrome. The prognosis for the child at this time is that she will be able to live a fairly long life, probably well into her 50s, but that the disability is severe enough that she probably will not be able to ever live on her own. She will be unable to work at anything but very low skill jobs, will never be able to control her own property, and is likely to need live-in care for most of her life. Henry and Wanda have chosen not to terminate the pregnancy, and they plan to take care of their child themselves by Wanda giving up her job and devoting herself 100% to the child's care.

These three significant changes in Henry's and Wanda's lives have brought them back to your office, in accord with your instructions, and you will need to think about more than a simple amendment or will codicil. Each of these changes will require that you draft a specialized trust instrument/amendment, as well as recognizing that other changes to their basic plan may be needed.

### Exercise 1—What to Do with Grandchildren and Potential In-Laws?

When Henry and Wanda first came to your office, they had two minor children and Henry had two grown children, Henry knew it was possible that Steve might have an illegitimate child, but Steve and Doris were focused on their careers and not families. That has changed. Doris has been involved with Patricia, her partner of many years and, through artificial reproductive technology, Doris has just given birth to twin boys, Brandon and Brock. Doris and Patricia have not married because Patricia has extensive student loans for which Doris does not want to be liable. But Patricia is in the process of going through a second-parent adoption which has a very unusual consequence on the inheritance rights of the boys. Henry needs to make some changes to his will and trust to ensure that Brandon and Brock will be entitled to inherit from him, to protect Doris's property in case she and Patricia marry and then divorce (which he thinks is likely), and to provide for Steve's child.

### *a. The Problem of Brandon and Brock*

Under the UPC § 2–119(a), children who are adopted are no longer treated as the legal children of their biological parents under the *fresh start provision*. This provision assumes that children who are adopted into new families will form new relationships in place of the old ones that are terminated as a result of the adoption. The only exception to the fresh start provision lies in UPC § 2–119(b), which provides that a parent-child relationship will continue to exist between a genetic parent and the adopted child, if the adoptive parent is the *spouse* of the genetic parent. This is the step-parent exception. Although same-sex marriages are now recognized in all states, many gay and lesbian couples have not gotten married and second parent adoptions in those states run the risk of not fitting within the safe-harbor of the step-parent exception, resulting in the complete cutting off of the children from their biological parents who are continuing to parent them. The fresh start also cuts off the children's inheritance rights in cases of opposite sex couples who choose not to marry but who parent together.[1] In this case, when Patricia successfully adopts Brandon and Brock, they will no longer count as the genetic children of Doris because the State of Sunshine does not have a special second-parent adoption provision that would allow an unmarried partner to adopt a partner's children without cutting off their inheritance rights. If Doris and Patricia decided to marry, they would fit within the step-parent exception. But Henry is not encouraging them to marry for a variety of reasons, not the least of which is that he really doesn't like Patricia.

This anomaly in inheritance laws is a result of the probate codes of many states not coming into line with family law codes that would treat Doris and Patricia both as parents, despite the lack of a valid marriage. But inheritance laws, including the UPC, continue to rely on the traditional categories of marriage, biology, and formal adoption, and do not usually allow functional children, foster children, or step-children to inherit. What this means for Henry and Doris is that they have to be explicit if they want Brandon and Brock to inherit from them once Patricia adopts them. They cannot rely on simple class gift language like "to my lineal descendants" or "to my children's issue." Because Brandon and Brock will not be considered Doris's children, anti-lapse protections may not apply and Brandon and Brock will not be able to inherit under intestacy from Henry, Doris, Janet, or Henry's mother. They will not have standing to intervene in any probate proceedings involving Doris' side of the family, nor will they receive the statutory priorities to be appointed administrator of Doris' estate. They probably would not be entitled to bring a wrongful death action if Doris were killed.[2]

Because of the cut-off effect, Henry needs to make amendments to his will and trust to ensure that Brandon and Brock will be treated as Doris' issue for all probate and inheritance purposes. He cannot rely on any statutory default rules. So go back through his will and trust and determine where changes need to be made. Also, Henry would like to make sure that Brandon and Brock receive trust benefits for their education and support, just as Gillian and Benjamin are receiving them. And he doesn't want them to take outright possession of any trust principal before they are of a sufficiently mature age.

---

[1] Although UPC § 2–116 permits a child to show that a parent/child relationship exists for inheritance purposes if an adult functioned as a parent, very few states have adopted this provision, while most have adopted some form of the fresh start provision that would result in the cut-off if the adoptive and biological parents are not married.

[2] For more information regarding the cut-off effect, see Laura Padilla, *Flesh of my Flesh but not my Heir: Unintended Disinheritance*, 36 BRANDEIS J. FAM. L. 219 (1997–1998).

### b. *What About Steve's Daughter, Rachel?*

Steve's illegitimate daughter Rachel, after having proven paternity, is entitled to inherit from Steve, Janet, and Henry regardless of the marital status of her parents. And usually this is what relatives want—that their lineal descendants be recognized and accorded full inheritance rights. Some relatives, however, may not be so generous. Although Henry and Steve are happy to have Rachel inherit from them, and Henry wants to make sure that Rachel is treated just like Brandon and Brock, Henry's mother is a bit old-fashioned. In her will devising property to Henry, she included a condition that her property would never be used for the benefit of any children born out of wedlock. As you recall from Chapter 6, Henry has a provision in his trust that any property he acquires will be given 3/4ths to his siblings and their issue, and his 1/4 will pass equally to his four children. As it happened, Henry's mother has since died, and her estate was quite a bit larger than expected. She had won a very large tort judgment against the nursing home where she was staying in her final years. Her estate was a little over $4 million, including the condo in Des Moines, and Henry's share of that property is $1 million. Divided four ways for his four children, each would take $250,000 in cash. And that is fine so long as grandma's property is paid out entirely to Henry's four children and is not put into further trust. But assume that Steve's share was held in trust until he became a bit more responsible, with alternate gifts to his issue. At the time, you didn't know that Henry's mother's will had this restriction on her property, but you do now. You need to redraft any provisions that might benefit Steve and/or his issue to ensure that none of Henry's mother's property can pass to Rachel, or to Brandon and Brock since they are non-marital children as well.

### c. *What About Patricia?*

Henry is not at all bothered by the fact that Doris has chosen to have children out of wedlock. But Henry knows Doris and knows enough of Patricia to be pretty convinced that their relationship isn't going to last, whether they marry or not. Henry is convinced that even if Doris and Patricia ever marry, upon a divorce Patricia will be entitled to an equitable share in Doris' property, including any property that Doris inherits from Henry or any trust property in which Doris has an irrevocable interest or a general power of appointment. If Doris dies instead of being divorced, Patricia would be entitled to an elective share in this property. Either way, divorce or death, Patricia is likely to be entitled to some of Henry's property, and he doesn't want her to have it.

Henry needs you to revisit his will and trust to ensure that if he dies soon, and Doris inherits from him, that none of that property will be treated as Doris' property for equitable distribution or elective share purposes if Doris and Patricia marry and their marriage turns sour.

So how do you draft these changes to ensure that Rachel, Brandon, and Brock are considered full legal grandchildren of Henry, but do not get any of Henry's mother's property, and that Patricia won't be able to get her hands on any of Henry's property or his mother's property through Doris? And of course, you want to keep all gifts to minors in trust until they are a responsible age. Fortunately, Brandon, Brock, and Rachel are all lives in being, so you don't need to worry about a rule against perpetuities problem in drafting trust interests for them. But the answer is probably to keep a lot of this property in trust with explicit instructions regarding Brandon's and Brock's rights to be treated as grandchildren for all inheritance purposes. You will need to create a sub-trust to segregate Henry's mother's property if any of that property could potentially be used to benefit non-marital descendants. And property Henry might have been willing to give to Doris outright might need to remain in trust until Henry knows a bit more about whether Doris' and Patricia's relationship is going to lead to marriage and is going to last, or not. And does Henry want Wanda to be the trustee of Doris' trust, or should Doris be the trustee, or someone else? If so, who?

Try your hand at redrafting the appropriate provisions from Henry's will and trust and discuss them with your classmates. There is no one-size-fits-all solution to any of these changes. You will need to discuss them with Henry and draft changes that best fit his wishes, while building in the requisite protections that you know should be there. At this point, flexibility is the name of the game. The grandchildren need to be provided for even if Steve is a loser, Patricia is a problem, and Brandon and Brock are not considered legal grandchildren. Who will make the best trustees, and should there be provisions to change trustees or trust terms if certain events occur in the future? Estate planning can be a lot like reading tea leaves, but if you know your clients well you are well on your way to mastering the arcane subject of divination.

### Exercise 2—Wanda's Sudden Fortune

Wanda's father died a year ago, leaving Wanda as the executor of his estate, the trustee of his discretionary trust, and his principal beneficiary. There are three major issues that you and she will need to address in her revised estate plan. First, she now has a lot more wealth that she inherited outright (an extra $2 million) that is currently sitting in a securities account in her name, with no beneficiary designation and which would be included in her probate estate were she to die tomorrow. You've got to think about elective share issues, as well as probate avoidance. That account should probably be put into Wanda's trust right away but it also means she is likely to change some of her will and/or trust dispositions now that she has a lot more wealth to dispose of. She had a very modest estate before this, and now she can make some significant changes in provisions for Susan, her half-sister Rosemary, her mother, her siblings, and her children. She might even want to give Henry some of it. Or, she might want Henry to waive his rights to all of this property through a post-nuptial agreement.[3]

Second, she is the discretionary trustee of the rest of her father's estate, which consists of another $2 million in trust over which she has a general power of appointment. She can appoint the property to herself, to her siblings, to her children, or she can ignore the power and not exercise it at all. If she fails to exercise the power of appointment, her father's trust directs that the trust corpus will pay equally to all his lineal descendants, by representation, upon Wanda's death. Wanda might want to release some or all this power to get it out of her own estate for possible estate tax purposes.

Third, Wanda has the discretion to use any or all this property for the benefit of any of her father's lineal descendants during her life for their health, education, maintenance, or support only. She will need to consider whether she can exercise her discretion for the benefit of her own children and under what circumstances or restrictions, and she will need to think about what to do if she becomes incapacitated and cannot serve as trustee for her father's trust.

Reproduced below is a copy of the relevant portions of Wanda's father's will and trust. In analyzing what to do with these three issues, discuss them with Wanda and advise her on the various implications of the different ways you could handle this new-found wealth. And then redraft her will and trust to reflect these changes.

---

[3] Pre-nuptial and post-nuptial agreements are beyond the scope of this book, although you should have an easy enough time finding some sample agreements on the internet if you choose to go down this path.

**Last Will and Testament of Alfred Doolittle**

This instrument, executed on the 14th day of January, 2020, is the last will and testament of Alfred Doolittle, and hereby revokes all previous wills.

I avow that I am of age and of sound mind and under no disability or undue influence. After payment of my just debts and funeral expenses, I direct my executor to pay the following bequests:

I. I give $1 million to each of my three children, Bernadette, Beverly, and William, to be theirs absolutely.

II. I give $2 million to my daughter Wanda, to be hers absolutely. Wanda is to receive more than her siblings because she has fewer assets than they have and I have spent less on her in her lifetime than I have spent on her siblings.

III. I give nothing to my wife or my daughter Rosemary because I have adequately provided for them through special trusts and other arrangements.

IV. I hereby appoint my daughter, Wanda, as personal representative of this, my estate, and if she is unable or unwilling to serve as personal representative, then I appoint her sister, Bernadette, as alternate personal representative.

V. All the rest and residue of my estate, including any lapsed gifts, shall pass into the Alfred Doolittle Revocable Trust, established by me this same date, except that if any of my children predecease me, leaving issue, then their issue shall take their bequest by representation.

Executed on the day above-mentioned.

*Alfred Doolittle*
Alfred Doolittle

*Sally Johnson*
Witness 1

*Jim Wilson*
Witness 2

**Alfred Doolittle Revocable Trust Established January 14, 2020.**

* * * * * *

**Article 8: Trustee**

Alfred Doolittle shall be the trustee of this trust. Upon the death or incapacity of Alfred Doolittle, the trustee of this trust shall be my daughter, Wanda Doolittle Higgins. If Wanda Doolittle Higgins is unable or unwilling to serve as successor trustee, then I appoint my daughter, Bernadette Doolittle, to serve as successor trustee. If neither of my daughters is able or willing to serve as trustee, then my four children, or their survivors if any has predeceased me, shall appoint a trustee.

**Article 9: Property Provisions**

1. Upon my death, all trust property, including property passing into this trust from my will executed this same date, shall be retained in trust and invested by my trustee. The income from one-third of the trust property shall be paid to my wife, Gloria, for her life.

2. The income of the remaining two-thirds of the trust property, or the income from all of the trust property upon the death of my wife Gloria, shall be payable to any of my lineal descendants as my trustee shall determine, in her sole and unfettered discretion. Any income not distributed shall be retained and reinvested as part of the corpus of this trust.

3. Upon the death of my wife Gloria, and the successor trustee, whichever later occurs, the entire trust corpus shall be payable to whoever and however my daughter Wanda directs in her will among my lineal descendants, including in further trust. If my daughter Wanda fails to appoint any of this trust property in her will, then it shall pass to my lineal descendants alive at the time of distribution, payable per stirpes.

* * * * * *

---

## Exercise 3—Wanda's and Henry's New Addition to the Family

As mentioned above, Henry and Wanda are about to have another child, only this baby has been diagnosed with a genetic abnormality that will prevent her from living an independent life. Now it is absolutely imperative that Henry and Wanda, together, make adequate provisions for this new child's support, and that you draft a *Supplemental Needs Trust*. This trust will need to be a separate trust from the trusts already established, with different trustees and different administrative terms. And you will need to make provisions for the payment of the child's needs, provide a spendthrift provision, and figure out a way to ensure that the child will not be disqualified from any government disability benefits without having to pay out every cent in the trust.

Although Wanda is planning on giving up working for pay, and she has enough money from her father's estate to cover all their likely expenses, she doesn't want to use every penny for this new baby to the detriment of Gillian and Benjamin. She also needs to designate successor trustees of the baby's trust in case anything happens to her or to Henry. A supplemental needs trust needs to do 5 things:

1. It must state that it is a supplemental needs trust and that it is intended to provide "supplemental and extra care" over and above that which the government provides. If the government provides nothing, the trust will provide for all of the beneficiary's needs. But if the government will provide certain benefits, there is no point eliminating the beneficiary's ability to receive those benefits simply by not drafting the trust accordingly. Thus, it needs to state that it provides *supplemental* and *extra care* and is not to be used for basic needs such as food, clothing and shelter.

2. It must state that it is not a basic support trust and it must not give the beneficiary any powers to withdraw from income or principal. Additionally, the trustee's powers must be entirely discretionary. If any distributions for the beneficiary are mandatory, then the beneficiary will be deemed to have control of the assets, and the trust assets can be considered when determining the beneficiary's eligibility for government assistance.
3. A self-settled supplemental needs trust (one funded by the beneficiary of the trust) should reference the relevant federal laws that allow for the creation of such a trust (the Omnibus Budget and Reconciliation Act—Obra-93 and appropriate provisions of the U.S. Code).
4. The trust must spell out the circumstances under which the trust will provide benefits and not provide benefits that meet the federal requirements. Otherwise, if the trust will pay out in ways or circumstances that might cause the beneficiary to lose benefits, the government may withhold those benefits.
5. The trust must be irrevocable, although it will need to include specific instructions regarding termination of the trust and disposition of any remaining assets upon the child's death. A third-party settlor trust needs an additional beneficiary who will take any remaining assets after the primary beneficiary's death. On the other hand, if a self-settled trust has assets remaining when the beneficiary dies, those assets are then available to the state agencies to pay back the cost of the beneficiary's care.

The sample third-party settlor supplemental needs trust reproduced below has a lot of the basic language in it, but it needs to be personalized for Henry and Wanda. You also need to do a bit of basic research to determine what laws authorize such trusts and include that language. And finally, you need to identify what property will go into the trust and under what conditions the trust terminates and who will take the property then.

SPECIAL NEEDS TRUST (CALIFORNIA)[4]

The Trustee will hold any trust share allocated under this Trust Agreement, or for the benefit of, the Settlors' *[son or* daughter*] [name of son or daughter]* in *FURTHER TRUST* for the special needs and benefit of *[name of son or daughter]* on the following terms:

1. The Trustee will pay to, or apply for the benefit of, *[name of son or daughter]* so much of the income and principal of this *Special Needs Trust* estate, up to the whole of it, as the Trustee (in the exercise of the Trustee's free and absolute discretion) deems necessary or desirable for *[*his *or* her*]* special needs *after* taking into consideration all other resources (including, but not limited to: Social Security, Medicare, SSI, MediCal, welfare benefits and other forms of federal and state aid and/or assistance for disabled persons) known by the Trustee to be available to and for *[name of son or daughter]*.

2. In this regard, the Settlors wish to acknowledge that *[name of son or daughter]* is emotionally disabled, which disability will likely continue. As a consequence, *[name of son or daughter]* will likely be in need of federal and/or state financial aid throughout *[*his *or* her*]* life. Such public benefits do not, however, currently provide adequately for all of one's basic living needs (such as dental care and outdoor recreation). Recognizing that limitation, the Settlors wish to explicitly state that the primary purpose of this Trust is to provide for *[name of son or daughter]*s *extra and supplemental* (and emergency) needs throughout *[*his *or* her*]* life (as the Settlors would if personally present) *in addition to,* and over and above, the benefits *[*he *or* she*]* may receive as a result of *[*his *or* her*]* disability, from any local, state or federal agency or from any private agency which provides services and/or benefits to handicapped persons.

3. In establishing this *Special Needs Trust* for their *[son's or daughter's]* benefit, the Settlors recognize that, after their death, it will be vitally important to *[name of son or daughter]* to continue to have programs supplemental to those now provided by public assistance in order to maintain a level of human dignity and humane care. If this Trust were to be invaded by creditors, subjected to any liens or encumbrances or cause public benefits to be terminated, it is likely that the trust corpus would be depleted prior to *[name of son or daughter]*s death, especially since the cost of care for emotionally disabled persons (not including emergency needs) is high. In this event *[name of son or daughter]* would not have resources to cover emergency needs or to provide needed supplements to basic benefits. These trust provisions should, therefore, be interpreted in light of these concerns and the Settlors' stated intent.

4. As used in this instrument the term "special needs" refers to the requisites for maintaining *[name of son or daughter]*s good health, safety and welfare when (in the free and absolute judgment of the Trustee) such requisites are not being provided by any public agency. "Special need" shall include (but not be limited to) dental care, health care not otherwise available, special equipment, training programs, education, housing, rehabilitation, travel needs, and recreation.

5. It is the Settlors' intent, as expressed in this Trust Agreement, that because *[name of son or daughter]* is emotionally disabled and may well continue to be unable to maintain and support *[*himself *or* herself*]* independently, the Trustee will (insofar as is practical) seek support and maintenance for *[name of son or daughter]* from all available resources including (but not limited to) Social Security and Supplemental Social Security (SSI) benefits, MediCal and Medicare benefits and whatever assistance might be available from time to time from appropriate regional centers for disabled persons. In making distributions to *[name of son or daughter]* for *[*his *or* her*]* special needs under this Trust Agreement, the Trustee will take into consideration the applicable resources and income limitations of the public assistance programs for which *[name of son or daughter]* is eligible at any given time.

6. No part of the corpus of this *Special Needs Trust* will be used to supplant or replace public assistance benefits of any agency (whether it be county, state, federal or other governmental agency or a private agency supported by such a state entity) which has a legal responsibility to serve persons with disabilities which are the same or similar to *[name of son or daughter]*s disability. For example, for purposes of determining *[name of son or daughter]*s

4 California Transactions Forms—Estate Planning, § 14:38 (2023).

MediCal eligibility, no part of the principal or undistributed income of the trust estate will be considered available to *[name of son or daughter]*.

7. In the event the Trustee is requested to release principal or income of the trust to or on behalf of *[name of son or daughter]* to pay for equipment, medication, services and/or programs which MediCal (or some other public agency) is authorized to provide were it not for the existence this Trust, or in the event the Trustee is requested to petition the court or any administrative agency for the release of trust principal or income for any such purpose, the Trustee is hereby authorized to deny the request and is hereby further authorized to take whatever administrative or judicial steps may be necessary to continue *[name of son or daughter]*s MediCal (or other public agency) eligibility, including obtaining instructions from a court of competent jurisdiction ruling that the trust corpus is *not* available to *[name of son or daughter]* for MediCal (or other public agency) eligibility purposes. Any expenses of the Trustee in this regard (including reasonable attorney fees) will, of course, be a proper charge to the trust estate.

8. Because this Trust is to be conserved and maintained for the special needs of *[name of son or daughter]* throughout *[*his *or* her*]* life, no part of the corpus of the trust (either principal or undistributed income) will be construed as a part of *[*his *or* her*]* "estate" or be subject to claims of voluntary or involuntary creditors (whether such claims be for the provision of care and services *[add, if applicable:* including, but not limited to, residential careby any public entity or otherwise).

9. The Trustee may, but need not, terminate this trust for *[name of son or daughter]*s benefit at any time following the Settlors' deaths that the Trustee (in the exercise of the Trustee's free and absolute discretion) finds that *[name of son or daughter]* has recovered from *[*his *or* her*]* disability without a significant possibility of relapse. The Trustee need *never* make this determination, and need not terminate the trust during *[name of son or daughter]*s lifetime.

10. Notwithstanding anything to the contrary contained in this Trust Agreement, in the event that the existence of this trust has the effect of rendering *[name of son or daughter]* ineligible for SSI, MediCal or any other program of public benefits, the Trustee is authorized (but not required) to terminate this further trust and distribute the then remaining balance of the same as if *[name of son or daughter]* had died on the day the Trustee elects to terminate the *Special Needs Trust*. It is the Settlors' wish (but not the Settlors' directive) that on such termination of the *Special Needs Trust* the trust beneficiaries will conserve, manage and distribute the then remaining proceeds of the trust estate for the benefit of *[name of son or daughter]* to ensure that *[*he *or* she*]* receives sufficient funds for *[*his *or* her*]* basic living needs when public assistance benefits are unavailable or insufficient.

This request pertaining to the management of trust proceeds after the termination of the trust for *[name of son or daughter]*s benefit is *precatory*, not mandatory.

In determining whether the existence of the trust has the effect of rendering *[name of son or daughter]* ineligible for SSI, MediCal or any other program of public assistance or benefits, the Trustee is granted full and complete discretion to initiate administrative and/or judicial proceedings for the purpose of determining eligibility before terminating the trust and all costs relating to such proceedings (including reasonable attorney fees) will, of course, be a proper charge to the trust estate.

11. On *[name of son or daughter]*s death, the Trustee will distribute the then remaining balance of the trust estate as follows:

> (a) First, the Trustee may (but need not) pay: any death taxes that may be due by reason of *[name of son or daughter]*s death (regarding assets passing in accordance with the terms of these trust provisions, or otherwise); all expenses of *[name of son or daughter]*s last illness and funeral; and all expenses related to the administration and distribution of *[name of son or daughter]*s estate (if any) and/or this trust *if* (in the opinion of the Trustee) other satisfactory provisions have not been made for the payment of such expenses.
>
> The Trustee will not, however, make any payments for expenses incurred prior to *[name of son or daughter]*s death if the Trustee reasonably determines that payment of the expenses were the obligation of any public agency which has a legal responsibility to serve persons with disabilities which are the same or similar to *[name of son or daughter]*s disability.
>
> (b) Next, the Trustee will distribute the then remaining balance of the trust estate to *[name of son or daughter]*s then living issue (if any), by right of representation, *subject, however,* to the CUTMA Trust

provisions set forth above in Section , for any such benefited issue who is under the age of *[same age (from 18 to 25) as established in CUTMA trust provisions, such as:* 25*]* at the time the gift to such issue vests under this Trust Agreement; and should there be no such issue, then to the Settlors' then living issue, by right of representation, *subject, however,* to the CUTMA Trust provisions set forth above in Section , for any such benefited issue who is under the age of *[same age (from 18 to 25) as established in CUTMA trust provisions, such as:* 25*]* at the time the gift to such issue vests under this Trust Agreement; and should there be no such issue, then as follows: *[describe distribution]*

12. In administering this special needs trust for *[name of son or daughter]*s benefit the Trustee will have all of the powers granted the Trustee in this Trust Agreement (particularly including the powers granted in Article *[insert article number of article setting forth rights and duties of trustees]*) *except* that the following caveat shall be observed: Any public assistance benefits payable to, or for the benefit of, *[name of son or daughter]* will be administered separately from the trust and will not be commingled with trust assets.

**Notwithstanding anything in this Trust Agreement to the contrary, the Trustee (if [he *or* she] is also a beneficiary, direct or contingent, of this Special Needs Trust) will not have any right, power, or authority to make or withhold any distribution under this Trust Agreement that would cause the value of the Special Needs Trust estate (or the income from it) to be taxed to the Trustee under state and/or federal income, gift, and/or death tax laws, specifically including, but not limited to, Section 2041 of the United States Internal Revenue Code [26 USCA § 2041].**

**IN WITNESS WHEREOF**, the parties have executed this instrument on the day and year first above written.

______________________________________

__________________________________, Grantor

______________________________________

__________________________________, Trustee

**SCHEDULE A**

The following assets are hereby transferred and conveyed to the Trustees as the initial Trust Estate to be held, administered and distributed in accordance with the terms of the foregoing Declaration of Trust:

- Cash [$ ]
- Other [ ]

## Lessons Learned

In this Chapter you have had to amend Henry's and Wanda's estate plans to deal with some important, but entirely expected, changes in their life situations. Henry now has to think a bit more about providing for the natural objects of his bounty as they grow and have children themselves. He has multiple generations he may need to provide for, and it's not as simple as giving the property away outright anymore. He also needs to tie up the property he is giving to Doris to prevent Patricia from getting it, either through a divorce settlement or an elective share. Although he isn't averse to Patricia enjoying his property while she and Doris are together, he doesn't want her walking away with it, to the detriment of his grandchildren, if they marry and divorce or Doris dies.

You have also had to amend Wanda's estates documents to deal with her greater wealth (including the effect that additional $2 million will have on Henry's elective share if Wanda predeceases him) and her power of appointment over her father's trust property. Wanda has the ability to dispose of this property by putting it in further trust, which may make a lot of sense. She can also put it into the supplemental needs trust you helped establish for Henry and Wanda for their soon-to-be new child.

Finally, you have made provisions for a special-needs child, a specialized trust that is very important if your clients have dependents who are likely to outlive them but will require care and assistance for their lives. From these exercises you should better understand how your clients' estate plans can easily change over time, what circumstances lead to the necessity for changes, and what kinds of changes make sense. What you should have also learned is that not every client needs all these instruments all of the time. We hope that you are beginning to get a feel for when simple instruments will suffice, and when you will need to dig a bit deeper into your estate planning toolbox to find the right tools to help your clients.

The key here is building flexibility into the plans because neither Henry nor Wanda can know for sure what the future holds for their minor children and grandchildren. With more assets, too, they may want to restructure their plan to spread their wealth more broadly and limit its distribution over time. You should know many of the tools for building flexibility into trusts, like discretion in the trustee, powers of appointment, and alternate gifts. Now is the time to put those tools to work.

P.S. Don't forget to do a new client retainer letter and keep track of your time for revising Henry's and Wanda's estate planning documents.

### *PRACTICE PROBLEMS*

If you are still looking for additional practice, try drafting some estates documents for:

1. Steve and his child Rachel.
2. Doris, Patricia, and their twins.
3. Rosemary, Wanda's older sister in the institution.

# CHAPTER 9

## PLANNING FOR THE POTENTIALLY TAXABLE ESTATE

We have postponed until this Chapter any consideration of tax matters because they are beyond the scope of this book and are more appropriately discussed in an advanced course on estate planning. Nevertheless, there are two considerations you will need to be aware of, even if you are drafting an estate plan for a non-taxable estate. These are tax apportionment provisions and the creation of a trust with Crummey powers to take advantage of the annual exclusion amount. The tax apportionment language is crucial in case your client wins the lottery days before her death or, as is more likely, earns or inherits enough property to place her estate into a potentially taxable status. This can also happen as a result of fortuitous circumstances, as when her small stock portfolio suddenly increases in value because her high tech stocks take off, or a meteorite lands on her Kansas farmland and it's full of valuable minerals. Virtually anything can happen to dramatically increase or decrease the value of one's estate. So it's always best to be prepared.

The use of *Crummey* powers[1] arises in the context of irrevocable trusts for beneficiaries who are given a limited power to withdrawal principal up to the amount of the annual exclusion ($17,000 in 2023). Even if the beneficiary doesn't withdraw the funds, the gift to a Crummey Trust counts as a present interest for gift tax purposes. For example, Henry could pass $17,000 to each of his four children each year, for a total of $68,000 per year. If he puts that amount into a trust each year for 10 years, giving each child a power of withdrawal, which they choose not to exercise, he will have transferred $680,000 into the trust with zero transfer tax consequences for him or for them. And if both spouses gift that amount, there could be a sizable trust in 20 or 30 years. Crummey powers are especially important in life insurance trusts in which the settlor intends the trustee to use the gift to pay the insurance premiums.

A gift to a Crummey trust, however is a gift of a present interest, and therefore qualifies for the annual exclusion, only if the beneficiary 1) is legally and technically capable of immediately possessing the gift, and 2) has a reasonable opportunity to possess the gift. One of the most common uses of Crummey powers is to give property to one's children annually while they are still minors so that there builds up a sizable sum that the child can use to buy a house or pay for college tuition. But many parents do not want to give their children a lump sum of money annually to be spent on whatever new gizmo or gadget catches their attention. Moreover, if the children had an unlimited power to withdraw at any time and for any purpose, the trust could not be limited to serve its intended purpose. An unlimited power to withdraw the funds would likely frustrate the trust settlor's intent to use a trust to gain favorable tax and probate benefits, and to postpone possession of the property until it has accrued substantial funds.[2] If those funds were used to purchase life insurance, and the beneficiary had an unlimited right to withdraw at any time, the life insurance trust would be in jeopardy.

---

1 Crummey powers are named after the famous case, *Crummey v. C.I.R.*, 397 F.2d. 82 (9th Cir. 1968).

2 For instance, there is no reason I cannot start making annual gifts of $17,000 to my children on the day they are born and continuing until they reach age 30. The fact that they aren't likely to understand the meaning of withdrawing the gift until they are 16 and want a new car doesn't mean the earlier gifts were not valid just because they didn't know about the money and could not logistically take possession of it. At age 18 they would be entitled to possession of the funds, or a later date if I use a trust. But the point is that I should be able to start early making these gifts, regardless of whether they are fully capable of understanding what they are and exercising their rights to unfettered possession. And perhaps more importantly, I should be able to put some limits on when and how they can withdraw the funds and still achieve favorable tax objectives. Why should I wait until they are 21 and make a lump sum gift of twenty years' worth of annual gifts which, at that time, would be potentially taxable if I can spread it out and avoid the tax?

In order to give the beneficiary a genuine power to withdraw, and to give the Settlor and Trustee some certainty, the IRS has determined that a gift with a lapsing withdrawal right may create a gift of a present interest, and qualify for the annual exclusion. In order to do so, the trustee must ensure that the beneficiary of the trust is aware of the withdrawal right and must give the beneficiary sufficient time to exercise that withdrawal right.

Most Crummey trustees will provide the beneficiary with written notice (the Crummey Notice) of a gift and of a 30 day withdrawal period. Additionally, some trustees will ask the beneficiary to sign and return a copy of the Crummey letter, in order to demonstrate that the withdrawal power is genuine. While written notice has never been required by the IRS, a Settlor who provides written notice has created proof of the beneficiary's awareness.

Although the decision to create a Crummey trust should be left to a qualified estate planner, which you are well on your way to becoming, whether or not to create one is beyond the scope of this course. However, you are likely to create many trusts with Crummey powers during the course of your legal career in estate planning, and therefore should be aware of the technical legal issues surrounding the powers and how to draft Crummey letters to the beneficiaries. Therefore, we are not focusing here on why you would create such a trust, or what financial considerations militate creating one, but on how to draft the Crummey letters if you do in fact create such a trust.

## The Law of Taxation of Gratuitous Transfers

As you are probably aware, the federal government imposes a tax on gratuitous transfers of property over a certain amount, whether that transfer occurs during life or at death. Some states also impose taxes on the transfer of property, while others impose taxes on the recipient of an inheritance. In 2023, the amount of property a person can transfer before the federal transfer tax is assessed is $12.92 million and that amount will increase yearly with inflation. Any estate that is valued below the federal exclusion amount will not incur any transfer taxes.

There are three kinds of federal transfer taxes: *gift* taxes (for transfers made during the donor's lifetime), *estate* taxes (for gifts made at the donor's death), and *generation skipping transfer* taxes (for gifts made to skipped generations designed to avoid transfer taxes that would be imposed on the skipped generation). All combined, a donor will pay one kind of transfer tax or another on any transfers over the lifetime exclusion amount. And the tax rate is quite high on such transfers—between 18–40% in 2023. You will probably have covered these in your Trusts and Estates course, or in a course on taxation of gratuitous transfers, if you are planning on specializing in estate planning in your career.

In addition to the lifetime exclusion of $12.92 million, any individual may transfer up to $17,000 annually to any other individual, without that sum being included in the donor's lifetime exclusion total. Thus, a donor could transfer $17,000 to 100 different people each year, for a total of $1.7 million, and that money would not be included as part of the $12.92 million lifetime exclusion amount, allowing the donor to pass tens of millions of dollars transfer-tax free if done over many years.

Although few people want to give 100 strangers a $17,000 gift every year just to avoid some taxes, the cumulative effect of the annual exclusion can make a big difference to an estate that is marginally over the $5.43 million lifetime limit. If a donor made a $17,000 gift to 10 children and grandchildren annually for 10 years, the effect would be the same $1.7 million. If it was done for 20 years, it would be over $3 million.[3] More importantly, if that $17,000 was used to purchase life insurance worth, say, $5 million, the effect on transfer taxes would be quite substantial because life insurance proceeds are taxable as part of the donor's estate if the policy is owned by the donor.

[3] This assumes that over the next 20 years inflation will cause the annual exclusion amount to increase.

Let's put this into perspective. If Henry purchased five $5 million life insurance policies on his own life, that would pay a total of $25 million to Wanda and his four children, that entire $25 million would be considered part of his gross taxable estate for estate tax purposes and would cause his estate to have to pay 40% on any amount over his $12.92 million lifetime exclusion.[4] That would be upwards of $4 million in taxes. Instead, Henry establishes a life insurance trust, to which he makes 5 individual gifts of $17,000 each to Wanda and his four children as beneficiaries, and they choose not to withdraw any of that money. The trust then purchases the five $5 million life insurance policies on Henry's life. Because Henry is not the owner of the policies, and the funds used to purchase the policies had already been given to the trust beneficiaries using the annual exclusion, the $25 million in life insurance passes transfer-tax free to Wanda and the children. Now those five $17,000 annual exclusion gifts make a tremendous difference to Henry's estate tax bill!

Life insurance trusts are not for everyone, but they are quite helpful in getting the proceeds of life insurance out of a donor's estate for estate tax purposes. So whether your client wants to establish a basic Crummey trust to transfer multiple years' worth of the annual exclusion amount out of your client's estate, or wants to use a Crummey power to establish a life insurance trust, Crummey powers are critical in properly leveraging the $17,000 annual exclusion amount.

Crummey powers are not particularly relevant if your client only has a $100,000 estate. And frankly they aren't that relevant if your client is Bill Gates and his estate is worth $70 billion, because it would be hard to use the miniscule annual exclusion to more than marginally decrease his estate taxes. But if your client's estate is between $10 and $15 million, a judicious use of the annual exclusion can mean the difference between paying a million or two in estate taxes and paying nothing.

But as noted at the outset, planning for tax minimization is beyond the scope of this book. You should take a specialized course on the taxation of gratuitous transfers where you can carefully study the different methods and criteria for moving property out of an estate to avoid transfer taxes. So we are not going to do any tax planning exercises for Henry and/or Wanda here. Instead, we are going to focus on drafting two important provisions of any estate plan that is, or could be, near the value of the lifetime exclusion. The first is the tax apportionment provision and the second is the drafting of Crummey powers and Crummey letters. The tax apportionment provision identifies the property from which any estate taxes will be paid and the Crummey powers and Crummey letters pertain to ensuring that the annual exclusion is properly used.

## Exercise 1—Tax Apportionment

When estates are large enough to be facing estate taxes, the estate pays the taxes before distributions to beneficiaries. In that sense, the estate tax is simply another debt against the estate. And in most estates, debts are paid out of the probate estate and, even more likely, out of the residuary property of the probate estate. This apportionment of the tax liabilities can cause real headaches if none of the property passing outside a will through a will substitute like a joint tenancy or a trust pays its share of estate taxes, because the tax burden is borne entirely by the residuary will beneficiaries. This may make sense if most of a decedent's estate is passing via a will and there are very few specific bequests, but it may not make sense if a decedent effectively uses numerous will substitutes.

To deal with the potential imbalance, the Uniform Estate Tax Apportionment Act (UETAA) apportions the tax burden across all the property that is included in the gross taxable estate *if* the decedent does not specify a different apportionment scheme. Thus, in the states that have some version of the UETAA, if property passing outside of probate (by, for example, joint tenancy or by

[4] Forget for the moment that the amounts to his spouse would be tax free under the unlimited marital deduction because that money will be part of Wanda's estate when she dies and will likely be taxed at that point.

POD designation), generates a tax liability, then that non probate property must pay its fair share of the estate tax. While this rule may balance the tax burden, there is no way for the estate to withhold taxes from the non-probate, non-trust assets. For instance, even though property held as joint tenancy must pay its taxable share, once the decedent joint tenant has died and the property has vested fully in the surviving joint tenant, it is difficult to claw back from the survivor money to pay the taxes. The UPC's §§ 3–9A–101 to 115 is modeled on the UETAA. Instead of placing all the liability for the estate tax on the residuary estate, the UPC apportions estate taxes to all recipients of taxable property. This means that *all* property is reduced pro rata, regardless of whether it is in a revocable trust, held as a joint tenancy, is in a securities account with a POD, is a specific bequest for the testator's 8-track tape collection in the will, or is the residuary devise of the will.[5]

The UETAA protects the will's residuary beneficiary, but arguably errs too much on the other side, assessing the taxes against every item of taxable property, from the non-liquid real estate to the run-down Saturn automobile. The Restatement 3d of Property § 1.1, comment g, explains that estate tax liability for non-probate property is assessed across *all* non-probate property, but estate tax liability for probate property is assessed solely against the residue, unless the decedent provided otherwise. That protects the 8-track tape collection and other specific and general devises in the will, but not the residuary and non-probate property. Not all states have adopted the UPC or the UETAA, however, and complications can arise when an estate owes estate taxes and property passing outside of probate is exempt from paying its share.

The solution for any potentially taxable estate is a tax apportionment provision in both the trust and the will, which means you need to effectively plan for the proper payment of taxes for any estate that is potentially taxable. And although a tax apportionment provision in the will or trust is effective to charge certain probate or trust property with any estate tax liabilities, it isn't effective to charge joint tenancy or POD property with those taxes. Thus, if you want joint tenancy property to pay its share, you will need to have the UETAA apply to that property. This can be complicated.

### Considerations

How do you decide what kind of tax apportionment provision to use? First, keep in mind that the first $12.92 million of property will pass tax free. So if your client's estate is valued at, say, $14 million, you are only looking at a little over $1,000,000 worth of property that is subject to tax and, at a 40% tax rate, that would in the neighborhood of $400,000. You probably would not want that sum to be pro-rated across all bequests and gifts in the estate.

You should also keep in mind that a donor can transfer an unlimited amount to a spouse transfer-tax free. Thus, if Henry's estate was worth $14 million and Wanda's was only going to be worth $2 million, you could transfer $2 million of Henry's property to Wanda and there would be no transfer tax liability for either estate. This cumulative effect means that a married couple can transfer, together, a combined $25.84 million before they run into transfer-tax problems.

But if your client is not married, or has an estate significantly over the lifetime exclusion amount, there is likely going to be some estate taxes due, and you will need to apportion them efficiently against the various property in the estate. At this point we won't use charitable gifts to avoid taxes altogether, but you should realize that any gifts to qualified charities are not subject to transfer taxes either, thus increasing the amount that can pass tax-free. But you may decide that charitable gifts should be altered if gifts to other individuals are sufficient to trigger a tax.

Ideally, if you know there is going to be a tax liability, you should plan for that and set aside some funds to pay it. A nice life insurance trust might do just the trick for setting aside funds to pay for estate taxes. And a provision in a revocable trust that all estate taxes are to be paid from trust

[5] Property passing to a spouse or a qualified charity, however, is excluded from being reduced since this property is not affecting the tax liability of the estate.

property will be effective to override the UETAA or your state law. But if you want all property to pay its share, then you will want to state that in the will and the trust, knowing that your stated provision will govern the will and trust property, and that the UETAA will be applicable to other property, like POD or joint tenancies. Remember, a will provision that states that all estate taxes will be paid from joint tenancy property will not be effective because the right of survivorship will have kicked in at the tenant's death, so the property is no longer in the estate or subject to the will provisions. You may have to figure out how to condition such property on the donee repaying the estate for her share of the estate taxes.

This means you should consider the following kinds of property and which ones should be assessed the taxes:

1. Specific bequests of property in the will
2. General bequests of cash in the will
3. Residuary property disposed of by the will either directly or through a pour-over into a trust
4. Trust property already in a revocable living trust, including real estate or securities accounts
5. Life insurance proceeds, whether in trust or not
6. Property over which the decedent has a power of appointment
7. Joint tenancy property with children or others
8. Joint tenancy or tenancy by the entirety property held with a spouse
9. Securities accounts held with POD designations
10. Bank accounts with POD designations
11. Property passing to a spouse or a charity that would otherwise be exempt from transfer taxes
12. Property over which an executor or trustee has immediate power to pay the taxes
13. Property which passes directly to beneficiaries and from whom the executor would need to reclaim a portion to cover the tax share of that property

Let's consider a possible estate tax scenario. Assume an unmarried decedent, Bob, has the following property:

- $500,000 worth of artwork
- $2,000,000 home titled in his own name
- $5,000,000 in a securities account designating his brother as beneficiary
- $5,000,000 in life insurance payable to his ex-wife
- $3,000,000 business he runs doing art appraisals/restoration
- $500,000 worth of personal property, including cars, jewelry, clothing, furnishings, etc.

Bob has a $16 million estate, which means he will likely owe taxes on the $3.08 million in excess of his lifetime exemption. Let's say the taxes amount to $1.2 million. As Bob's estate is currently held, the securities account and the life insurance will pass automatically to the beneficiaries outside of probate, and the rest of the property ($6 million) will pass through probate. All of Bob's property is responsible for the estate tax since none of it is exempt. This means that if each item paid it's fair share, 7.5% of each gift will need to be held back to pay the estate taxes ($1.2 million/$16 million). But we will have a hard time collecting on the securities and life insurance which together are responsible for $750,000 in taxes. Instead of trying to claw that property back, Bob could use an apportionment clause in his will to provide that all his estate taxes will be payable from the sale of his home, or from the sale of the business. Bob needs to think about where he would get this $1.2 million. If we ask only the probate property to pay that $1.2 million tax, then 20% of each item of probate property would need to be held back, meaning $100,000 of artwork, $100,000 in personal property, $400,000 from the equity in the home, and $600,000 from the business. Or, Bob could change his life insurance to pay $1.2 million to his estate to pay the tax, leaving only $3.8 million to pass to his ex wife. The point is that if all property has to pay its fair share of the tax, then much of it will have to be sold, including some art, a part of the business and the home, and some of the personal property. Imagine taking 20% of the value of every lamp, chair, plate, appliance, and other items of personal property. But a good tax apportionment provision tells the executor which property Bob would like to have sold to pay the taxes and. if he wants the life insurance or securities account beneficiaries to pay their fair share, he should only give them 92.5% of those assets, and have the remaining 7.5% pay to his estate.

Most likely your client has certain property she wants to have pass without tax liabilities to particular beneficiaries as part of her lifetime exemption amount, and has other property that she may be giving to others against which she wants the taxes to be assessed. In that case, you need to be sure to provide appropriate apportionment language in these gifts to identify which property is subject to paying the taxes and which is not.

Here are a few sample apportionment provisions:

- Upon the death of the Grantor, the Trustee shall, to the extent that the assets of the Grantor's estate * * * are insufficient, pay * * * reasonable expenses of administration of his estate, * * * all income, estate, inheritance, transfer and succession taxes, including any interest and penalties thereon, which may be assessed by reason of the Grantor's death, without reimbursement from the Grantor's Executor or Administrator, from any beneficiary of insurance upon the Grantor's life, or from any other person; . . . . *Lurie v. C.I.R.*, 425 F.3d 1021 (7th Cir. 2005).
- I direct my Trustees to pay from the principal of my residuary estate, but in no event from that portion of my estate constituting the marital Trust 'A' as hereinabove set up in my Will, all taxes in the nature of estate, inheritance, succession and transfer or other similar taxes of every kind levied or assessed upon legacies, gifts and devises given herein or in any Codicil hereto, and in respect to any other assets which may be included in or added to my estate for the purpose of calculating such taxes. *Est. of Bertolet*, 397 A.2d 776 (Pa. 1979).
- I direct my Executors, hereinafter named, to pay out of the principal of my residuary estate, . . . all estate, inheritance, transfer and succession taxes, imposed upon or payable with respect to any property or interest in property which may be included as part of my estate for the purposes of said taxes, at such time and in such manner as my Executors in their sole discretion shall determine, and no part thereof shall be collected from or pro-rated among any persons receiving or in possession of, or receiving the benefit of, the property or interest in property taxed; it being my particular intention that the bequest to my wife under Article Fifth hereof and the bequest and devise for the benefit of my wife under Article Thirteenth hereof shall be free of all such taxes. In the absolute discretion of my Executors, such taxes may be paid immediately, or the payment of taxes on future or remainder interests under the residuary clause hereof may be postponed until the time possession thereof accrues to

the beneficiaries, in which event such taxes shall be paid out of the principal of the trust subject thereto. *In re Fleischman's Est.*, 388 A.2d 1077 (Pa. 1978).

- In making this bequest/devise, I hereby direct that all state and federal taxes together with costs of administration attributable to same shall be a charge against said bequest/devise. The same shall also be the beneficiary of any legislation granting tax relief to any family-owned business. *Gallagher v. Est. of Stepfield*, 2013 Ohio 3113 (Ct.App.Ohio, 2013).
- I direct my said Executrix to pay out of the principal of my residuary estate as hereinafter given, devised and bequeathed, any and all estate, inheritance, succession, legacy, transfer or similar death taxes, including any interest or penalties thereon, which may be levied or assessed in respect to any property or interest therein passing under this my Last Will and Testament or any Codicil thereto. I specifically direct that such taxes which shall become due and payable in respect to any other property required to be included in my gross estate for the purpose of computation of such taxes shall be apportioned against, and paid out of, such other property[.] *Steinhof v. Murphy*, 991 A.2d 1028 (R.I. 2010).
- I direct that any estate, succession, inheritance, death or transfer tax arising by reason of or in any way in connection with my death, be paid out of my estate as an expense of administration thereof, without apportionment or contribution. *Bunting v. Bunting*, 760 A.2d 989 (Ct.App. 2000).

Here is a provision for recouping taxes from property that may have already transferred to a beneficiary.

- "except that the amount, if any, by which the estate and inheritance taxes shall be incurred as a result of the inclusion of property in which the grantor has a qualifying income interest for life, over which the grantor may have a power of appointment, or that is not held as a part of or payable to the grantor's estate or trust following the grantor's death, shall be paid by the person holding or receiving that property."[6]

After a thorough review of Henry's and Wanda's property and their estate plans, we want you to draft an appropriate tax apportionment provision in both the trust and the will that you have drafted. If you choose to focus on Wanda's estate plan, in light of the property she received from her father's estate, be sure to account for all the property in his estate that she can dispose of and that might be considered part of her gross taxable estate. Look up additional tax apportionment provisions if you don't feel that these are adequate.

Remember, Wanda's father has died and Wanda has inherited about $4 million worth of assets, both in the form of the Montana property and in cash and securities. She is also the trustee of her father's trust and has a power to appoint over $10 million in assets among her siblings and their children. Depending on the scope of your class, you might want to focus solely on the tax apportionment language of Wanda's will and trust, or you might want to go further and make some tax planning decisions with Wanda. It is also important to realize that if Wanda inherited this property, and she is passing a significant amount of it to Henry at her death, that Henry's estate documents may need to be amended to reflect the potential for inheriting sizable wealth from Wanda if she predeceases him. If that happens, his estate may become taxable.

---

[6] David Berek, Tax Apportionment in Estate Planning: Drafting Clauses to Preserve Dispositive Provisions, available at http://media.straffordpub.com/products/tax-apportionment-in-estate-planning-drafting-clauses-to-preserve-dispositive-provisions-2015-01-20/reference-material.pdf.

### Exercise 2—Crummey Powers

Crummey powers are a result of the famous case (in the tax world anyway) of *Crummey v. C.I.R.*[7] In that case, the trust settlors, a husband and wife, put money into a trust over a number of years naming their four children as beneficiaries, and taking an exemption of $3,000 per child per year under the annual exclusion amount. (In 1962 and 1963 the annual exclusion amount was only $3,000 per person but each of them gave that amount for a total of $6,000 per child.) Each child was given a power to withdraw a portion of his or her gift each year by the trust terms. The trust provided as follows:

> . . . With respect to such additions, each child of the Trustors may demand at any time (up to and including December 31 of the year in which a transfer to his or her Trust has been made) the sum of Four Thousand Dollars ($4,000.00) or the amount of the transfer from each donor, whichever is less, payable in cash immediately upon receipt by the Trustee of the demand in writing and in any event, not later than December 31 in the year in which such transfer was made. Such payment shall be made from the gift of that donor for that year. If a child is a minor at the time of such gift of that donor for that year, or fails in legal capacity for any reason, the child's guardian may make such demand on behalf of the child. The property received pursuant to the demand shall be held by the guardian for the benefit and use of the child.[8]

The I.R.S. refused to grant the exemption for three of the children in the tax year 1962, and for two of the children in the tax year 1963, because they were under the age of 21 and could not, under California law, legally exercise their right to withdraw the funds themselves. They had no legal guardians other than their parents, who were the trust settlors and obviously had no intention of exercising the power for their children. The I.R.S. treated the transfers into trusts as future interests in the trust principle when the children came of age or the trust would pay out. The Ninth Circuit reversed the Commissioner, however, and held that even though the children were minors, their guardians did have the power to withdraw the funds, and the fact that the trust settlors were the guardians was not relevant! The court explained:

> Given the trust, the California law, and the circumstances in our case, it can be seen that very different results may well be achieved, depending upon the test used. Under a strict interpretation of the *Stifel* test of examining everything and determining whether there is any likelihood of present enjoyment, the gifts to minors in our case would seem to be 'future interests'. Although under our interpretation neither the trust nor the law technically forbid a demand by the minor, the practical difficulties of a child going through the procedures seem substantial. In addition, the surrounding facts indicate the children were well cared for and the obvious intention of the trustors was to create a long term trust. No guardian had been appointed and, except for the tax difficulties, probably never would be appointed. As a practical matter, it is likely that some, if not all, of the beneficiaries did not even know that they had any right to demand funds from the trust. They probably did not know when contributions were made to the trust or in what amounts. Even had they known, the substantial contributions were made toward the end of the year so that the time to make a demand was severely limited. Nobody had made a demand under the provision, and no distributions had been made. We think it unlikely that any demand ever would have been made.[9]

The court held that because the children were legally entitled, through a guardian, to withdraw the funds and spend them as they wished, they were given a present interest in the property and

[7] *Crummey v. C.I.R.*, 397 F.2d 82 (9th Cir. 1968).

[8] Id. at 83.

[9] Id. at 87–88.

therefore it counted as a completed gift of the money up to the annual exemption amount, even if the right to withdraw eventually lapsed. The parents could therefore place into a long-term trust $24,000 per year tax-free by utilizing the annual exemption. So long as the children had a *legal* right to withdraw, the gift was deemed a present transfer, and the fact that the parent/guardians had no intention of exercising the power to withdraw on behalf of their children did not make the transfer illusory.

Since that decision, the I.R.S. and the courts have developed some explicit rules on Crummey powers so that trust settlors don't come quite as close to the line as the petitioners did in the *Crummey* case.

1. Effective gifts can be made to minor children who can be given the power to withdraw through a guardian.
2. The children need not be aware of their power of withdrawal so long as the guardian knows (this permits settlors to make gifts to very small children who would not understand the nature of the gift).
3. There is no conflict of interest if the trust settlor is also the guardian and makes a decision for the minor beneficiaries not to withdraw.
4. The adult beneficiary or the guardian of a minor beneficiary must have a reasonable time within which to exercise the right of withdrawal (30 days is usually deemed reasonable).
5. It is not necessary that the right of withdrawal continue indefinitely; a lapsing right of withdrawal may still constitute a present transfer of a present interest.

You will find that Crummey provisions and Crummey notices are very important in your trust practice. As mentioned earlier, Crummey powers are important in the context of life insurance trusts to remove the proceeds of life insurance from the insured decedent's estate. But to effectively navigate the Scylla and Charybdis of the I.R.S.'s rules on Crummey powers, you need to master two skills. First, you must draft the appropriate trust language to create the right of withdrawal and provide for its lapse if it is not exercised according to explicit terms. Second, you must draft appropriate Crummey notices from the trustee to the beneficiaries to satisfy the present interest test.

For this exercise, we want you to draft a Crummey provision for Wanda's trust that would allow her three children the power to withdraw trust principal at the rate of the annual exclusion and accounting for the fact that the exclusion amount will increase periodically. Then, we want you to draft Crummey notices to the three children for the current tax year. We have included a sample Crummey notice below. And you may use the language from the *Crummey* case, reprinted above, as a sample for the trust provision. You should do some additional research, however, into other trust and notice language, thinking particularly about the fact that Wanda's children are minors and that their legal guardian is Wanda herself.

In drafting the Crummey notice, you will note that this sample is very simple. Is it advisable to include language regarding the rights of guardians to sign for the minor beneficiary? Should there be any reference in the notice to limits in the trust agreement? Should it explain what Crummey rights are? Should it specify the withdrawal limit as being based on the annual gift exclusion? Should it include language to exercise the right to withdraw? Do a little research on this and draft accordingly.

### Sample Crummey Notice

The notice below is a very simple Crummey notice, which provides the beneficiary with actual notice of his or her right to withdraw the gift, and provides for a reasonable opportunity to exercise the right. This notice would be sent out to the beneficiary shortly after the gift is made, in order to ensure that it is timely.

**CRUMMEY NOTICE**

**TO:** Beneficiary name and address

**DATE:** 00/00/20__

**RE: Settlor's Irrevocable Trust (the "Trust")**

This notice is being sent to you as beneficiary of the Trust. As beneficiary, you may withdraw funds gifted to the Trust.

Please be advised that on 00/00/00, a contribution of $X.00 was made to the Trust. Subject to the limitations set forth in the Trust, you may withdraw up to $X.00 of this amount no later than the 30th day after the date of this notice. If you wish to make a withdrawal, please provide me with a written request for the amount to be withdrawn. If you do not wish to make a withdrawal, please sign the statement below and return it to me at your earliest convenience.

______________________________

Trustee

I have been notified of my right to withdraw a portion of the noticed addition to the Trust, and I do not wish to exercise this right.

Dated: ______________________

______________________________

Beneficiary

## Lessons Learned

The two exercises in this Chapter are aimed at two common issues that arise in the estate plans for potentially taxable estates. Although the lifetime exclusion of $12.92 million is currently so high that fewer than 1% of estates are likely to face any transfer taxes, you will be surprised how many of your clients will come to you adamant that they want to eliminate their death taxes and that your estate plan must show evidence of that. Crummey powers are a terrific way to do some sensible tax planning which might, or might not, prove valuable in the long run. It may very well be that your client worth $20 million when he comes into your office will spend $10 million on an expensive heart transplant and thus not die with a taxable estate. Similarly, that modest estate may hit the jackpot and be worth millions at the client's death. Planning sensibly to deal with tax apportionment and to utilize Crummey powers are basic requirements of skilled estate planning.

But if you aim to be an estate planner for the rich and famous, you will need to take some advanced tax courses, as well as a course on advanced trust planning. Most Trusts and Estates courses simply don't have the time to cover complex trusts, like GRATs and GRITSs or CRATs and CRUTs, which are common features of the estate plans for very wealthy clients. Today you are ready to write a basic will and revocable living trust. But if you have enjoyed the exercises in this book, and you continue your education in trusts and estates, you will be well positioned on that first day of practice to dig right in and start putting your client's affairs in order. That is a sign of a good day's work!